ITALIAN ENVIRONMENTAL LITERATURE

ITALIAN ENVIRONMENTAL LITERATURE
AN ANTHOLOGY

■

EDITED BY
PATRICK BARRON & ANNA RE

■

FOREWORD BY JOHN ELDER

PREFACE BY REBECCA WEST

ITALICA PRESS
NEW YORK
2003

COPYRIGHT © 2003 BY PATRICK BARRON AND ANNA RE

ITALICA PRESS, INC.
595 MAIN STREET
NEW YORK, NEW YORK 10044

LIBRARY OF CONGRESS CATALOGING-IN-PUBLICATION DATA

Italian environmental literature : an anthology / edited by Patrick Barron & Anna Re.
    p. cm.
    English and Italian.
    Includes bibliographical references.
    ISBN 987-0-934977-70-8 (pbk. : alk. paper)
        1. Italian literature--20th century. 2. Italian literature--19th century.
3. Environmental policy--Literary collections. 4. Ecology--Literary collections.
5. Nature--Literary collections. I. Barron, Patrick, 1968- II. Re, Anna, 1970-
PQ4204.A9185 2003
850.8'355--dc21

2003001567

Cover Photo: Lama dei Peligni, Abruzzo, on the east flank of the Majella Massif. Photo © Patrick Barron.

Printed in the U.S.A. and E.U.
5 4 3 2 1

For a complete list of titles in this series
visit our website at
www.ItalicaPress.com

CONTENTS

Map of selected locations mentioned in the anthology. (By Manuela Mariani and Patrick Barron.)

FOREWORD
by John Elder

Environmental thought and writing in America have long profited from their dialogue with Italy's literature of the earth. From a certain perspective, the modern environmental movement might even be said to have begun in Italy. It was in this ancient land and culture, after all, while serving as Abraham Lincoln's ambassador, that George Perkins Marsh wrote his 1864 masterpiece *Man and Nature*. His book, which Lewis Mumford has characterized as "the fountainhead of the conservation movement," was the first to argue in a scientifically informed way that human actions could inflict significant, long-lasting damage on natural systems. In its critique of deforestation, especially, Marsh's book contributed to the 1873 Timber Culture Act, the 1885 founding of Adirondack State Park, and the 1891 Forest Reserves Act. The last of these, in William Cronon's words, "created national forests as we know them today." Marsh's writing also strongly influenced the establishment of Yellowstone in 1872 as the first national park in the world. I am convinced that these benefits all flowed directly from the inspiration of Italian landscapes and culture in Marsh's life, and from the ways in which they helped him take a much longer view of the ravaged mountains in his native Vermont.

Indeed, one of the gifts Italy offers to American writers and thinkers has always been a deeper and more complex historical vision. In exploring the dialogue of nature and culture, Italian authors frequently look back, not only to past writers such as Lucretius and Virgil, but also to the mythic, pastoral, and agricultural history of the peninsula. For them, as for the Laguna Pueblo writer Leslie Marmon Silko in our own day, a long-settled landscape may best be mapped by "a bundle of stories." With the help of such "story-maps" we may pursue a more satisfying and sustainable way of life. The reverberant, mythic aspect of the past in Italian literature is especially striking in the poetry included here (and in many instances translated so beautifully by Patrick Barron). Not just the animals, but also the trees, the rain, the seasons, the sky, death, rivers, and the poets' own bodies, become conduits for ancient and mysterious powers of the earth. Natural phenomena for these poets can embody history and divinity as well as the laws of physics. In the prose selections here, too, there is often a similar sense of mighty forces immanent in the mundane details of our surroundings.

All of the represented authors have lived and written within the past century and a half. One of the realities of Italian life in this period – extending right up through the decade after World War II – has been the dire poverty of many country people. Living at the edge of starvation may sometimes lend an hallucinatory vividness to sensory perception, as it did so many years earlier for the voluntarily famished St. Francis. In addition, though, the pervasive fact of such deprivation often leads to a heightened concern for social and economic justice in writers like Grazia Deledda and Carlo Levi. This model of integrating natural landscapes into a broader political discourse can be especially helpful to American environmentalists today, as we try to relate both our wilderness movement and our transcendentalist tradition in nature writing more directly to such historical realities as the Civil War, the Great Depression, and the persistence of racial polarization in our society. An awareness of social conditions that shape both landscapes and the fate of rural communities contributes to the highly sophisticated and strategic rhetoric of the environmentalists with whom this collection ends.

Finally, it is important to note the highly localized nature of many of these entries, in time as well as in space. In this regard, as the present-day bioregionalist Giuseppe Moretti regularly explores in the review *Lato Selvatico*, the traditional Italian experience of landscape and seasons has a marked affinity with the American bioregional movement. Not only are ecology and culture seen as mutually reinforcing expressions of a watershed, but their connections are also most clearly revealed through attentiveness to a single, closely defined place on earth. The astounding originality of a poet like Andrea

Zanzotto is inseparable from lifelong fidelity to the rural district where he was born. Sometimes the pieces in this collection — poetry and prose alike — seem a litany of sacred place names and a calendar of holy days. Such passionate affiliation with a landscape may remind readers of such contemporary figures as Terry Tempest Williams and Rick Bass in our own literature. Through such connections and many more, this remarkable anthology fosters and renews the dialogue between Italian and American literature that has long proven so fruitful, and that has never been more urgent than it is today.

Middlebury College

PREFACE
by Rebecca West

Like the natural world, Italian literature gives us a rich abundance that is difficult to tame. Literary historians and critics have attempted to do so by creating taxonomies: periods, movements, schools, styles, and dominant thematics. In recent literature, as in past writing, however, we find texts that resist classification, books that flow between genres, between the fictional and factual, between dialects and standard Italian, between oral traditions and literary language. It is all the more appropriate, then, that in the twenty-first century we find new ways of gathering texts together so as to make them available and decipherable to non-native and native readers alike. This anthology, organized as a contribution to "ecological" and "environmental" approaches to literature, gives to specialist readers, that is, students and scholars of Italian literature, a new way of appreciating both known and lesser-known Italian poems and prose writing from the late nineteenth and twentieth centuries, while introducing these writers to non-specialists from within a framework of concerns that illuminate many essential aspects of the geography, history, and social-political realities of post-unification Italy. A country known for its wealth of artworks, through time Italy has also offered visitors, whether young aristocrats on the Grand Tour or backpacking students, exceptional natural splendors; from the majestic Dolomite mountains in the North to the lush Riviera seacoast, from the poetically lovely Tuscan and Umbrian countrysides to the astounding wildness of Sicilian and Sardinian sea and landscapes, this small country is filled with diverse natural environments that have contributed to the shape of its equally diverse literature. Italy has its share of urban problems as well, as anyone who has experienced Milanese, Roman, or Neapolitan traffic and pollution knows. The waters threaten to engulf Venice, as the automobiles threaten to engulf other large and small cities, yet one travels only short distances to find idyllic nature, flourishing wildlife, and flora of exceptional beauty. The contrasts are extreme, and if Italy can be defined in a word, then it might be "kaleidoscopic." Its literature, tied as it is to natural, regional, and dialectal roots, offers readers inroads into understanding more fully the motherland that has nurtured its themes, inflections, styles, and multiplicious voices.

As Patrick Barron writes in the Introduction to this anthology, nature, the nonhuman, and the human are inextricably related. As humans shape their environments, so do environments shape human existence. To recuperate this essential connection is one of the admirable goals of ecocriticism, which is inherently global, or should be. We live in spaces as well as in time, and if temporally-conditioned approaches to knowledge in such fields as historiography, literary studies, and art history, to name but a few, have tended to dominate academic research and creative work, the last several decades have seen a shift to spatially-oriented methodologies that acknowledge the importance of place as well as time in our collective human story. Massive migrations, the internet, and other phenomena of our age move both people and ideas through space with amazing speed, and effect immediate changes on the environment that are surely transforming the inner lives of humans as much as the places in which we live and die. With its exceptionally rapid transformation from an agrarian country to an industrial and technological power, modern Italy is particularly suited to environmental studies. Reading the poems and prose pieces included in this volume, I was struck by the alternation of what has been called by critic Gerald Graff the contrasting postmodern tones of "celebratory" and "apocalyptic" type. Especially since the unification of their country, Italian writers have both welcomed and feared the progressive spirit that has marked modern Italian history, have both believed in and viewed with deep suspicion the idea of a fully modern, fully unified Italy. Reflecting the transformations of their land, while also recording the disappearance of ancient landscapes and ways of life, many writers of the last century have shown in their works the ways in which human souls as well as the Italian environment have been inalterably changed by so-called progress, but also by indifference, corruption, and thoughtlessness. What people collectively care about matters tremendously in the shaping of both environment and national identities; literature gives us a priceless record of those shared hopes, dreams, and even nightmares. In this anthology we read words that convey the Italian sensitivity to the value of natural beauty and of nonhuman life, and we also read words that portray the suffering caused by harsh, unforgiving landscapes and poverty, by rapacious industrialization, and by humanity's cruelty to itself, to the earth, and to the other creatures that share the globe with us. These poems and prose pieces speak of the connections between nature and culture with the power of creative artistry, which often surpasses the impact of expository writing, due to literature's capacity to endure, to shift, and to grow in meanings through generations of readers.

Among the writers included in this collection is Gianni Celati, who in the 1980s worked closely with the late photographer Luigi Ghirri, one of Italy's most important contemporary artists of the landscape. The writer and photographer traveled through the Po valley together in the 1980s, and their mutual interest in ways of seeing and representing the external world resulted in a very fruitful collaborative exchange on many topics including humankind's place in and response to the environment. Celati became more and more interested in pursuing work as a video artist, and Ghirri developed his talents as a writer about photography and landscape, almost as if their work in the verbal and visual realms began to merge into a new art form made up of aspects of both: art always centered on the shared narrational potential of words and images. In 1997, three of Ghirri's short essays, collectively entitled "Paesaggi" (Landscapes) were published in the journal *Almanacco delle prose: Il semplice*, co-edited by Celati. The first, 'L'omino sul ciglio del burrone" (The little man on the edge of the gorge), describes Ghirri's love for photographs in old geographic atlases and on postcards of illustrations in which a little human figure was always to be found contemplating vast natural landscapes (waterfalls, mountains, gorges, etc.) or monuments like the Roman Forum or the Tower of Pisa. Ghirri explains: "The little man's was a state of continual contemplation of the world, and his presence in the images endowed them with a special attraction. Not only was [the little man] a meter for measuring the illustrated marvels, but thanks to this unity based on a human measure an idea of space was restored to me: I saw in this way and I believed, by means of the little man, that I was able to understand the world and space."[1] Ghirri felt that the little man accompanied him as he went about exploring fascinating unknown places in the external world, although he was never able to give him a face or a precise identity. Nonetheless, he was there in Ghirri's imagination, always looking, contemplating, and measuring the world. When Ghirri began to photograph, he continued to look at other contemporary photographs of landscapes, but he did not succeed in finding the little man in them. He comments: "Stupendous scenery, backdrops, and spaces increasingly deserted and incomprehensible followed one on the other, became fragmented, multiplied in an increasingly vertiginous way. But all of this seemed to me to be uninhabitable, or better, the places were dissolved."[2] The photographer's conclusion is that, with the disappearance of the little man, the possibility of representation had also disappeared, leaving instead only a "simulacrum" of places. To my mind, Ghirri's moving essay powerfully conveys the place of the human within the environment, natural or manmade as it may be. We are not here to dominate the external world, his words imply, but to look upon it, contemplate it, and measure it in relation to our own measure as "omini" or "little beings." As an environmental sensibility also makes clear, we are here to cherish and to protect the natural and nonhuman elements of our shared globe, or simulacra might well be all we shall have to leave to future generations.

1. "Quello dell'omino era uno stato di continua contemplazione del mondo, e la sua presenza nelle immagini conferiva a queste un fascino particolare. Non solo era il metro per misurare le meraviglie rappresentate, ma grazie a questa unità di misura umana mi restituiva l'idea dello spazio: io vedevo in questo modo e credevo, attraverso l'omino, di comprendere il mondo e lo spazio" (p. 44).
2. "Scenari stupendi, fondali, spazi sempre più deserti e incomprensibili si susseguivano, si frantumavano, si moltiplicavano in modo sempre più

This anthology gives abundant evidence of the importance of environmental and ecological themes to Italian literature of the last century and a half. In addition, it gives readers the opportunity to think about the modern Italian literary tradition from a new perspective in which dominant schools, trends, and names are much less important than are aspects of language, sensibility, and the ethos of both individual writers and a national collectivity. I am grateful to the editors for embarking on the relatively new journey along the path of environmental approaches to national and, eventually, global literary traditions, and particularly pleased that they chose to focus on modern Italian literature, which "naturally" lends itself to this approach. Delving into this collection, I am sure that readers will make many discoveries, as I have, about a land and a cultural inheritance that are all too often viewed as having been thoroughly discovered, albeit in stereotypes of Italian sun, song, and spaghetti. Nature and culture are both astoundingly complex realms within the small "boot" called the Italian nation, as this most welcome anthology makes clear.

The University of Chicago

vertiginoso. Ma tutto questo mi sembrava inabitabile, o meglio, i luoghi erano dissolti" (p. 44).

ACKNOWLEDGEMENTS

Our deepest thanks to all those who gave us assistance, encouragement, and inspiration during the long process of bringing this project to fruition. At the University of Nevada, Reno, Cheryll Glotfelty, Michael Branch, and Scott Slovic believed in our ability to write this book and provided invaluable help from start to finish; for all of their care, we are most grateful. Franco Manca generously lent his expertise on many authors, including Giuseppe Dessì, Pier Paolo Pasolini, and Corrado Govoni, and has long been a source of inestimable support. We are particularly grateful for the collaborative spirit of the community of faculty and graduate students at the Literature and Environment program at the University of Nevada, Reno, as well as that of many members of the Association for the Study of Literature and Environment (ASLE). Special thanks go to the editorial staff of *ISLE: Interdisciplinary Studies in Literature and Environment*, in whose pages the initial translations for the anthology first saw light. We owe gratitude to the many translators and writers who generously allowed us to include their work in this book. Among many, we give special thanks to Gianni Celati, Andrea Zanzotto, Tonino Guerra, Mario Rigoni Stern, Jolanda Insana, Mariella Bettarini, Luciana Notari, Monica Sarsini, Nicola Licciardello, Giuseppe Moretti, Khaled Fouad Allam and Studio Azzurro, Fulco Pratesi, Virginio Bettini, Charles Wright, William Weaver, Cinzia Sartini Blum, Lara Trubowitz, Jessie Bright, Martha King, and Umberto Mariani.

In particular, Anna thanks Loredana Lucarini, Giorgio Nebbia, and Massimo Scalia for their help in choosing many of the texts of the environmental writers, and Stash Luczkiw, Deberah Catts Petrini, and Rosemary Romiti for their help in translating them.

Patrick gives special thanks to Nida Caselli for her invaluable suggestions for many of the more stubborn sections of the translations, and for her help in tracking down elusive dialectal words; to George Hart, Chris Greger, and Erika Vals-ecchi for their helpful editorial suggestions; to Mark Long for the invitation to present a paper related to this book at the American Literature Association Conference in Los Angeles; to Gary Snyder for introducing him to Giuseppe Moretti and Nicola Licciardello; to Byron Smith, Kalmia Smith, Whitney Smith, Annie Blanton, Bridget Barron, and Vaughan Barron for their loving support and unfailing belief in him; and to Manuela Mariani for her many valuable editorial and graphic contributions to this book, and above all, for her love and wonderful companionship.

INTRODUCTION
by Patrick Barron

One of the most visible and significant developments in literary studies of the past ten years has been ecological literary criticism, or as it is now widely known, ecocriticism. Cheryll Glotfelty, in the introduction to *The Ecocriticism Reader: Landmarks in Literary Ecology*, defines ecocriticism as "the study of the relationship between literature and the physical environment," and states that "all ecological criticism shares the fundamental premise that human culture is connected to the physical world, affecting it and affected by it. Ecocriticism takes as its subject the interconnections between nature and culture, specifically the cultural artifacts of language and literature. As a critical stance, it has one foot in literature and the other on land; as a theoretical discourse, it negotiates between the human and the nonhuman."[1]

Since the early 1990s, which saw the establishment of the Association for the Study of Literature and Environment (ASLE), and the journal *ISLE: Interdisciplinary Studies in Literature and Environment*, ecocriticism has continued to emerge and develop.[2] Numerous anthologies and critical studies of environmental literature have been published, from John Elder

---

1. Cheryll Glotfelty, and Harold Fromm, eds., *The Ecocriticism Reader: Landmarks in Literary Ecology* (Athens: University of Georgia Press, 1996), xviii–xix. Scott Slovic ("Forum on Literatures of the Environment," *PLMA* 114 [October 1999]: 1089–1104) offers a similar, if slightly more specific definition, that ecocriticism "is the study of explicitly environmental texts by way of any scholarly approach or, conversely, the scrutiny of ecological implications and human-nature relations in any literary text, even texts that seem, at first glance, oblivious of the nonhuman world" (1102). His inclusive claim for ecocriticism rebuts the continuing, disparaging attitude that the study of environmental literature is limited to "hackneyed pastoral or wilderness texts" or driven by "nostalgic" yearnings.
2. The website for the journal *ISLE: Interdisciplinary Studies in Literature and Environment* is: <http://www.unr.edu/artsci/engl/isle>; the website for the

and Robert Finch's *The Norton Book of Nature Writing* and William Cronon's *Uncommon Ground: Rethinking the Human Place in Nature*, to Lawrence Buell's *The Environmental Imagination* and Karla Armbruster and Kathleen Wallace's *Beyond Nature Writing*.[3] An early critical focus on nature writing, especially on nonfiction personal essays and wilderness-oriented literature, has expanded to include feminist, multicultural, and "canonical" works in all genres — from poetry to the novel. In addition to analyzing writing traditionally associated with environmental literature, such as that by Gilbert White, Henry David Thoreau, Barry Lopez, and Annie Dillard, ecocritics have begun to examine the work of authors as diverse as Chaucer, Frederick Douglass, Larry Eigner, and Toni Morrison. With this enlargement and diversification of attention to environmental literature written in English, the need to extend ecocriticism beyond national borders has become increasingly apparent.

In his 1998 collection of critical studies of world environmental writing, *Literature of Nature: An International Sourcebook*,[4] Patrick Murphy argues that ecocriticism needs to become more comparative. Cross-cultural study is an important and necessary development for the continued vigor and growth of all environmental literary studies. Although extensive, *Literature of Nature* is a globally-scaled overview,

---

Association for the Study of Literature and Environment (ASLE) is: <http://www.asle.umn.edu>.

3. John Elderand Robert Finch, eds., *The Norton Book of Nature Writing* (New York: W. W. Norton, 1990); William Cronon, ed., *Uncommon Ground: Rethinking the Human Place in Nature* (New York: W. W. Norton, 1995); Lawrence Buell, *The Environmental Imagination: Thoreau, Nature Writing and the Formation of American Culture* (Cambridge, MA: Harvard University Press, 1995); Karla Armbruster and Kathleen Wallace, eds., *Beyond Nature Writing: Expanding the Boundaries of Ecocriticism.* (Charlottesville: University Press of Virginia, 2001). For a comprehensive list of recent publications in the field, please refer to the ASLE bibliography: <http://www.asle.umn.edu/pubs/biblio/biblio.html>, and the *ISLE* Bibliography of Recent Scholarship in Literature and Environment: <http://www.unr.edu/artsci/engl/isle/Bib.htm>.

4.Patrick Murphy, ed., *Literature of Nature: An International Sourcebook.* (Chicago: Fitzroy Dearborn, 1998).

and necessarily omits many national literatures, including Italian. An important next step in this international development of ecocriticism is the appearance of anthologies that represent the environmental literatures of specific countries, thereby helping to open cross-cultural windows. The comparative exchange at work in the study of international environmental literature counters the unfortunate tendency of American cultural criticism to operate in a kind of nationalist isolation. It also underlines the fact that actual environmental problems are no respecters of national boundaries and provides important comparative models that may generate new insights into specific national literatures and their accompanying landscapes. A key contribution then, of *Italian Environmental Literature: An Anthology* is to introduce a wide range of Italian environmental literature to English-speaking audiences, with the hope that it will spark comparative ecocritical study between Italian and the many English-language literary traditions, from American to British. Above all, we hope that the anthology will provide an intriguing taste of the rich Italian environmental literary tradition of the past century and a half.

Another contribution of this anthology is to provide illuminating sources of comparison within Italian literature to the uniquely American predilection for so clearly and passionately distinguishing between the wild and domestic. An increased sophistication in these matters is needed. Environmental literature from Italy — a country that has gone through several millennia of environmental upheaval, as well as the civilization-wilderness cycle numerous times — has much to offer U.S. audiences. Literary attention to urban nature and the human place *in* nature (as opposed to simply visiting it) is slowly gaining momentum. However, by focusing exclusively upon American literature, many studies that set out to analyze the intersections between nonhuman and human nature often ignore a wide variety of texts that express the deep familiarity with place evident in cultures that have remained rooted to vernacular landscapes for many centuries. Works by Italian writers such as Gianni Celati, Andrea Zanzotto, and Tonino Guerra, make clear that people change as their landscapes change, with one influencing the other.

When this process is slow, with relatively low levels of human transience and sudden environmental damage, the resulting layers in a landscape's palimpsest of human activity are interwoven in complex patterns. In these authors' work, the boundaries between the nonhuman and human become blurred and porous, making it difficult to imagine humankind as separate from the earth.

George Perkins Marsh's pioneering book *Man and Nature, or Physical Geography as Modified by Human Action*,[5] which is often cited as a cornerstone text of the U.S. environmental movement (and which helped ground work in a variety of fields, from forest ecology and cultural geography to hydrology and environmental literature) is based upon Marsh's observations of the Italian landscape during his long residence in Italy during the mid-nineteenth century. Examining the fall of the Roman Empire in the environmental context of deforestation, erosion, the abandonment of land, increasing technological power, greed, and simple ignorance, Marsh developed a complex analysis of the manifold, long-term relationships between developed nations and their respective landscapes. In Italy Marsh was able to identify and correlate the overlaying strata of landscapes that, by turns, had been well-cared for, ravaged, rehabilitated, and abandoned to the healing process of slow regeneration.

The selections in this anthology explore a wide range of Italian landscapes, wild and urban, mountainous and flat, northern and southern, and all characterized by the complex relationships of human beings and the land that so attracted and stimulated Marsh. Italy is rife with overlaying human and nonhuman signs of residence and alteration, even if at first glance particular landscapes appear to be the clear domain of either nature or culture. For example, in the most isolated corners of the high Abruzzese Apennines, which look more like the Arctic than the Mediterranean, it is not uncommon to stumble across the ruins of a shepherd's stone hut, or even

5. George Perkins Marsh, *Man and Nature or, Physical Geography as Modified by Human Action* [1864]. ed. by David Lowenthal (Cambridge, MA: Harvard University Press, 1965).

an abandoned medieval monastery, tucked into the cliffs in the fashion of Anasazi pueblos. Not far from the chaotic metropolis of Rome, in what from a distance appear to be largely uninhabited, forested hills, are innumerable Etruscan necropolises, ancient town sites, and labyrinths of abandoned roads cut deep into the volcanic earth. Conversely, Rome itself, with its polluted air and traffic jams, has one of the highest proportions of urban green space to built space in Italy; less than a hundred miles to the east lives the largest, and perhaps last population of Apennine brown bears, in the Parco Nazionale d'Abruzzo. The irregular field patterns in rural farming areas throughout Italy seem to meld into the chaotic, yet strangely ordered clusters of dwellings in nearby villages; rural and urban aspects of vernacular landscapes are distinctly linked through the overlapping, long-evolved spatial organizations of land and housing. It is particularly telling that in Italy there is plenty of beautiful "wilderness," but in the Italian language there is no equivalent of the word.[6]

Certainly Italy's relatively late entrance as a dominant international, economic, and industrial force in the mid-twentieth-century has by now brought many ills that threaten its environmental health, from air and water pollution to urban sprawl and the seemingly endless proliferation of the automobile. Many of its vernacular landscapes, from the small-scale farms of the Po Valley that have given way to corporate agriculture, to small agrarian villages swallowed up by the expansion of major cities such as Bologna, Milan, and Florence, are in danger of erasure. The landscapes of mountainous villages on marginal agricultural lands throughout the length of the Italian peninsula, many of which were abandoned during the large-scale migrations to large urban centers and foreign countries that took place throughout the twentieth century, are now verging on partial, if not complete, disappearance. Many local traditions, dialects, and practices are on the decline. On the other hand, with the abandonment of medium- to high-altitude farm

---

6. The term "wilderness" is best approximated in Italian by *regione selvaggia* (wild region), or *territorio incolto* (uncultivated territory).

and grazing lands, many endangered animals, such as the wolf and chamois, have regained habitat and are on the comeback. Numerous national parks, often styled in part on American models, have been established in the past two decades, from the Parco Nazionale della Majella in Abruzzo to the Parco Nazionale delle Foreste Casentinesi in Tuscany.

Clearly, the past fifty years have brought many social and environmental upheavals to Italy. The writers in this anthology, for the most part from the late nineteenth and the twentieth centuries, chronicle this recent, immense change and offer rare glimpses into specific cultures and locales where slow transformation of, and rootedness in, the land have long been the rule, but where massive and damaging alterations such as deforestation and overgrazing, from Roman times to the present day, have also occurred. Some of the authors, such as Corrado Alvaro and Nuto Revelli, reveal what it was like to live as a poor sharecropping peasant, or an indebted shepherd tending the cattle and sheep of the local petty nobility. Others, from Ignazio Silone and Carlo Levi to Italo Calvino and Pier Paolo Pasolini, describe the effects of the extensive pre- and post-fascist land "reforms," as well as the massive and chaotic proliferation of cities following the Second World War, especially of Rome and Milan. Still others, such as Laura Conti and Antonio Cederna, speak out against past and continuing environmental abuses, from air and water pollution to the destruction of wild animal habitats. It is uncertain what will become of either Tonino Guerra's beloved yet crumbling rural landscapes, his "abandoned places," or the (by now vastly extended) dystopian cityscapes of Italo Calvino's *Marcovaldo*. As in the rest of the industrialized and "developing" world, environmental crises in Italy continue largely unabated. However, in a country that has borne witness to innumerable human-caused shifts in environmental conditions, including many cycles of land through the stages of urban development and total abandonment to the elements (on both large and local scales), a certain wry and subtle environmental wisdom is at play in the work of many of Italy's best writers.

These authors carry, as do most of Italians up to the very present, deep connections to their particular native regions.

Fantasies of escape from what is regional or provincial, no matter how drab the present scene may appear, tend to end with disappointment, back at the point of departure. Neither pastoral nor urban idealism is an easy retreat. The oftentimes painful memories of severe poverty and the trials of sharecropping for many older, current, and former rural inhabitants are too recent to allow indulgence in Arcadian reveries. Likewise, most urban dwellers in Italy do not enjoy the easy mobility for which Americans are by now famous. In place of the disposable tract house is the fixed and small postwar apartment. Many Italians do not move often, and apart from the many immigrants of the early to mid-twentieth century (and some current-day, highly skilled, "temporary immigrants"), usually live most of their lives in their regions of birth. These patterns are changing, but have until recent times accounted for the survival of numerous local customs, dialects, and culinary traditions, despite widespread modernization and the threat of cultural homogenization due to, among other influences, the television.[7] There is an underlying rootedness, at once happily familiar yet uneasily enclosing, evident in all of the writers included here. This inescapable and binding connection, with pointed lessons for those of us less attached to any particular place, is eloquently expressed in the last two lines of Andrea Zanzotto's poem "Ormai" ("By now"):

Here all that's left is to wrap the landscape around the self and turn your back.[8]

7. For further reading on the cultural geography of Italy, see John A. Agnew, *Place and Politics in Modern Italy* (Chicago: University of Chicago Press, 2002); and Russell King, *The Industrial Geography of Italy* (New York: St. Martin's Press, 1985), and "Italy: From Sick Man to Rich Man of Europe," *Geography* 77.2 (1992): 153–69.
8.   *Qui non resta che cingersi intorno il paesaggio*
       qui volgere le spalle.
Translated from Andrea Zanzotto, *Dietro il paesaggio* (Milano: Mondadori, 1951), 18.

EDITORIAL CRITERIA

Our primary aim in choosing the selections in this anthology was to represent, as fully as possible within our limited space, the wide range of Italian environmental literature of the late nineteenth and twentieth centuries, by writers from regions throughout Italy, from the north to the south, including Sicily and Sardinia. We have broadly defined environmental literature as writing in any genre that explores and expresses the relationships between humanity and the landscape, and between the human and nonhuman. As a result, we have not restricted ourselves to any one genre, and have divided the anthology into the two major sections of poetry and prose, followed by a shorter, final section of environmental writing – work based in the sciences with the specific moral or political goal of raising ecological awareness. We have chosen these broad categories, rather than organizing the anthology into geographical, historical, or thematic sections, which would have more narrowly restricted our choices.

Some selections do not clearly fit any particular genre, such as Nuto Revelli's transcribed stories of the rural inhabitants of Piemonte or Dino Campana's "La Verna," which ranges wildly from poetry to poetic prose. We have placed these pieces where they seemed to fit most comfortably, with the understanding that genres are approximations that never exist in isolation. We felt it particularly important to include both famous and lesser-known authors, and have provided short introductions and notes to each with basic biographical, historical, and cultural background information.

Although the anthology begins with selections from the late nineteenth century, the roots of these and the later pieces that follow stretch back to the influence of much earlier writers, such as Lucretius and Virgil. It is upon these authors' work, as well as that of other ancient Roman and Greek writers, such as Varro, Tibulus, Columella, Theocritus, and Horace, that pastoral, and thus more generally environmental, traditions in Italian literature are based. From Giovanni Pascoli's early book of verse, *Myricae*, which takes its title from a line in Virgil's

Fourth Eclogue, to Eugenio Montale's and Andrea Zanzotto's own versions of (post-) modern eclogues, the presence of these ancient writers remains strong.

And yet, even if a clear attachment to native landscapes is readily apparent in many recent writers' work, neither an idealized belief in Arcadia nor an unwavering Epicurean faith in human liberation through the understanding of nature is a common feature. Although Pascoli certainly found succor in exploring the "sweet" fields of his native Romagna, themes of death and loss permeate his work; Lucretius's conviction that if nature could speak then it would affirm that "Death is a matter, then, of no concern," would most likely have fallen on deaf ears. Ignazio Silone's troubling depiction in *Fontamara* of rural life in Abruzzo during fascism recalls more Meliboeus's forced exile by Roman authorities than Tityrus's happy rural leisure in Virgil's *First Eclogue*. Montale's "Egloga" is by no means idyllic, but rather an exploration into aspects of our attachment to the earth that are dark, mysterious, and ultimately disturbing. Likewise, in Zanzotto's *IX Ecloge*, bucolic themes are turned on their heads. As Giuseppe Ungaretti observed, Zanzotto's landscape is "a country of idyllic enchantments disfigured by tragedy."[9] Within this tension, at once embracing and critical of past traditions, is an ongoing investigation of the deep relationship of humanity to particular landscapes, especially in the spirit of George Perkins Marsh's warning that humanity "has too long forgotten that the earth was given to [it] for usufruct alone, not for consumption, still less for profligate waste."[10] There may no longer be much confidence that a golden age ever existed (or will exist), but a continuing drive to revitalize and better understand our complex ecological relationships with the earth — often with a

---

9. Giuseppe Ungaretti, "Piccolo discorso sopra *Dietro il paesaggio* di Andrea Zanzotto," in *Vita d'un uomo: Saggi e interventi* (Milano: Mondadori, 1982), 699.
10. Marsh, *Man and Nature*, 36.

clear lineage to ancient writers' attempts to do the same — appears in the work of each author included in this book.

As with all anthologies, we were unfortunately forced to leave out many contemporary pieces, to say nothing of the many writers from before the late-nineteenth century, from Dante Alighieri and Ludovico Ariosto to Ugo Foscolo and Giacomo Leopardi.[11] Limitations on space, the difficulty of paring down certain works to the dimensions required for an anthology, and of course our own personal tastes and inclinations, all contributed to the long formative process represented by the final table of contents. We realize that there are myriad examples of any one genre of Italian environmental literature (from one or more centuries) that might fill numerous anthologies. In fact, it is our hope that *Italian Environmental Literature: An Anthology* helps to inspire other efforts in the collection and study of Italian environmental literature.

After a number of years of work in relative isolation, with similar ideas of editing an anthology in mind, it was only through a fortuitous meeting that this book began to take shape, thanks to Michael Branch, Cheryll Glotfelty, and Scott Slovic of the Literature and Environment Graduate Studies Program of the Department of English at the University of Nevada, Reno, who first introduced me to Anna, and then later provided much helpful advice and encouragement. When Anna and I initially compared lists of authors, we were pleasantly surprised to find many common names, thus confirming our private hunches that a loose-knit, yet clearly discernible, tradition of Italian environmental literature not only existed, but contained recognizable key figures. Since then, in our sifting, organizing, sorting, and consideration of many writers, we have identified myriad recurrent themes. These range from the seasons, as in Pascoli's and Gabriele D'Annunzio's celebrations of the rain and Luciana Notari's

---

11. For an excellent discussion of environmental, specifically arboreal, themes in the work of many early (Italian) writers, including Dante and Boccaccio, see Robert Pogue Harrison, *Forests: The Shadow of Civilization* (Chicago: University of Chicago Press, 1992).

winter landscapes, to animals, as in Mario Rigoni Stern's poignant meditations on crows, and in Guerra's elegy to anachronous oxen, sent to the butchers with little thanks for their long labor. And yet, none of these themes is representative of the anthology as a whole, which exhibits a very diverse collection of preoccupations concerning the relationships of humans and the land. If this book is similar to what Zanzotto refers to as "Un libro di Ecloghe" ("A book of eclogues"), then it is our hope that it both answers a few of his exclamatory questions (and raises more of the same kind):

A diagram of the "soul"? A land that is always
sprouting feathers and raving of green and of springtimes?
Jugglers and astrologers intent on escape,
on freeing butterflies among ethereal wheels?
Three hundred thousand parts joined along a knife blade,
the bitter jumbled machine which disrupts the future?[12]

We hope too, as in the final lines of Eugenio Montale's poem "L'anguilla" ("The eel"), that the selections provide both the inspiration and means to recognize the subtle and beautiful connections between humans, the land, sea, rivers, and animals — to catch a glimpse, in whatever form it takes, of

the green spirit that seeks
life where only
parching drought and desolation sting,
the spark that says
everything begins when everything seems
cinder and buried, twisted wood;
brief rainbow, iris,
twin to the one your lashes enclose

---

12. *Un diagramma dell'«anima»? Un paese che sempre*
    piumifica e vaneggia de verde e primavere?
    Giocolieri ed astrologi all'evasione intenti,
    a liberar farfalle tra le rote superne?
    Trecentomila parti congiunte a fil di lama,
    l'acre tricosa macchina il futuro disquama?
Translated from Andrea Zanzotto, *IX Ecloghe* (Milano: Mondadori, 1962), 7–8.

and you set gleaming, undiminished, amidst the sons
of men, immersed in your mud — can you
not see her as sister?[13]

NOTE ON THE TRANSLATIONS

Whenever possible, especially in the case of prose works, we
have used well-proven translations, such as William Weaver's,
Eric Mosbacher's, and Frances Frenaye's incomparable rendi-
tions of works by Italo Calvino, Ignazio Silone, and Carlo
Levi. Close in time and style to the heart of the original texts,
these translations have achieved a classic status of their own.
Others less well-known, such as Charles Wright's translation
of Dino Campana's "La Verna," are matchless for their sheer
virtuosity of language and form; they were extremely welcome
discoveries. With such texts, we felt it unnecessary to produce
additional translations. Many other works had simply never
been translated, such as the selections by Mario Rigoni Stern,
Carlo Cassola, Corrado Govoni, and Laura Conti.

We have presented the poetry below in facing dual-language
format. The generous addition of newly translated poetry is
based on the belief that poetry benefits from multiple trans-
lations, especially because its transformation into another
language is so approximate and interpretive. In each new
translation there is a fresh release of the concentrated energy
stored in the original language. Much is lost and much is

---

13. *l'anima verde che cerca*
    vita là dove solo
    morde l'arsura e la desolazione,
    la scintilla che dice
    tutto comincia quando tutto pare
    incarbonirsi, bronco seppellito;
    l'iride breve, gemella
    di quella che incastonano i tuoi cigli
    e fai brillare intatta in mezzo ai figli
    dell'uomo, immersi nel tuo fango, puoi tu
    non crederla sorella?

Translated from Eugenio Montale, *La bufera e altro* (Milano: Mondadori,
1957), 85–86.

gained in the rendering of any poem across linguistic bound-aries; however, a poem's impact and meanings, even through the inevitable alteration that translation brings, should come across as forcefully as possible in the "reincarnation" of the original. Likewise, multiple meanings must not be sacrificed for the sake of a mere "sound" line that minimizes potential readings. The music must come through, as well as the word play. I have done my best to enter into the "kinetics" of poetry, in agreement with Charles Olson's claim that "poetry must, at all points, be a high energy-construct and, at all points, an energy-discharge."[14]

The process of translating has thus been a long one, reserved for extended periods of concentration and pooled time and energy. Translating is at once maddening and extremely sat-isfying; certain words and phrases that seem intractable for months, will suddenly come clear in a burst of insight and inspiration. Others remain elusive. In the end, we hope that our work comes across in the spirit of Edith Hamilton's eloquent description of this labor of love:

> There are few efforts more conducive to humility than that of the translator trying to communicate an incom-municable beauty. Yet, unless we do try, something unique and never surpassed will cease to exist except in the libraries of a few inquisitive book lovers.[15]

14. Charles Olson, "Projective Verse" in *Selected Writings*, ed. by Robert Creeley (New York: New Directions, 1966), 16.
15. Edith Hamilton, Introduction to *Three Greek Plays* (New York: W.W. Norton, 1937), 16.

POETRY

GIOVANNI PASCOLI
(1855–1912)

Born in San Mauro di Romagna at mid-century, Giovanni Pascoli studied literature under Giosuè Carducci at the University of Bologna. In 1867 his father was mysteriously murdered, a tragedy followed shortly afterward by the deaths of a sister, his mother, and two brothers. These events would deeply affect Pascoli, inflicting a terrible wound, and sharply ending at an early age his sense of childhood innocence. Graduating from the university in 1882, Pascoli went on to teach Latin and Greek in a series of high schools and universities, and eventually, in 1906, replaced Carducci as professor of Italian literature in Bologna. His verse, written in both Latin and Italian, shows a deep absorption in the life of the country and strong ties to the rural landscapes of his youth. While recognizing in nature comfort, beauty, and tenderness, Pascoli's work is never far from the bewildering and painful interplay of life and death. The smallest creatures are directly related to the most distant creations in a poetic language dedicated to an ecstatic and mysterious relationship with physical reality. His early collection *Myricae* (Tamarisks) takes its title from a line in Virgil's *Fourth Eclogue*: "arbusta iuvant humilesque myricae" ("the small trees and humble tamarisks"). The poems of this collection are celebrations of the minute and particular, from hedges, flowers and rain to poplars, townsfolk and frogs. At the heart of much of his work is the concept of the "fanciullino," the poetic, childlike sensibility that exists in everyone, but is most present in children and poets. His other works include *Poemetti, Canti di Castelvecchio* (Songs from Castelvecchio), *Poemi conviviali* (Banquet songs), and *Nuovi poemetti*. His works of criticism on Dante include *Minerva oscura* (Dark Minerva), *Sotto il velame* (Under the veil), and *La mirabile visione* (The wondrous vision).

3

PIOGGIA *

Cantava al buio d'aia in aia il gallo.
E gracidò nel bosco la cornacchia:
il sole si mostrava a finestrelle.
Il sol dorò la nebbia della macchia,
poi si nascose; e piovve a catinelle.
Poi fra il cantare delle raganelle
guizzò su campi un raggio lungo e giallo.

Stupìano i rondinotti dell'estate
di quel sottile scendere di spille:
era un brusìo con languide sorsate
e chiazze larghe e picchi a mille a mille;
poi singhiozzi, e gocciar rado di stille:
di stille d'oro in coppe di cristallo.

VESPRO

Dal cielo roseo pullula una stella.

Una campana parla della cosa
col suo grave dan dan dalla badia;
onde tra i pioppi tini in color rosa
suona un continuo scalpicciar per via:
passa una lunga e muta compagnia
con fasci di trifoglio e lupinella.

Una fanciulla cuce ed accompagna,
canterellando, dalla nera altana,
un canto che s'alzò dalla campagna,
quando nel cielo tacque la campana:
s'alzò da un olmo solo in una piana,
da un olmo nero che da sé stornella.

* All poems in this section are from Giovanni Pascoli, *Myricae* (Livorno: Giusti, 1903).

4

RAIN

In the dark from yard to yard sang the cock.
And in the woods cawed the rook:
the sun showed itself in patches through the clouds.
It gilded the fog of the maquis,
then hid itself; the rain crashed down.
Then amidst the song of tree frogs
flashed a long yellow beam over the fields.

Summer swallows were astonished at
that thin descent of needles:
it was a buzzing with languid draughts
and wide patches and thousands of patterings;
then drizzlings, slow drippings of droplets:
of golden droplets in crystal bowls.

VESPERS

From the rose sky surges a star.

A bell speaks of the thing
with its grave *dan dan* from the abbey;
waves amidst the poplars tinted rose,
a continuous tramping sounds on the road:
a long and silent company passes by
with bundles of clover and sainfoin.

A young woman sews and accompanies,
singing softly, from the black terrace,
a song which rises from the countryside
when in the sky the bell falls silent:
it arises from a solitary elm in a field,
from a black elm that sings by itself.

LA DOMENICA DELL'ULIVO

Hanno compiuto in questo dì gli uccelli
il nido (oggi è la festa dell'ulivo)
di foglie secche, radiche, fuscelli;

quel sul cipresso, questo su l'alloro,
al bosco, lungo il chioccolo d'un rivo,
nell'ombra mossa d'un tremolìo d'oro.

E covano sul musco e sul lichene
fissando muti il cielo cristallino,
con improvvisi palpiti, se viene
un ronzìo d'ape, un vol di maggiolino.

SERA D'OTTOBRE

Lungo la strada vedi su la siepe
ridere a mazzi le vermiglie bacche:
nei campi arati tornano al presepe
                    tarde le vacche.

Vien per la strada un povero che il lento
passo tra foglie stridule trascina:
nei campi intuona una fanciulla al vento:
                    Fiore di spina!

THE SUNDAY OF THE OLIVE TREE

Today the birds have finished
the nest (today is the festival of the olive)
of dry leaves, stalks, twigs;

that on the cypress, this on the laurel,
in the woods, along the gurgling of a streambank,
in the shade, a shimmering of gold plays.

They nest on moss and lichen
silently watching the crystalline sky
with sudden heartbeats, for the approaching
buzzing of bees, the flight of a beetle.

OCTOBER EVENING

Along the road you see on the hedge
red berries laughing in clusters:
across plowed fields the cows are slowly
                    returning to the manger.

Down the road comes a poor man who drags his slow
step through the rustling leaves:
In the fields a young girl is singing to the wind:
                    "Flower of thorns!"

ARANO

Al campo, dove roggio nel filare
qualche pampano brilla, e dalle fratte
sembra la nebbia mattinal fumare,

arano: a lente grida, uno le lente
vacche spinge; altri semina; un ribatte
le porche con sua marra pazïente;

ché il passero saputo in cor già gode,
e il tutto spia dai rami irti del moro;
e il pettirosso: nelle siepi s'ode
il suo sottil tintinno come d'oro.

NOVEMBRE

Gemmea l'aria, il sole così chiaro
che tu ricerchi gli albicocchi in fiore,
e del prunalbo l'ordorino amaro
    senti nel cuore...

Ma secco è il pruno, e le stecchite piante
di nere trame segnano il sereno,
e vuoto il cielo, e cavo al piè sonante
    sembra il terreno.

Silenzio, intorno: solo, alle ventate,
odi lontano, da giardini ed orti,
di foglie un cader fragile. È l'estate,
    fredda, dei morti.

THEY ARE PLOWING

In the field, where the vines
are shining red in the rows, and from the thickets
the morning fog seems to smoke upward,

they are plowing: shouting slowly, one drives
the slow cows ahead; others sow; one turns down
the edges with his patient hoe;

and the knowing sparrow is glad in his heart,
spying all from the rough branches of the mulberry;
and the robin: one hears his light song
jingling like gold in the hedges.

NOVEMBER

Crystalline air, the sun so clear
that you seek the flowering apricots,
and from the prune the bitter scent
                        you feel in the heart…

But dry is the prune, and the stiffened plants
in black plots underscore the fair weather,
and empty the sky, and hollow to the pounding foot
                        seems the ground.

Silence, all around: alone, to the gusts,
far-off songs, from gardens and orchards,
of leaves a fragile falling. It is the summer,
                        cold, of the dead.

Translations by Patrick Barron

GABRIELE D'ANNUNZIO
(1863–1938)

Poet, novelist, dramatist, journalist, soldier, and political fire-brand, Gabriele D'Annunzio was a controversial, complex, and highly influential figure. Often associated with the European Decadence, his enthusiastic welcoming of early fascism, and his zealous interpretations of Nietzsche's concept of the "superman," D'Annunzio's fame as a public figure has much diminished since the early twentieth century. His importance to Italian letters, however, remains great, especially in his ground-breaking experimentation with language, his two early masterworks, *Canto novo* (New song) and *Alcyone* (Halcyon), and books such as *La figlia di Iorio* (The daughter of Iorio) and *Il piacere* (The child of pleasure). Untangling the "barbarian" from the "decadent," the man of action from the aesthete in D'Annunzio is a bewildering task. He was born in Pescara on the coast of Abruzzo — a mountainous region whose rugged landscapes and ancient customs greatly influenced much of his literary production. Later he studied in Cicognini di Prato and Rome, fought in the First World War, and achieved a measure of fame in 1919 when with a small force he seized Fiume and remained as dictator until 1921. D'Annunzio's first works of verse began to appear in the late 1870s and show an aesthetic mysticism based on a mix of sensual and naturalistic inspiration. His best poems search out a direct communication with the vital energies of nature. This communion, a desire to dissolve the human self into the external environment, requires as much a physical as a spiritual connection to the very things of the earth. The force of this harmonious, entangled stream of human and nonhuman life tears apart traditional verse structures and produces the musical, unrefined, and evocative poetic forms for which D'Annunzio is best known.

11

LA PIOGGIA NEL PINETO*

*Taci. Su le soglie
del bosco non odo
parole che dici
umane; ma odo
parole più nuove
che parlano gocciole e foglie
lontane.
Ascolta. Piove
dalle nuvole sparse.
Piove su le tamerici
salmastre ed arse,
piove su i pini
scagliosi ed irti,
piove su i mirti
divini,
su le ginestre fulgenti
di fiori accolti,
su i ginepri folti
di coccole aulenti,
piove su i nostri volti
silvani,
piove su le nostre mani
ignude,
su i nostri vestimenti
leggieri,
su i freschi pensieri
che l'anima schiude
novella,
su la favola bella
che ieri
t'illuse, che oggi m'illude,
o Ermione.*

* All poems in this section are from Gabriele D'Annunzio, *Alcyone* (Verona: Arnoldo Mondadori, 1927).

THE RAIN IN THE PINEWOOD

Hush. On the edge
of the wood I don't hear
words that you would call
human, but hear
newer words
that speak drops and leaves
far away.
Listen. It's raining
from scattered clouds.
It's raining on the tamarisks,
dry and salty,
raining on the pines,
scaly and bristly,
raining on the sacred
myrtle,
on the gleaming gorse
of clustered flowers,
on the thick junipers
of redolent berries,
raining on our sylvan
faces,
raining on our bare
hands,
on our light
clothes,
on the new thoughts
that the freshened soul
puts forth,
on the excellent fable
that yesterday
deluded you, as today deludes me,
O Hermione.[1]

Odi? La pioggia cade
su la solitaria
verdura
con un crepitìo che dura
e varia nell'aria
secondo le fronde
più rade, men rade.
Ascolta. Risponde
al pianto il canto
delle cicale
che il pianto australe
non impaura,
né il ciel cinerino.
E il pino
ha un suono, e il mirto
altro suono, e il ginepro
altro ancóra, stromenti
diversi
sotto innumerevoli dita.
E immersi
noi siam nello spirito
silvestre,
d'arborea vita viventi;
e il tuo volto ebro
è molle di pioggia
come una foglia,
e le tue chiome
auliscono come
le chiare ginestre,
o creatura terrestre
che hai nome
Ermione.

Ascolta, ascolta. L'accordo
delle aeree cicale
a poco a poco

Do you hear? The rain is falling
on a solitude
of green
with a rustling that lasts
and varies in the air
as the leaves
are more sparse, less sparse.
Listen. Responding
to the rain is the song[2]
of the cicadas
whom no southern rain
frightens,
nor ashen sky.
And the pine
has a sound, and the myrtle
another sound, and the juniper
yet another, instruments
all distinct
under innumerable fingers.
And we are immersed
in the sylvan
spirit,
of animate arboreal life;
and your enraptured face
is wet with the rain[3]
like a leaf,
and your hair[4]
is redolent as
the bright junipers,
O terrestrial creature
whose name is
Hermione.

Listen, listen. The singing
of the airy cicadas
little by little

15

più sordo
si fa sotto il pianto
che cresce;
ma un canto vi si mesce
più roco
che di laggiù sale,
dall'umida ombra remota.
Più sordo e più fioco
s'allenta, si spegne.
Sola una nota
ancor trema, si spegne,
risorge, trema, si spegne.
Non s'ode voce del mare.
Or s'ode su tutta la fronda
crosciare
l'argentea pioggia
che monda,
il croscio che varia
secondo la fronda
più folta, men folta.
Ascolta.
La figlia dell'aria
è muta; ma la figlia
del limo lontana,
la rana,
canta nell'ombra più fonda,
chi sa dove, chi sa dove!
E piove su le tue ciglia,
Ermione.

Piove su le tue ciglia nere
sì che par tu pianga
ma di piacere; non bianca
ma quasi fatta virente,
par da scorza tu esca.
E tutta la vita è in noi fresca

grows softer
under the rain
that grows stronger;
but a hoarser song
mixes in
and rises from down below,
from the wet and distant shadows.
More muffled and more faint
it slackens, it dies out.
One note only
still trembles, dies out,
rises, trembles, dies out.
The voice of the sea is not heard.
But over the leafy fronds
the pattering is heard
of silver rain
that cleans,
a pattering that varies
as the leaves
are more sparse, less sparse.
Listen.
The daughter of the air
is mute; but the daughter
of the distant mud,
the frog,
sings in the deepest shadows,
who knows where, who knows where!
And it is raining on your eyelashes,
Hermione.

It is raining on your black eyelashes
so that it seems you are crying
but out of pleasure; not white
but almost made green,
you seem to emerge out of bark.
And in us all life is fresh,

aulente,
il cuor nel petto è come pèsca
intatta,
tra le pàlpebre gli occhi
son come polle tra l'erbe,
i denti negli alvèoli
son come mandorle acerbe.
E andiam di fratta in fratta,
or congiunti or disciolti
(e il verde vigor rude
ci allaccia i mallèoli
c'intrica i ginocchi)
chi sa dove, chi sa dove!
E piove su i nostri volti
silvani,
piove su le nostre mani
ignude,
su i nostri vestimenti
leggieri,
su i freschi pensieri
che l'anima schiude
novella,
su la favola bella
che ieri
m'illuse, che oggi t'illude,
o Ermione.

DITIRAMBO III

O grande Estate, delizia grande tra l'alpe e il mare,
tra così candidi marmi ed acque così soavi
nuda le aeree membra che riga il tuo sangue d'oro
odorate di aliga di résina e di alloro,
laudata sii,
o voluttà grande nel cielo nella terra e nel mare
e nei fianchi del fauno, o Estate, e nel mio cantare,

redolent,
the heart in the breast is like a peach,
still growing,
between their lids the eyes
are like pools of water in grass,
the teeth in their sockets
like unripe almonds.
And we go from thicket to thicket,
now joined, now apart
(and the rough green vigor
binds our ankles
entangles our knees)
who knows where, who knows where!
And it is raining on our sylvan
faces,
raining on our bare
hands,
on our light
clothing,
on the new thoughts
that the freshened soul
puts forth,
on the excellent fable
that yesterday
deluded you, as today deludes me,
O Hermione.

DITHYRAMB III

To you, great Summer, great delight of the alps and sea,
between marbles so candid and waters so sweet,
nude, your airy limbs pulsing with golden blood
redolent of seaweed, of resin and of laurel,
praise be,
O great pleasure in the sky, in the earth and in the sea
and in the flanks of the faun, O Summer, and in my song,

laudata sii
tu che colmasti de' tuoi più ricchi doni il nostro giorno
e prolunghi su gli oleandri la luce del tramonto
a miracol mostrare!

Ardevi col tuo piede le silenti erbe marine,
struggevi col tuo respiro le piogge pellegrine
tra così canditi marmi ed acque così soavi
alzata; e grande eri, e pur delle più tenui vite
gioiva la tua gioia, e tutto vedeva la tua pupilla
grande: le frondi delle selve e i fusti delle navi,
e la ragia colare, maturarsi nelle pine
le chiuse mandorlette e la scaglia che le sigilla
pender nel fulvo, e l'orme degli uccelli nell'argilla
dei fiumi, l'ombre dei voli su le sabbie saline
vedea, le sabbie rigarsi come i palati cavi,
al vento e all'onda farsi dolci come l'ìnguine e il pube
amorosamente,
imitar l'opre dell'api,
disporsi a mo' dei favi
in alveoli senza miele,
e l'osso della seppia tra le brune carrube
biancheggiar sul lido, tra le meduse morte
brillar la lisca nitida, la valva
tra il sughero ed il vimine variar la sua iri,
pallida di desiri la nube
languir di rupe in rupe
lungh'essi gli aspri capi
qual molle donna che si giaccia co' suoi schiavi,
scorrere la gómena nella rossa
cùbia, sorgere la negossa
viva di palpitanti pinne, curvarsi al peso vivo
la pertica, la possa
dei muscoli gonfiarsi nelle braccia vellute,
una man rude
tendere la scotta,

praise be
to you who have heaped with your richest gifts our day
and over the oleanders stretch the sunset out
showing a miracle!

You scorched with your foot the silent sea grass,
you dried with your breath the wandering rains
between marbles so candid and waters so sweet
arisen; and you were huge, and even the tiniest lives
enjoyed your joy, and your enormous eye saw
everything: the fronds of the forests and the boles of ships,
and the resin flowing, maturing in the pines,
the enclosed almond seeds and the scales sealing them
hanging and tawny, and the tracks of birds in the clay
of the rivers, you saw the shadows of flights over the salty sands
ridged like hollow palates,
pleasant to wind and wave like groin and pubis
lovingly,
sands imitating the work of bees,
arranged like honeycombs
in honeyless hives,
and the cuttlefish bone among brown carobs
whitening on the shore, among dead medusae
the bright fishbone gleaming, the shellfish
iridescent among cork and osiers,
the clouds pale with desire
languishing from crag to crag
along which the rough capes
like a voluptuous woman lying down with her slaves,
and the cable running through the red
hawsepipe, the fishing net rising
alive with pulsating fins, the pole
bending with the living weight, the strength
of muscles swelling on shaggy arms,
a rough hand
tending to the sheet,

al garrir della vela forte
piegarsi il bordo come la gota del nuotatore,
la scìa mutar colore,
tutto il Tirreno in fiore
tremolar come alti paschi al fiato di ponente.

O Estate, Estate ardente,
quanto t'amammo noi per t'assomigliare,
per gioir teco nel cielo nella terra e nel mare,
per teco ardere di gioia su la faccia del mondo,
selvaggia Estate
del respiro profondo,
figlia di Pan diletta, amor del titan Sole,
armoniosa,
melodiosa,
che accordi il curvo golfo sonoro
come la citareda
accorda la sua cetra,
dolore di Demetra
che di te si duole
ne' solstizii sereni
per Proserpina sua perduta primavera!
O fulva fiera,
o infiammata leonessa dell'Etra,
grande Estate selvaggia,
libidinosa,
vertiginosa,
tu che affochi le reni,
che incrudisci la sete,
che infurii gli estri,
Musa, Gorgóne,
tu che sciogli le zone,
che succingi le vesti,
che sfreni le danze,
Grazia, Baccante,
tu ch'esprimi gli aromi,

22

to the fluttering of the sail,
the ship's side bending like a swimmer's cheek,
the wake changing color,
all the Tyrrhenian in flower
shimmering like high pastures in the breath of the west wind.

O Summer, burning Summer,
we loved you enough to become like you,
to be enraptured with you in the sky, in the earth and in the sea,
to joyously burn with you on the face of the earth,
wild Summer
of deep breath,
beloved daughter of Pan, love of the titan Sun,
harmonious,
melodious,
who tunes the curving, sonorous gulf
as the musician
tunes his lyre,
the sorrow of Demeter[5]
who for you grieves
in the serene solstices
for Persephone her lost spring![6]
O tawny beast,
O flaming lioness of the Ethers,
giant, wild Summer,
libidinous,
vertiginous,
you who fire the loins,
who aggravate the thirst,
who infuriate the passions,
Muse, Gorgon,[7]
you who loosen the belts,
who gird the garments up
who unleash the dances,
Grace, Baccante,
you who express the scents,

tu che afforzi i veleni,
tu che aguzzi le spine,
Esperide, Erine,
deità diversa,
innumerevole gioco dei vènti
dei flutti e delle sabbie,
bella nelle tue rabbie
silenziose, acre ne' tuoi torponi,
o tutta bella ed acre in mille nomi,
fatta per me dei sogni che dalla febbre del mondo
trae Pan quando su le canne sacre
delira (delira il sogno umano),
divina nella schiuma del mare e dei cavalli,
nel sudor dei piaceri,
nel pianto aulente delle selve assetate,
o Estate, Estate,
io ti dirò divina in mille nomi,
in mille laudi
ti loderò se m'esaudi,
se soffri che un mortal ti domi,
che in carne io ti veda,
ch'io mortal ti goda sul letto dell'immensa piaggia
tra l'alpe e il mare,
nuda le fervide membra che riga il tuo sangue d'oro
odorate di aliga di résina e di alloro!

you who strengthen the poisons,
you who sharpen the spines,
Herperis, Erinys,[8]
diverse deity,
endless game of the winds
of the waves and of the sands,
beautiful in your silent
rages, acrid in your torpors,
O beautiful and acrid in a thousand names,
made for me of the dreams Pan pulls from the feverish world[9]
when he raves on his sacred reeds
(the raving of human dreams),
divine in the spume of the sea and of horses,
in the sweat of the pleasures,
in the redolent plaint of the thirsty pines,
O Summer, Summer,
I will call you divine in a thousand names,
in a thousand praises
I will praise you if you answer my prayers,
if you suffer a mortal to master you,
to see you in the flesh,
to permit me, a mortal, to relish you on the bed of the
    immense shore
between the alps and the sea,
nude, your fervent limbs pulsing with golden blood
redolent of seaweed, of resin and of laurel!

Translations by Patrick Barron

CORRADO GOVONI
(1884–1965)

Born in Ferrara to a farming family, and resident in Rome for many years, Corrado Govoni was entirely self-educated. He first took part in the crepuscular movement, and then later futurism, contributing to Filippo Tommaso Marinetti's *Poesia*, as well as avant-garde journals, such as *Lacerba* and *La Voce*. While a writer of novels, plays, and short stories, Govoni was above all a poet, publishing numerous collections from *Le fiale* (The phials) in 1903 to *I canti del puro folle* (Songs of pure madness) in 1959. One of the most characteristic features of his poetry is a predilection for concentrated, impressionistic images, often of landscapes. He was particularly interested in the visual content of words, or the phonic simulation of the seen. Rich in colors, shadows, and lights, his poetry challenges the many ways in which we observe — and in large part invent — our surroundings.

PAESAGGIO *

La casina si specchia in un laghetto,
pieno d'iris, da l'onde di crespone,
tutta chiusa nel serico castone
d'un giardino fragrante di mughetto.

Il cielo dentro l'acque un aspetto
assume di maiolica lampone;
e l'alba esprime un'incoronazione
di rose mattinali dal suo letto.

Sul limitare siede una musmè
trapuntando d'insetti un paravento
e d'una qualche rara calcedonia:

vicino, tra le lacche ed i netzkè,
rosseggia sul polito pavimento,
in un vaso giallastro una peonia.

CREPUSCOLO FERRARESE †

Il mao si stira sopra il davanzale
sbadigliando nel vetro lagrimale.

Nella muscosa pentola d'argilla
il geranio rinfresca i fiori lilla.

La tenda della camera sciorina
le sue rose di fine mussolina.

I ritratti che sanno tante storie
son disposti a ventaglio di memorie.

Nella bonaccia della psiche ornata

---

*From Corrado Govoni, Le fiale (Firenze: Lumachi, 1903).
†From Corrado Govoni, Fuochi d'artifizio (Palermo: Ganguzza-Lajosa, 1905).

LANDSCAPE

The little house is reflected in a lake
full of irises and wide rippled waves,
all enclosed in the silky setting
of a garden redolent of lily of the valley.

The sky inside the waters becomes red
as raspberry, bright as majolica;
and the dawn displays a coronation
of morning roses from its bed.

On the edge sits a geisha
embroidering a fan with insects
and a rare form of chalcedony:

Nearby, among the lacquers and the netsuke,
on the polished floor in a yellowish vase,
a peony is reddening.

FERRARESE TWILIGHT

The cat stretches himself on the windowsill
yawning in the teary glass.

In the mossy clay pot
a geranium refreshes the lilacs.

The curtain in the room hangs out
its roses of fine muslin.

The portraits that know many stories
are arranged to fan the memory.

In the calm of the psyche[10]

il lume sembra una nave affondata.

Sul tetto d'una prossima chiesuloa
sopra una pertica una ventarola

agita l'ali come un uccelletto
che in un laccio pei piedi sia stretto.

Altissimi, per l'aria, dai bastioni
capriolano fantastici aquiloni.

Le rondini bisbigliano nel nido.
Un grillo dentro l'orto fa il suo strido.

Il celo chiude nella rete d'oro
la terra come un insetto canoro.

Dentro lo specchio, tra giallastre spume
ritorna a galla il polipo del lume.

La tristezza si appoggia a una spalliera
mentre le chiese cullano la sera.

LA PRIMAVERA DEL MARE*

Anche il mare ha la sua primavera:
rondini all'alba, lucciole alla sera.
Ha i suoi meravigliosi prati
di rosa e di viola,
che qualcuno invisibile, là, falcia
e ammucchia il fieno
in cumuli di fresche nuvole.
Si perdon le correnti
come pallide strade
tra le siepi dei venti,
da cui sembra venire, nella pioggia,
come un amaro odore

*Corrado Govoni, *L'inaugurazione della primavera* (Firenze: La Voce, 1915).

30

the light seems a sunken ship.

On the roof of a nearby church
a weathercock on its perch

ruffles its wings like a small bird
whose feet are caught in a noose.

High above, in the air, from sticks
spin fantastic kites.

The swallows whisper in their nests.
A cricket in the garden strikes up its cry.

The sky encloses in a golden net
the earth like a singing insect.

Inside the mirror, amidst yellowish spume
the polyp of light floats to the surface.

Sadness leans back into the seatback
while the churches lull the evening.

THE SPRINGTIME OF THE SEA

The sea too has its springtime:
sparrows in the dawn, fireflies at night.
It has its marvelous
pink and violet meadows,
in which someone invisible, mows
and stacks the hay
in heaps of fresh clouds.
The currents disperse
like pale roads
amidst the hedges of the winds,
from which seems to come, in the rain,
the bitter odor

di biancospino in fiore.
E certo, nella valle più lontana,
un pastore instancabil tonde
il suo gregge infinito di onde,
tanta è la lana
che viene a spumeggiare sulla riva.
Verdognolo e lillastro, come l'arcobaleno
gemmeo elastico refrigerante:
d'accordo con il cielo
profondo arioso concavo specchiante,
come il cristallo con il fiore;
tutto abbandoni e improvvise malinconie,
come il primo amore.
Così fresco ed azzurro,
come se trasparissero
dalle sua limpidità
le sue tacite foreste
sottomarine
avvinghiate di alghe serpentine;
quest'edera senza foglie;
scorse dai freddi scivolii
di pesci di maiolica e d'argento,
alati come uccelli muti,
tra i coralli irrigiditi:
questi pesci sempre fioriti.
Son le rondine, fisse, le conchiglie.
E le lucciole, enormi, son le seppie morte,
lanterne sorde
di palombari annegati,
fari di naufraghi pericolati.
Una barca, con un'immensa vela,
sembra qualche straccione
fermo in una crocevia sotto l'ombrello
in attesa che passi l'acquazzone.

of hawthorn in flower.
And surely, in the farthest valley,
an untiring shepherd shears
his endless flock of waves;
much is the wool
that foams upon the shore.
Pale green and violet, as a rainbow
gem-like elastic chilling:
in harmony with the sky
deep airy concave reflective,
like crystal with flowers;
all forlorn and sudden melancholy,
like first love.
So refreshing and blue,
as if gleaming forth
from its limpidity
its silent underwater
forests
grasped by serpentine algae;
this ivy without leaves;
slid through by cold glidings
of fish of majolica and silver,
winged like mute birds,
amidst stiffened coral:
these fish always in flower.
The swallows, fixed, are the shells.
And the fireflies, enormous, are the dead cuttlefish,
deaf lanterns
of drowned divers,
beacons of precarious shipwrecks.
A boat, with an immense sail,
seems an enormous rag
halted at a crossroads under an umbrella
waiting for the downpour to pass.

Translations by Patrick Barron

DINO CAMPANA
(1885–1932)

The "wild man" of Italian poetry, Dino Campana is best known for his 1914 book *Canti Orfici* (Orphic songs), which he self-published and hawked in Florentine and Bolognese cafes. In this work, a delirious, poetic journey back to his homeland, Campana explores sight, space, and primordial existence in the language of familiar objects and scenes exploded into dizzying visions. His ecstatic revelations of the intertwinings of soul and body, of the physical world and the spirit, untiringly search out the authentic and real — rooted in a musical and visual poetic exploration of his native Tuscany, and of bordering Romagna. Campana is one of the earliest poets to delve into and yet also transcend the chaotic existence of industrialized society — a dexterity of thought, which is constantly at work in his wanderings through the countryside and towns of the northern Apennines. After a series of breakdowns, in 1918 Campana was permanently committed to an asylum, where he died in 1932.

LA VERNA *

I. LA VERNA (DIARY)

15 September (on the road to Campigna)

Three girls and a donkey on the mule track coming down the mountain. Complimentary wisecracks from the road workers.

---

*All texts in this section are from Dino Campana, *Orphic Songs*, trans. by Charles Wright (Oberlin, Ohio: Oberlin College, 1984).

The donkey who rolls in the dirt. Laughter. Mountain profanities. The rocks and the river.

. . . .

Castagno, 17 September

The Falterona is still wrapped in fog. I can only see rocky run-offs that vein its sides, then lose themselves in a fog-sky which alternating waves of sunlight fail to thin out. Rain has made the gray mountain a slick darkness. In front of the fountain the people of Castagno have been sitting a long time now waiting for the sun, weighed down by the long night of rain in their flooded hovels. A girl in broken shoes walks by saying submissively, "one day the flooding will carry us all away." The swollen stream in its dark noise remarks on all this misery. I look on oppressed at the steep rocks of the Falterona: I will have to climb, and climb. In the presbytery I find a tablet to Andrea del Castagno. The type of the local girls suddenly strikes me: wooden face, deep set dark eyes, cave-like dark tones on faded yellowish tones: contrasted with such a simple antique Tuscan grace in the profile and neck as to render them quite pleasant! perhaps. How different the evening at Campigna: how mystical its landscape, how beautiful the poverty of its hovels! How enchantingly the stars rose for me in the sky and how fateful: against the distant backdrop of the web of valleys the barbarous valley disappeared in, the same mist the restless stream came out of dark with meaning! I felt the stars flow up and settle back luminously on that mystery. Raising my eyes to the highest peak of the rock mountain cut in a toothy semicircle onto the violet twilight, solitary and magnificent arc strained to the breaking point by catastrophe under the restless piling up of rocks out to the ambush of the infinite, I was not ravished I was not ravished to discover lights more lights in the sky. And, while time was disappearing in vain for me, a song, the long waves of a triple chorus rising then flung out from the rocks, restrained at last on the golden borders of night by their own echo which sunk them again

35

into the strong breast of the landscape pushing them back and away, lost forever.

The song was brief: a pause, a sudden and mysterious comment, and the mountain again took on its catastrophic dream. The brief song: the three young girls had expressed desperately, in a millenary cadenza, their brief, dark pain and were then silenced in the night. All the windows in the valley were lit up. I was alone.

The fog has lifted: I go out. The good, homey smell of lavender and washing that small Tuscan villages have makes me happy again. The church has a portico of small squared columns made of whole stones, bare and elegant, simple and austere, truly Tuscan. Among the cypresses I notice other porticos. On one hillside a cross opens its arms to the vast flanks of the Falterona, dark booty, which in turn lays bare its own rocky structure. The grasses burn in the graveyard with a pale red-ochre flame.

— On the Falterona (Giogo)

The Falterona green black and silver: the formal sadness of the Falterona that swells up like an enormous petrified breaker, that leaves behind a cavalry of cracks and splits and chinks in the rock down to the sandy boiling up again of hills there on the Tuscan plain: Castagno, little stone houses scattered about half-way up the mountain, windows I saw lit up: thus to the creatures of this cubist landscape, in a light barely gilded by the inner eye among thin vegetable-like hairs the rectangle of the head in a line occultly fine out of the delicate features the smile of the blonde Ceres shows through: the clear gray eyes limpid under the black line of the eyebrow: sweetness of the lip line, serenity of the eyebrow memory of the Tuscan poetry that once was.

(You had already understood O Leonardo, O divine primitive!)

— Campigna, forest of the Falterona

(The quadrangular houses made out of living stone by the Lorenas remain empty, and the avenue of linden trees gives a romantic overtone to the solitude where the mighty of the earth have built their homes. Evening slides down from the Alpine crest and collects itself in the green bosom of the spruce trees.)

From the avenue of linden trees I watched a solitary star catch fire on the Alpine spur of rock and the ancient forest shadows coagulate and the deep-ditched rustlings of silence. From the sharp peak in the sky, over the drowsy mystery of the forest going down the avenue of lindens I spotted my old friend the moon who rose up in a new red dress of coppery smoke: and I greeted my friend again without surprise as though the savage depths of the crag were waiting for her to surge up out of the unknown landscape. Meanwhile I went on down the avenue of lindens protected from all enchantments while you rose and disappeared my sweet friend moon, a solitary and smoky vapor over the barbaric clefts and slices. And I didn't look up again at your strange face but wanted to keep on walking a long time down the avenue if I had heard your red aurora in the breathing of the night life of the forest.

Stia, 20 September

In the hotel an old Milanese gentleman talks of his distant love affairs to a white-haired lady who has a face like a baby's. Calmly she explains the vagaries of the heart to him: he is still amazed and becomes distressed: here in this old village enclosed in the woods. I have left Castagno: I climbed the Falterona slowly following the course of the fast-flowing stream: I rested in the angelic purity of the high mountain glazed over and brilliant from dark shadings left from the recent rains, sparkling against the sky in the clear and luminous contours that once made me dream standing in front of the

37

hills in old paintings. I stopped in the houses of Campigna. I went down interminable valleys wild and deserted seeing the sudden background of a promised landscape, a distant and isolated castle: and at the end Stia, white and elegant among the greenery, melodious with her serene castles: the first greeting of happy life in a new town: the poetry of Tuscany still alive in the piazza sonorous with tranquil voices, watched over by the old castle: the ladies on their balconies leaning their pure profiles languidly in the evening: the hour of grace in the day, of rest and forgetfulness.

Outside all is quiet: the brotherly conversation of the gentleman continues:

Comme deux ennemis rompus
Que leur haine ne soutient plus
Et qui laissent tomber leurs armes!

21 September (near La Verna)

I saw a turtle dove break off from the mystical solitudes and glide toward the open immensity of the valleys. The Christian landscape marked by crosses bent over by the wind was mysteriously quickened by it. The dove glided endlessly on its outstretched locked wings, light as a little boat on the ocean. Goodbye, dove, O goodbye! The soaring rock columns of La Verna rose up into peaks gray in the twilight, all ringed around by the dark forest.

The hospitality of the local peasants was enchantingly Christian. I was covered with sweat and they offered me water. "You will arrive at La Verna within an hour if God wishes it." A little girl watched me a bit sadly I thought, her black eyes amazed under an enormous straw hat. In all an unconscious absorption and a convent-like serenity sweetened each feature of their faces. I'll remember the little girl for a long time and her tranquil know-everything eyes under her nunnish hat.

Higher up on the interminable stubble always higher the natural rock towers rose up and up supporting the little house that looked like a convent its windows lit and relit by rays of the setting sun.

The fortress of the spirit was rising, enormous rocks thrown in heaps and piles by a violent law toward the sky, then soothed by nature before it had covered them with green forests, soothed later still by an infinite spirit of love: the purpose which had soothed over the jarring blows of the ideal that had tortured it, and to which they were the sacred, pure and supreme emotions of my life.

22 September (La Verna)

"Francesca B. O divine St Francis pray for me poor sinner. 20 August 189..."

I had gone through the forest remembering something that made me feel my first traumatic anxiety again. I kept remembering the victorious eyes, the line of the eyebrows: perhaps she'd never known about it: and now I found her at the end of my pilgrimage that broke out in a confession so sweet, up there and so far away from everything. It was written halfway down the corridor where the Via Crucis branches out from the life of St Francis: (through the gratings the frozen breath rises from the grottoes below). Halfway down, in front of the simple figure of love her heart had opened into a cry into a tear of passion, and destiny had been perfected.

Deep grottoes, rocky fissures where stone steps went down down into unremembering shadow, colossal steeps and bas-reliefs of columns cut in the living rock: and in the church the angel, sweet purity that the lily shares and the Virgin elects, and a fluffy cloud turns blue in the sky and a classical amphora encloses the earth and the lilies: who appears in the proper foreshortening the one the dream appears in, and in

the white cloud of her beauty rests an instant knee on the earth up there like that next to heaven:. . . . .
. . . .
solitary little streets among the tall columnars of trees, content with a slight ray of sun . . . until I arrived there, in front of the veiled immensity of the landscape where a divine nocturnal sweetness revealed itself to me in the morning, the green completely covered with a bright shine which shaded over and slowly diminished out to infinity: still full of the power of its chains outlined against the lingering darkness. Caprese, Michelangiolo, she whom you bent over on her knees so tired of walking, who bends and bends and never rests, in her arcane pose so like the ancient sisters, like the ancient barbarous queens hurling forever in the whirlwind of Dante's song, barbarous queen under the whole weight of the human dream. .
. . . .

The corridor, filled with the iced breath from the caves, is covered completely with the Franciscan legend. The saint appears as the shadow of Christ, resigned, born in the land of Humanism, who accepts his destiny in solitude. His renunciation is simple and sweet: from his loneliness he chants his hymn to nature with great faith and fidelity: Brother Sun, Sister Water, Brother Wolf. A beloved Italian saint. Now they have redone his chapel carved out of the living rock. A walnut tableau runs completely around it where with melancholic power a monk . . . from Bibbiena inlaid half-figures of saintly monks. The bizarre simplicity of the white design is raised up time and again when the golden light of sunset tries to spill over from the close glass window into the penumbra of the chapel. Those simple designs then take on a bizarre and nostalgic fascination. White on the rich walnut surfaces seems to elevate the hieratic profiles of the slight claustral landscape they rise from beheaded, figures of a saintliness made wholly spirit, the enigmatic and rigid lines of great unknown souls. A decrepit monk drags himself in the late hour through the half-light in front of the altar, silent in his shaggy robe, and prays the prayers of 80 years of devotion. Outside the sunset muddies and darkens. Threatening iron-colored streaks lower and weigh down on the mountains facing us in the distance. The dream approaches its end and the spirit suddenly alone seeks out a support some faith in the sad hour. Far off one sees the mysterious lookouts and warriors of the Casentino castles slowly go under. All around us a vast silence stretches out a vast emptiness in the false light from the cold glitterings still flickering under the pressure of darkness. And my memory suddenly flashes back to the gentle ladies with white arms down there on their balconies: as though in a dream: as though in a chivalrous dream.

I go out: the main piazza is deserted. I sit on the low wall. Figures wander by, and the dim lights vamp and go out: the monks take leave of the pilgrims. A breath of wind continuous and soft blows down from the wood above, but one hears neither its rustling on the dark mountainside nor its flow through the grottoes. A bell from the little Franciscan church tolls through the sadness of the monastery: and it seems like the day of the great shade, the day in tears that it is dying.

II. RETURN

I LEAP (into space, out of time)

Water wind
The purity of first things —
Man's work on the element
Of water — nature that blankets
Layers of rock on top of layers — the wind
That plays around in the valleys — and the shadow of wind
The cloud — the far-off admonition
Of the river in the valley —
And the ruin of the mountain's spur — the landslide
Victory of the elements — the wind

That plays around in the valley.
Up the long valley that rises in terraces
The little stone house in the exhausted greenery:
The white image of the element.

The Telluric melody of the Falterona. Telluric waves. The last asterisk of the Falterona's song gets lost in the clouds. On the distant hillside the triumphant line of young firs glistens, the advance guard of young giants grouped together for battle, radiant in the sunlight strung out along the long torrential slope. Behind them, in the rustling of the black woods extending their encampments farther and farther down the valley the enormous rock folds and turns in on itself grotesquely, like a pachyderm with four hooves under its dark huge body: La Verna. I cross and I go across it.

Campigna: barbarous country, always vanishing, night country, mystic nightmare of chaos. Your one inhabitant offers up the true night of the ancient human animal in all its gestures. In your troubled mountains the element of the grotesque is outlined: a lout and a fat whore flee under the flying clouds. And your white sides like the clouds, triangular, curved like full sails: barbarous country, vanishing always, night country, mystic nightmare of chaos.

. . . .

I'm resting now for the last time in the solitude of the forest. Dante, his poetry of ascendance, comes back whole in my memory. O pilgrim, O pilgrims who go out searching so seriously. Catherine, bizarre daughter of the barbarous mountain, of the rocky shell of the winds, how sweet is your weeping: how sweet it is when you were present at the painful scene of the mother, the mother who now had her last son dead. One of the pious women around her, kneeling tried to console her: but she didn't want to be consoled, but she who had thrown herself to the ground wanted to cry out all her grief. Figure out of Ghirlandaio, last daughter of the Tuscan poetry that once was, you got down then from your horse you then were watching: you who arose in the overflowing waves of your own hair, arose with your own company, as in the ancient poetic fables: already having forgotten the love of the poet.

Monte Filetto, 25 September

A nightingale sings in the limbs of the walnut tree. The hill is too beautiful against the too-blue sky. The river sings its own sweet selfsame song as best it can. It's been an hour now that I've watched the space below and the road halfway up the hill that leads there. Up here the hawks live. The fine summer rain patterned a fine tune on the walnut leaves. But the leaves of the acacia tree dear to the night submitted without a sound like a green shadow. The blue opens up between these two trees. The walnut stands in front of my room's window. At night it seems to gather all of the darkness up and curve its shadowy melody of leaves like a harvest of songs about its milky round and almost human trunk: the acacia knows how to outline itself like an illusion of smoke. The stars were pirouetting on the deserted hill top. No one is coming down the street. I like to watch the empty countryside with its scattered trees from my balcony, the soul of solitude beaten out by the wind. Today when the wind and the whole landscape were so sweet after the rain I thought of the young ladies in de Maupassant and Jammes their pale oval faces inclined over the tapestries and engravings full of memories. The river takes up its lullaby again. I walk away. I look back at the window once more: the slope is a little golden painting among the quick cries of the hawks.

Near Campigna (26 September)

To render the landscape, virgin country that only the tame river in the valley fills with noises of a quivering freshness, painting would never be enough, you need water, the element itself, the tractable melody of water that spreads out among the draws

43

and ravines from the ample gorge of its own bed, that sweet as the ancient voices of the wind presses down the valleys in regal curves: because here she is truly queen of the landscape.

.   .   .   .

Valdervé is a hillside entirely Alpine which drops down suddenly over the crags and ravines and buries its pedestal in the water like the fang of a lion. The water turns here with clear deep thrashing sounds leaving the high pastoral scenery with its great trees and hills.

.   .   .   .

Here are the rocks, strata upon strata, monuments of that solitary tenacity which console the anxious hearts of all men. And my destiny seemed sweet to me fleeing towards the far-spangled illusory fascinations that still stream down from the blue mountains: and to hear the susurration of waters under the bare-faced rocks, still breath-fresh from the depths of the earth. Thus I know a music sweet in my memory and never remember one note of it: I know that it's called Departure or Return: I know a painting lost among the splendor of Florentine art with its message of sweet nostalgia: it's the prodigal son under the shade trees of his father's house. Literature? I don't know. My memory, water is like this. After the spiritual backdrops that have no spirit, after the beaten gold of twilight, sweet as the song of encompassing darkness is the song of water under the rocks: the way the essence is sweet in the black splendor of the eyes of Spanish virgins: and the chords of Spanish guitars . . . Ribera, where did I see your dances like bitter songs? Your whip-flick satire about the dance of victorious songs? And against your other face, the horseman of death, your other face that is the heart's deep core, the heart's dance, satyr girdled about with vines dancing on the holy obscenity of Silenus? Naked skeletal imprints, against the raw rock wall of a cave one hot afternoon phantoms, of the stone.   .   .   .

.   .   .   .

I listen. The fountains have gone silent under the voice of the wind. From the rocks a little string of water runs down to a hollowed-out place. The wind slacks off and softens the bite of distant sorrow. Here I am turned. From among the twilit rocks a black horned immobile shape watches me I too immobile with its golden eyes.

. . . .

Down there in the twilight the plain of Romagna. O woman I've dreamed over, woman adored, strong-minded woman, your profile ennobled by a memory of Byzantine stillness, noble and mythic head in strong smooth lines gilded by the enigma of sphinxes: twilit eyes in a landscape of towers dreamed there on the banks of the war-torn plain, on the banks of rivers drunk down by the savage earth there where Francesca's cry is lost forever: from my childhood a liturgical voice over and over intoned in prayer slowly and movingly: and you from that rhythm sacred to me and much moved arose, already restless with vast plains, with distant miraculous destinies: my hope reawakens on the endlessness of the plain or the sea when I feel a breath of grace flutter: nobility incarnate and golden, golden depth of your eyes: huntress, lover, mystic, benign in human nobility ancient Romagna.

. . . .

Water from the mill flows slowly and invisibly into the millstream. I see a boy again, the same boy, stretched out down there on the grass. He appears to be sleeping. I think back on my own childhood: how long it's been since magnetic rays from the stars spoke to me for the first time about the endlessness of the dead! . . . Time has passed, growing thicker and larger, and gone: just so the water goes by, not moving at all for the boy down there: leaving behind it a silence, the millrace deep and unchanged: conserving the silence just as every day the shadow . . .

That boy or merely some likeness projected by my own nostalgia? So still down there: just like my own corpse.

Marradi (Ancient vault. Covered mirror)

Morning shines on the tops of all the mountains. High on the pinnacles of a desolate triangle the castle catches the light, higher and farther away. Venus goes by, crouched down in a two-wheeled cart on the street next to the convent. The river unknots in the valley: broken and lowing softly from time to time it sings and rests in huge blue mirrors: it runs more quickly along the black walls of rock (a red cupola, far off, laughs out with its lion), and the bell towers crowd together and in the blackening restlessness of the rooftops in sunlight a long veranda which has scribbled a many-colored comment with its arches!

Near Marradi (October)

I've fallen in with good people. The window of my room gives out on the winds: and the . . . and the son, poor little bird with sweet features and indecisive spirit, poor little bird who drags a broken leg, and the wind that beats at the window from the cloud-crowded horizon, the mountains high and far away, the monotonous rumble of the wind. In the distance snow has fallen . . . the silent landlady makes up my bed again helped by her young servant girl. Monotonous sweetness of the patriarchal life. End of the pilgrimage.

IMAGES FROM THE JOURNEY AND THE MOUNTAIN

After the stronger, second soul had broken our chains
In the deaf, night-long struggle,
We woke up crying and it was blue morning:
They sailed like the shadows of heroes:
Out of the dawn no shades fell in the pure silences
Out of the dawn
In the pure thoughts
No shades fell

Out of the dawn no shades:
Crying: swearing our faith to that blue
· ·
· ·

The woman sitting above the last steep ascent
Near the old house seems like a pale young girl still:
At her feet the valleys unknot uncertainly
Toward the high solitudes of the horizons:
So kind so old she hears the cuckoo singing.
And her simple heart tested over the years
By the melodies of the earth
Listens quietly: the notes
Come on, ambiguous and unbroken like veins in a silk veil.
The swollen stream had risen out of the dark woods
And in sluggish eddies and suck-pools skims the rock edges,
Wrapping around the light blue of the air . . .
And the cuckoo lets fall, more slowly still, two veiled notes
Into the pale blue silence
· ·
· ·

The air laughs: the valley trumpet
Blasts at the mountains: the outriders
Break loose: they move in quick leaps and bounds: our hearts
Leap also: they shout and cross over the bridges.
And from the heights to the infinite dawns.
Vigilant, they come down anxiously through the mountains,
Trembling and beautiful in the living fountains,
The echoes of our two submissive hearts . . .
They have crossed over in a long procession:
I don't know what drinking song they raise
In the air: and behind them the mountain thunders down:
· ·

And one makes out their green song.
· ·

To go, *from the waters to the whirlpools* down

The valley's slope, *in the muffled whisper caressing me*:
To follow down the valley's descent
A tired wing that beats and turns: to go
Desolate through valleys until, in a serenity
Of pale blue, rising out of the harsh rocks
A gray various village looms over me
Appearing and disappearing in alternating thoughts,
Above the barren dream, the sky cleared off!
O if like the stream that collapses
And rests in the smooth blue of itself,
If so at your walls the spirit declines
To nothing in its fatal going away,
If at your walls I could stretch out
In a crystalline peace, in a similar peace,
And mirror the memory of a divine
Lost serenity O you immortal
Spirit! O You!

. . . .
. . . .

Intent on the mysterious chorus of the wind
In roads of long tranquil waves,
Mute and glorious the harvest unbuttons the blouse
Of her golden lights in front of my very eyes.
O Hope! O Hope! By the tens of thousands
The summer fruits glisten and shine! a chorus
Enchanted, melodious in its own murmur,
Which lives by a myriad of sparks . . . !

Here is the night: and here to watch me
And lights and lights: and I far away and alone:
The harvest is quiet, toward infinity
(The spirit is quiet) poems go silently
Into the night: into the night: I mean: only
Shadow that comes back, that once was divided . . .

Translations by Charles Wright

GIUSEPPE UNGARETTI
(1888–1970)

Giuseppe Ungaretti was born in Alexandria, Egypt to parents from Lucca who were the proprietors of a bakery in the Arab quarter of Moharrem Bey. In 1912, he made his first trip to Italy, en route to Paris — where he took up residence and studied at the Sorbonne. There he met Giorgio De Chirico, Fernand Lèger, Blaise Cendrars, Georges Braque, Amedeo Modigliani, and Pablo Picasso, and became a close friend of Guillaume Apollinaire. He was inducted into the Italian army in 1915 and wrote poetry at the front. His first book of verse, *Il porto sepolto* (The buried port), was published in 1916 in a small edition of eighty-seven copies, subsidized in large part by the critic Renato Serra. Of the great trio of hermetic poets, including Salvatore Quasimodo and Eugenio Montale, Ungaretti was key in establishing the importance of the poet's inner vision, the use of bizarre and allusive imagery, and the need to explore realities requiring the paring down of traditional poetic language to its essential, primordial roots. Much of his best verse offers intense, private glimpses into an "authentic" reality, and personal revelations of the human condition. Throughout his work, Ungaretti searches for organic analogies to unite the external, physical world of things with that of personal sensations, emotions, and thoughts. In addition to many works of poetry, including *L'allegria* (The joy), *Sentimento del tempo* (The feeling of time), *Il dolore* (The grief), and *Un grido e paesaggi* (A cry and landscapes), Ungaretti translated works by William Shakespeare, Jean Racine, Luis de Gongora, and Stephané Mallarmé.

49

I FIUMI*

Cotici il 16 agosto 1916

Mi tengo a quest'albero mutilato
abbandonato in questa dolina
che ha il languore
di un circo
prima o dopo lo spettacolo
e guardo
il passaggio quieto
delle nuvole sulla luna

Stamani mi sono disteso
in un'urna d'acqua
e come una reliquia
ho riposato

L'Isonzo scorrendo
mi levigava
come un suo sasso

Ho tirato su
le mie quattr'ossa
e me sono andato
come un acrobata
sull'acqua

Mi sono accoccolato
vicino ai miei panni
sudici di guerra
e come un beduino
mi sono chinato a ricevere
il sole

Questo è l'Isonzo
e qui meglio

*From Giuseppe Ungaretti, *L'Allegria* (Milano: Preda, 1931).

THE RIVERS

Cotici, August 16, 1916

I hold fast to this mutilated tree
deserted in this doline
that has the languor
of a circus
before or after the show
and watch
the quiet passage
of clouds across the moon

This morning I stretched out
in an urn of water
and like a relic
rested

The flowing Isonzo
polished me
like one of its stones

I pulled up
my flesh and bones
and made my way
like an acrobat
into the water

I crouched down
near my clothes
filthy with war
and like a Bedouin
bent down to receive
the sun

This is the Isonzo
and here I better

mi son riconosciuto
una docile fibra
dell'universo

Il mio supplizio
è quando
non mi credo
in armonia

Ma quelle occulte
mani
che m'intridono
mi regalano
la rara
felicità

Ho ripassato
le epoche
della mia vita

Questi sono
i miei fiumi

Questo è il Serchio
al quale hanno attinto
duemil'anni forse
di gente mia campagnola
e mio padre e mia madre

Questo è il Nilo
che mi ha visto
nascere e crescere
e ardere d'inconsapevolezza
nelle estese pianure

Questa è la Senna
e in quel suo torbido
mi sono rimescolato
e mi sono conosciuto

recognized myself
a soft fiber
of the universe

My torment
is when
I don't feel myself
in harmony

But those hidden
hands
that knead me
give me
rare
happiness

I went over
the stages
of my life

These are
my rivers

This is the Serchio
from whose waters have drawn
perhaps two thousand years
of my farming people
and my father and my mother

This is the Nile
who saw me
born and growing
burning with unknowing
in the wide plains

This is the Seine
in whose murk
I was remingled
and came to know myself

Questi sono i miei fiumi
contati nell'Isonzo

Questa è la mia nostalgia
che in ognuno
mi traspare
ora ch'è notte
che la mia vita mi pare
una corolla
di tenebre

CON FUOCO*

1925

Con fuoco d'occhi un nostalgico lupo
Scorre la quiete nuda.

Non trova che ombre di cielo sul ghiaccio,

Fondano serpi fatue e brevi viole.

QUIETE*

1929

L'uva è matura, il campo arato,

Si stacca il monte dalle nuvole.

Sui polverosi specchi dell'estate
Caduta è l'ombra,

Tra le dita incerte
Il loro lume è chiaro,
E lontano.

Colle rondini fugge
L'ultimo strazio.

*From Giuseppe Ungaretti, *Sentimento del Tempo* (Firenze: Vallecchi, 1933).

These are my rivers *River in Egypt*
counted in the Isonzo *and flower in Italy.*

This is my nostalgia
that in each one
gleams through
now that it is night
and my life seems to me
a corolla
of shadows

WITH FIRE

1925

With eyes of fire a nostalgic wolf
Stalks the naked quiet.

He finds nothing but the shadows of sky on ice.

Ephemeral serpents fuse with brief violets.

QUIET

1929

The grape is ripened, the field plowed,

The mountain breaks free from the clouds.

The shadow has fallen
On the dusty mirrors of summer,

Between uncertain fingers
Their gleaming is clear,
And distant.

With the swallows escapes
The final agony.

55

TU TI SPEZZASTI*

1

I molti, immani, sparsi, grigi sassi
Frementi ancora alle segrete fionde
Di originarie fiamme soffocate
Od ai terrori di fiumane vergini
Ruinanti in implacabili carezze,
— Sopra l'abbaglio della sabbia rigidi
In un vuoto orizzonte, non rammenti?

E la recline, che s'apriva all'unico
Raccogliersi dell'ombra nella valle,
Araucaria, anelando ingigantita,
Volta nell'ardua selce d'erme fibre
Più delle altre dannate refrattaria,
Fresca la bocca di farfalle e d'erbe
Dove dalle radici si tagliava,
— Non la rammenti delirante muta
Sopra tre palmi d'un rotondo ciottolo
In un perfetto bilico
Magicamente apparsa?

Di ramo in ramo fiorrancino lieve,
Ebbri di meraviglia gli avidi occhi
Ne conquistavi la screziata cima,
Temerario, musico bimbo,
Solo per rivedere all'imo lucido
D'un fondo e quieto baratro di mare
Favolose testuggini
Ridestarsi fra le alghe.

Della natura estrema la tensione
E le subacquee pompe,
Funebri moniti.

*From Giuseppe Ungaretti, *Il Dolore* (Milano: Mondadori, 1947).

YOU SHATTERED

1

The myriad, enormous, scattered, gray stones
Still quavering in secret slings
Of smothered originating flames
Or in the terrors of virgin torrents
Crashing down in implacable caresses
— Rigid on the dazzling sands
On an empty horizon, don't you remember?

And where it leaned, opening toward the only
Gathering of shadows in the valley,
The araucaria, swollen with longing,[11]
Its lonely fibers twisted into the hard flint
More refractory than the other damned,
Its mouth cool with butterflies and grass
Where it severed from its roots,
— Don't you remember it, delirious, mute
Above three spans of rounded rock
In perfect balance
Magically present?

From branch to branch, light gold-crested wren,
Your eager eyes drunk with astonishment,
You won its speckled summit,
Reckless and musical child,
Simply to see again on the glimmering bed
Of a deep and tranquil ravine
Fabulous tortoises
Reawakening amidst the seaweed.

From nature outermost tension
And the underwater processions,
Funeral admonitions.

2

Alzavi le braccia come ali
E ridavi nascita al vento
Correndo nel peso dell'aria immota.

Nessuno mai vide posare
Il tuo lieve piede di danza.

3

Grazia, felice,
Non avresti potuto non spezzarti
In una cecità tanto indurita
Tu semplice soffio e cristallo,

Troppo umano lampo per l'empio,
Selvoso, accanito, ronzante
Ruggito d'un sole ignudo.

TERRA *

Potrebbe esserci sulla falce
Una lucentezza, e il rumore
Tornare e smarrirsi per gradi
Dalle grotte, e il vento potrebbe
D'altro sale gli occhi arrossare...

Potresti la chiglia sommersa
Dislocarsi udire nel largo,
O un gabbiano irarsi a beccare,
Sfuggita la preda, lo specchio...

Del grano di notti e di giorni
Ricolme mostrasti le mani,
Degli avi tirreni delfini

*From Giuseppe Ungaretti, *Il Dolore* (Milano: Mondadori, 1947).

58

2

You raised your arms like wings
And gave birth back to the wind
Running in the weight of the motionless air.

No one saw your foot, so light
In dance, ever touch the ground.

3

Happy grace,
You couldn't have not shattered
In a blindness so unbending,
You, simple breath and crystal,

Too-human flash for the profane,
Sylvan, relentless, humming
Roar of a naked sun.

EARTH

It might be a gleaming on
The scythe, and from the caves
Sound might return and fade away
And the wind might redden
The eyes with other salt…

You might hear the sunken
Keel shifting places in the sea,
Or an angry seagull, his prey
Fled, pecking at the mirror…

The grain of nights and days
Overflowed your outstretched hands,
You saw painted on the secret

Dipinti vedesti a segreti
Muri immateriali, poi, dietro
Alle nave, vivi volare,
E terra sei ancora di ceneri
D'inventori senza riposo.

Cauto ripotrebbe assopenti farfalle
Stormire agli ulivi da un attimo all'altro
Destare,
Veglie inspirate resterai di estinti,
Insonni interventi di assenti,
La forza di ceneri — ombre
Nel ratto oscillamento degli argenti.

Il vento continui a scrosciare,
Da palme ad abeti lo strepito
Per sempre desoli, silente
Il grido dei morti è più forte.

Immaterial walls of Tyrrhenian
Ancestors the dolphins, then saw them
Flying after ships, alive,
And earth, you are still made of the ashes
Of untiring inventors.

Cautious, the rustling in the olive trees
Might, at any moment, wake the dozing
Butterflies,
Inspired wakes, you will remain, of the dead,
Sleepless interventions of the absent,
The force of ashes — shadows
In the rapid oscillation of silver leaves.

The wind continues to blast,
From palms to firs the uproar
Forever desolate, silent,
The clamor of the dead is louder.

Translations by Patrick Barron

EUGENIO MONTALE
(1896–1981)

Born in Genoa to affluent parents, Eugenio Montale initially studied accounting, but often was unable to attend class due to poor health. His true education came from his older sister Marianna, a philosophy student, and from independent study. An autodidact of impressive breadth and depth, Montale spent long hours in the Genoa library, reading widely in philosophy, the arts, music, language, and literature. At the age of nine, his father built a summer villa in Monterosso on the coast of Liguria, near La Spezia. This rough edge of the Mediterranean coast was the formative landscape that entered into Montale's work and being. It is central to his first book of poetry, *Ossi di seppia* (*Cuttlefish Bones*), and figures prominently in later verse and writings. Later, after Montale had moved to Florence where he worked as an editor, and then as the director of a research library, he acknowledged a certain, stifling parochialism to his "extended childhood" on the Ligurian coast. The tension between the world of nature and the world of human ideas remains high in all of his work. It indicates a difficult and tenuous boundary between a near spiritual, yet introverted "imprisonment in the cosmos," and the "terra firma of ideas, tradition, humanism."[12] Breaches in this marginal zone, the poetic "miracles" Montale so cherished, offer rare glimpses of the interpenetrating of place and ideas, of country and city, of the nonhuman and human. Montale's other works include *Le occasioni* (*The Occasions*), *La bufera e altro* (*The Storm and Other Poems*), *Quaderno di traduzioni* (Notebook of translations), *Satura*, and *Quaderno di quattro anni* (Notebook of four years).

*Meriggiare pallido e assorto**
presso un rovente muro d'orto,
ascoltare tra i pruni e gli sterpi
schiocchi di merli, frusci di serpi.

Nelle crepe del suolo o su la veccia
spiar le file di rosse formiche
ch'ora si rompono ed ora s'intrecciano
a sommo di minuscole biche.

Osservare tra frondi il palpitare
lontano di scaglie di mare
mentre si levano tremuli scricchi
di cicale dai calvi picchi.

E andando nel sole che abbaglia
sentire con triste meraviglia
com'è tutta la vita e il suo travaglio
in questo seguitare una muraglia
che ha in cima cocci aguzzi di bottiglia.

■

*Portami il girasole ch'io lo trapianti**
nel mio terreno bruciato dal salino,
e mostri tutto il giorno agli azzurri specchianti
del cielo l'ansietà del suo volto giallino.

Tendono alla chiarità le cose oscure,
si esauriscono i corpi in un fluire
di tinte: queste in musiche. Svanire
è dunque la ventura delle venture.

Portami tu la pianta che conduce
dove sorgono bionde trasparenze

*From Eugenio Montale, *Ossi di seppia* (Milano: Mondadori, 1948).

Sit out the noon, pale and engrossed
beside a red-hot garden wall,
listen, amidst thorns and briars
to chattering blackbirds, rustling snakes.

In the cracks of the earth or on the vetch
spy lines of red ants
that now divide, now weave together
on top of tiny sheaves.

Watch through the leaves the distant
throbbing of the sea's scales
as the quavering screaks of cicadas
rise up from the bald peaks.

And going into the blinding sun
feel with sad wonder
how all of life and its suffering
is contained in following a wall
in whose top are the jagged shards of bottles.

■

Bring me the sunflower so that I may plant it
in my land, parched by the salty sea winds,
and let it show all day long, to the blue glimmerings
of the sky, the longing of its yellow face.

Things dark incline towards brightness,
bodies waste away in a stream
of colors, into music. To disappear
is thus the destiny of destinies.

Bring me the plant that leads to
where blond transparencies rise up

e vapora la vita quale essenza;
portami il girasole impazzito di luce.

■

Riviere, *
bastano pochi stocchi d'erbaspada
penduli da un ciglione
sul delirio del mare;
o due camelie pallide
nei giardini deserti,
e un eucalipto biondo che si tuffi
tra sfrusci e pazzi voli
nella luce;
ed ecco che in un attimo
invisibili fili a me si asserpano,
farfalla in una ragna
di fremiti d'olivi, di sguardi di girasoli.

Dolce cattività, oggi, riviere
di chi s'arrende per poco
come a rivivere un antico giuoco
non mai dimenticato.
Rammento l'acre filtro che porgeste
allo smarrito adolescente, o rive:
nelle chiare mattine si fondevano
dorsi di colli e cielo; sulla rena
dei lidi era un risucchio ampio, un eguale
fremer di vite,
una febbre del mondo; ed ogni cosa
in se stessa pareva consumarsi.

Oh allora sballottati
come l'osso di seppia dalle ondate
svanire a poco a poco;

*From Montale, *Ossi di seppia.*

and life evaporates as essence;
bring me the sunflower crazed with light.

∎

Seacoasts,
a few blades of swordgrass are enough
hanging from a ledge
above the delirium of the sea;
or two pale camellias
in deserted gardens,
and a blond eucalyptus plunging
amidst rustlings and crazed flights
into the light;
and then in an instant
invisible threads snake around me,
butterfly in a web
of quivering olive trees, gazing sunflowers.

Sweet captivity, today, seacoasts
for the man who almost surrenders
as if reliving an old game,
never forgotten.
I remember the bitter philter you offered
a bewildered adolescent, O coasts:
in the bright mornings the hillcrests
fused with the sky; on the sand
of the beaches a heavy undertow sucked, a correspondent
frenzy of life,
a fever of the world; and every thing
seemed to consume itself.

O tossed about then
like the cuttlefish bones by the waves
to vanish bit by bit;

diventare
un albero rugoso od una pietra
levigata dal mare; nei colori
fondersi dei tramonti; sparir carne
per spicciare sorgente ebbra di sole,
dal sole divorata...
                              Erano questi,
riviere, i voti del fanciullo antico
che accanto ad una rósa balaustrata
lentamente moriva sorridendo.

Quanto, marine, queste fredde luci
parlano a chi straziato vi fuggiva.
Lame d'acqua scoprentisti tra varchi
di labili ramure; rocce brune
tra spumeggi; frecciare di rondoni
vagabondi...
                 Ah, potevo
credervi un giorno o terre,
bellezze funerarie, auree cornici
all'agonia d'ogni essere.
                              Oggi torno
a voi più forte, o è inganno, ben che il cuore
par sciogliersi in ricordi lieti — e atroci.
Triste anima passata
e tu volontà nuova che mi chiami,
tempo è forse d'unirvi
in un porto sereno di saggezza.
Ed un giorno sarà ancora l'invito
di voci d'oro, di lusinghe audaci,
anima mia non più divisa. Pensa:
cangiare in inno l'elegia; rifarsi;
non mancar più.
                    Potere
simili a questi rami
ieri scarniti e nudi ed oggi pieni

to become
a gnarled tree or a stone,
polished by the sea; to fuse
with the colors of the sunset; to dissolve as flesh
and reemerge, a spring drunk on the sun,
devoured by the sun...
                              These, coasts,
were the vows of the ancient child
who next to a rusting balustrade
slowly died smiling.

How much, shores, these cold lights
speak to that tormented one who fled you.
Blades of water glimpsed through the fissures
of swaying branches; dusky rocks
in the foam; arrows of wandering
swifts...
                    O earth, if I could
believe in you one day,
funeral wonders, gilded frames
the agony of every being.
                              Today I return
to you stronger (or deceived) even though the heart
seems to dissolve in pleasant — and atrocious – memories.
Sad soul of the past,
and you, new will that calls me,
perhaps it's time to unite you
in a serene harbor of wisdom.
And one day there'll be once more the call
of golden voices, of audacious enticements,
soul no more divided. Think:
to change elegy into hymn; to be remade;
to lack no more.
                         To be able
like these branches
yesterday fleshless and bare, and today full

di fremiti e di linfe,
sentire
noi pur domani tra i profumi e i venti
un riaffluir di sogni, un urger folle
di voci verso un esito; e nel sole
che v'investe, riviere,
rifiorire!

EGLOGA[*]

Perdersi nel bigio ondoso
dei miei ulivi ara buono
nel tempo andato — loquaci
di riottanti uccelli
e di cantanti rivi.
Come affondava il tallone
nel suolo screpolato,
tra le lamelle d'argento
dell'esili foglie. Sconnessi
nascevano in mente i pensieri
nell'aria di troppa quiete.

Ora è finito il cerulo marezzo.
Si getta il pino domestico
a romper la grigiura;
brucia una toppa di cielo
in alto, un ragnatelo
si squarcia al passo: si svincola
d'attorno un'ora fallita.
È uscito un rombo di treno,
non lunge, ingrossa. Uno sparo
si schiaccia nell'etra vetrino.
Strepita un volo come un acquazzone,
venta e vanisce bruciata

[*]From Montale, *Ossi di seppia.*

70

of quiverings and sap,
to feel within us
tomorrow amidst the fragrances and winds
a resurgence of dreams, a wild rush
of voices towards an outcome; and in the sun
that swathes you, seacoasts,
to flower anew!

ECLOGUE

To lose myself in the undulant gray
of my olives was good
in times past — loquacious
with quarrelsome birds
and singing creeks.
How the heel sank
into the cracked earth,
among the silver blades
of slender leaves. Disconnected
thoughts came into my mind
in the too quiet air.

The marbled blue is now gone.
The umbrella pine has shot up
to break the grayness;
a patch of sky burns
up high, a spiderweb
rips apart at my step: from around me
a failed hour releases its grasp.
The rumbling of a train emerges,
not far off, and intensifies. A shot
smashes into the vitreous air.
A flight of birds beats down like a deluge,
an armful of your bitter rind

una bracciata di amara
tua scorza, istante: discosta
esplode furibonda una canea.

Tosto potrà rinascere l'idillio.
S'è ricomposta la fase che pende
dal cielo, riescono bende
leggere fuori...;
                    il fitto dei fagiuoli
n'è scancellato e involto.
Non serve più rapid'ale,
né giova proposito baldo;
non durano che le solenni cicale
in questi saturnali del caldo.
Va e viene un istante in un folto
una parvenza di donna.
È disparsa, non era una Baccante.

Sul tardi corneggia la luna.
Ritornavamo dai nostri
vagabondari infruttuosi.
Non si leggeva più in faccia
al mondo la traccia
della frenesia durata
il pomeriggio. Turbati
discendevamo tra i vepri.
Nei miei paesi a quell'ora
cominciano a fischiare le lepri.

L'ANGUILLA *

L'anguilla, la sirena
dei mari freddi che lascia il Baltico
per giungere ai nostri mari,

---

*From Eugenio Montale, *La bufera e altro* (Milano: Mondadori, 1957).

72

blows away and vanishes, burned;
instant: far off
explodes a furious baying.

Soon the idyll can be reborn.
The phase that hangs from the sky
is recomposed, light streamers
extend out...
                    the thicket of beans
is obliterated, enfolded in them.
Swift wings no longer serve,
nor bold proposals help;
only the solemn cicadas withstand
these saturnalias of heat.
For an instant in the dense brush
an image of a woman comes and goes.
She disappears; she was no Baccante.

Later, the moon grows horns.
Returning from our
useless wanderings,
no trace
of the afternoon's long frenzy
could be read on the face
of the world. Troubled,
we went down amidst the briars.
In my parts that's the time
when the hares begin to hiss.

THE EEL

The eel, the siren
of cold seas who leaves the Baltic
to reach our seas,

ai nostri esuarî, ai fiumi
che risale in profondo, sotto la piena avversa,
di ramo in ramo e poi
di capello in capello, assottigliati,
sempre più addentro, sempre più nel cuore
del macigno, filtrando
tra gorielli di melma finché un giorno
una luce scoccata dai castagni
ne accende il guizzo in pozze d'acquamorta,
nei fossi che declinano
dai balzi d'Appennino alla Romagna;
l'anguilla, torcia, frusta,
freccia d'Amore in terra
che solo i nostri botri o i disseccati
ruscelli pirenaici riconducono
a paradisi di fecondazione;
l'anima verde che cerca
vita là dove solo
morde l'arsura e la desolazione,
la scintilla che dice
tutto comincia quando tutto pare
incarbonirsi, bronco seppellito;
l'iride breve, gemella
di quella che incastonano i tuoi cigli
e fai brillare intatta in mezzo ai figli
dell'uomo, immersi nel tuo fango, puoi tu
non crederla sorella?

our estuaries, rivers
rising up, deep from under the enemy flood
from branch to branch,
twig to twig, tapering
ever more inward, snaking into the granite
heart, threading
slimy capillaries until one day
light gleaming off the chestnut trees
ignites her slither in pools of dead water,
in the gorges flowing off
the Apennine escarpments to Romagna;
the eel, a torch, a whip,
arrow of Love on earth
whom only our gullies or desiccated
Pyrenean brooks lead back
to Elysiums of fecundity;
the green spirit that seeks
life where only
parching drought and desolation sting,
the spark that says
everything begins when everything seems
cinder and buried, twisted wood;
brief rainbow, iris,
twin to the one your lashes enclose
and you set gleaming, undiminished, amidst the sons
of men, immersed in your mud — can you
not see her as sister?

Translations by Patrick Barron

SALVATORE QUASIMODO
(1901–1968)

Born the son of a stationmaster in Ragusa at the turn of the century, Salvatore Quasimodo spent his childhood in eastern Sicily, ranging from Roccalimera to Messina. He studied engineering in Palermo and then later in Rome, where in the early 1920s he began to read widely in literature and to learn Greek. Qualifying as a surveyor in 1926, he returned to the south in Reggio Calabria where he wrote his first poems. In this period he encountered the influential circle of writers based in Florence that included Montale, Elio Vittorini, Arturo Loria, and Alessandro Bonsanti. By the late 1930s he left engineering definitively, and in 1940, accepted a teaching position in Milan. Much of his verse centers on his native homeland and is characterized by a spontaneous warm exuberance coupled with a deeply entrenched undercurrent of painful isolation. Childhood memories, the Sicilian landscape, a lost communion with physical reality, and a lost innocence are all themes that dominate his poetry. His works include *Acque e terre* (Waters and lands), *Oboe sommerso* (Sunken oboe), *Ed è subito sera* (And suddenly it's evening), *Il falso e vero verde* (The true and false green), *La impareggiabile terra* (The incomparable earth), and *Lirici greci* (Greek lyrics).

ALLA MIA TERRA[*]

Un sole rompe gonfio nel sonno
e urlano alberi;
avventurosa aurora
in cui disancorata navighi,
e le stagioni marine
dolci fermentano rive nasciture.

Io qui infermo mi desto,
d'altra terra amaro
e della pietà mutevole del canto
che amore mi germina
d'uomini e di morte.

Il mio male ha nuovo verde,
ma le mani sono d'aria
ai tuoi rami,
a donne che la tristezza
chiuse in abbandono
e mai le tocca il tempo,
che me discorza e imbigia.

In te mi getto: un fresco
di navate posa nel cuore:
passi nudi d'angeli
vi s'ascoltano, al buio.

CAVALLI DI LUNA E DI VULCANI[†]

Alla figlia

Isole che ho abitato
verdi su mari immobili.

D'alghe arse, di fossili marini
le spiagge ove corrono in amore

---

[*]From Salvatore Quasimodo, *Oboe sommerso* (Genova: Edizioni di Circoli, 1932).
[†]From Salvatore Quasimodo, *Ed è subito sera* (Milano: Mondadori, 1942).

TO MY EARTH

A swollen sun bursts into sleep
and trees howl;
adventurous aurora
where you, unanchored, sail off,
and mild marine seasons
ferment nascent shores.

I here, infirm, awake,
bitter with another earth
and from the mutable piety of the song
that germinates love in me
of men and of death.

My pain bears new green,
but the hands are of the air
on your branches,
on women whom sadness
shut in desolation
and time never touches,
that rips my bark and turns me gray.

In you I throw myself: a coolness
of naves settles in the heart:
naked steps of angels
sound there, in the dark.

HORSES OF MOON AND OF VOLCANOES

To my daughter

Islands on which I have lived
green on immobile seas.

Of burnt seaweed, of marine fossils
the beaches where run loving

cavalli di luna e di vulcani.

Nel tempo delle frane,
le foglie, le gru assalgono l'aria:
in lume d'alluvione splendono
cieli densi aperti agli stellati;

le colombe volano
dalle spalle nude dei fanciulli.

Qui finita è la terra:
con fatica e con sangue
mi faccio una prigione.

Per te dovrò gettarmi
ai piedi dei potenti,
addolcire il mio cuore di predone.

Ma cacciato dagli uomini,
nel fulmine di luce ancora giaccio
fanciullo a mani aperte,
a rive d'alberi e fiumi:

ivi la latomìa l'arancio greco
feconda per gl'imenei dei numi.

RIDE LA GAZZA, NERA SUGLI ARANCI*

Forse è un segno vero della vita:
intorno a me fanciulli con leggeri
moti del capo danzano in un gioco
di cadenze e di voci lungo il prato
della chiesa. Pietà della sera, ombre
riaccese sopra l'erba così verde,
bellissime nel fuoco della luna!
Memoria vi concede breve sonno;
ora, destatevi. Ecco, scroscia il pozzo
per la prima marea. Questa è l'ora:
non più mia, arsi, remoti simulacri.

*From Quasimodo, *Ed è subito sera.*

horses of moon and volcanoes.

In the season of landslides,
the leaves, the cranes assail the air:
In the light of the flood shine
skies dense and open to the stars;

the doves fly
from the naked shoulders of children.

Here the earth is finished:
with strain and with blood
I make myself a prison.

For you I must throw myself
at the feet of the powerful,
soften my marauding heart.

But driven off by men, again
I crouch down in the flash of light,
a child with open hands,
on the banks of trees and rivers:

there the quarry makes the Greek orange tree
fruitful for the mating of the gods.

THE MAGPIE LAUGHS, BLACK UPON THE ORANGE TREES

Maybe it is a true sign of life:
around me children dance with light
movements of the head in a game
of cadences and voices along the meadow
of the church. Piety of the evening, shadows
rekindled upon the grass so green,
so very beautiful in the fire of the moon!
Memory grants you a brief rest;
but now, stir yourself. Look, the well churns
for the first tide. This is the hour:
never again mine, burnt, remote simulacrums.

E tu vento del sud forte di zàgare,
spingi la luna dove nudi dormono
fanciulli, forza il puledro sui campi
umidi d'orme di cavalle, apri
il mare, alza le nuvole dagli alberi:
già l'airone s'avanza verso l'acqua
e fiuta lento il fango tra le spine,
ride la gazza, nera sugli aranci.

PREGHIERA ALLA PIOGGIA *

Odore buono del cielo
sull'erbe,
pioggia di prima sera.

Nuda voce, t'ascolto:
e ne ha primizie dolci di suono
e di rifugio il cuore arato;
e mi sollevi muto adolescente,
d'altra vita sorpreso e d'ogni moto
di subite resurrezioni
che il buio esprime e trasfigura.

Pietà del tempo celeste,
della sua luce
d'acque sospese;

del nostro cuore
delle vene aperte
sulla terra.

ED È SUBITO SERA †

Ognuno sta solo sul cuor della terra
trafitto da un raggio di sole:
ed è subito sera.

---

*From Quasimodo, *Oboe sommerso.*
†From Salvatore Quasimodo, *Acque e terre* (Milano: Edizione di Solaria, 1930).

And you, wind from the south thick with orange blossoms,
drive the moon where the children
sleep naked, force the foal to fields
damp with the tracks of mares, open
the sea, lift the clouds from the trees:
already the heron approaches the water
and slowly sniffs the mud amidst the thorns,
the magpie laughs, black upon the orange trees.

PRAYER TO THE RAIN

The good scent of the sky
on the grass,
early evening rain.

Naked voice, I listen to you:
and from you come the first sweet sounds
and in you the plowed heart takes refuge;
and you comforted me, mute adolescent,
surprised by another life and by every motion
of resurrections undergone
that the dark expresses and transfigures.

Sacredness of celestial time,
of its light
of suspended waters;

of our heart
of our open veins
on the earth.

AND SUDDENLY IT'S EVENING

Everyone stands alone on the heart of the earth,
transfixed by a ray of sun:
and suddenly it's evening.

Translations by Patrick Barron

DARIA MENICANTI
(1914–1995)

Daria Menicanti was born in Piacenza and died in Milan in 1995. She graduated from the University of Milan with a thesis on the poetry of John Keats. There she studied aesthetics under the supervision of Antonio Banfi. Menicanti's work with Banfi brought her into contact with a large group of young philosophers, including Enzo Paci, Giulio Preti, and Remo Cantoni. She and Preti married in 1937 and were divorced in 1951. Menicanti's interest in the relationship between philosophy, politics, and literature would eventually lead her to a meeting with Vittorio Sereni. Sereni was a respected poet of the *linea lombarda* school and had close ties to the publishing house Mondadori. Impressed by her poetry, he brought her work to the attention of Mondadori's editors. In 1964 they published her first collection of verse, *Città come*. Selections of other work have been translated into English in *Contemporary Italian Women Poets, The Defiant Muse* and *Italian Women Poets of the Twentieth Century*. Her work has also appeared in several Italian anthologies including *Donne in poesia, Poesia italiana del Novecento*, and *Poesia erotica italiana del novecento*. Over the years, she contributed to such journals as *Paragone, Inventario, Lunarionuovo, Salvo Imprevisti*, and *Resine*. She translated works by Nôel Coward, Paul Géraldy, John Keats, Paul Nizan, Sylvia Plath, Betty Smith, Dylan Thomas and Michael Tournier.*

---

*Introductory note by Cinzia Sartini Blum and Lara Trubowitz is from Cinzia Sartini Blum and Lara Trubowitz, eds., *Contemporary Italian Women Poets* (New York: Italica Press, 2001), 289.

CAMALEONTE*

> ...he is nothing and he is all:
> he is the chameleon poet
>
> — John Keats

Ma sono — oltre che me — sono sul guscio
d'un fiore il mite grillo
dell'estate inquilino —
o l'urlo abbandonato dell'ossesso
sul marciapiede riverso —
o sono cane
lupino che abbaia alla strada
avventato ai cancelli —
o, lungo i cornicioni,
gatta sottile ignara di padroni —
o, ancora, per i viali e gli alberati
la ribalda che vende una sapiente
sfioritura di sé —
o, perché no? — la pioggia
calma e solenne dopo il temporale
d'una giornata cieca —
o la siepe recisa
d'arte a regola in sangue dolorante
atroci amputazioni —
o questa stessa strada che alle soglie
di via Marcello agghinda
di edicole e mercati i suoi cantoni.
Tutto questo e — di nuovo —
la brace che si spegne dentro sé.

aprile 1962

*From Daria Menicanti, *Città come* (Milano: Mondadori, 1964), translation from Blum and Trubowitz, *Contemporary Italian Women Poets*, 3.

CHAMELEON

> ...he is nothing and he is all:
> he is the chameleon poet[13]
>
> — John Keats

But I am — other than me — I am the gentle cricket
on the shell of a flower
summer's tenant —
or the forsaken howl of the possessed
supine on the sidewalk —
or I am lupine
dog barking at the street
hurled against the gates —
or, along eaves,
slender cat unaware of masters —
or, again, along avenues and tree-lined roads
the rogue who sells her skillful
withering —
or, why not? — the rain
calm and solemn after the storm
of a blind day —
or the hedge cut off
by expert hand in aching blood
atrocious amputations
or this very street that at the threshold
of Via Marcello dresses up
its corners with kiosks and markets.
All this and — again —
the embers that inside are dying out.

April 1962

EPIGRAMMA PER UN VERME*

*Un verme tranquillo e bavoso
d'un roseo infantile fa il traghetto
del viale.
Mi domando perché poi
mi faccia quasi tenerezza...Ah, sì:
è perché ti assomiglia, mio diletto*

SE*

*Con l'ultimo giardino la strada
s'insabbia, s'impaluda in un'orchestra
di rane. Steso, chiaro
mi arriva lo stagno con bruschi
cespugli, con piante leggère.
C'è un'aria di abbandono e di rivalsa
intorno alle paludi: se ne vive
ciascuno della vita e della morte
dell'altro: e questo bel verde innocente
della felce ricciuta si fa —
come il resto — da un lungo cimitero.
 E qui ritrovo quel mio divenire
infinito con tutta l'altra terra
e la saggezza ironica: sapere
d'essere sostituibile sempre.
 — Se questo, dico all'improvviso, questo
fosse il mio ultimo giorno —
E subito di tutto m'innamoro
tanto ogni cosa mi risembra bella
nella sua fuga, ogni spiro, ogni insetto.
E quel tuo viso stesso*

*From Daria Menicanti, *Poesie per un passante: 1969–1976* (Milano: Mondadori, 1978), translations from Blum and Trubowitz, *Contemporary Italian Women Poets*, 7.

EPIGRAM FOR A WORM

A worm tranquil and slobbering
rosy like an infant makes the crossing
over the avenue.
I wonder why on earth
it gives me almost tender feelings...Ah, yes:
it's because it resembles you, my darling

IF

With the last garden the road
becomes silted, swamped in an orchestra
of frogs. Outstretched, clear
the pond reaches me with brusque
bushes, with light plants.
There is an air of surrender and revenge
around swamps: everyone
lives off the life and death
of another: and this beautiful innocent green
of the curly fern grows —
like the rest — from a long cemetery.
Here I recover my becoming
infinite with all other earth
and the ironic wisdom: the knowledge
of always being replaceable.
— If this, I suddenly say, this
were my last day—
And with all things I fall in love at once
so beautiful each thing again appears
in its flight, every breath, every insect.
And your very face

— che ieri non riuscivo più a vedere —
ecco ridiventarmi fiore e festa.
O vita, o cara mia felicità.
Mi sento nuovamente buia e calda
come una linfa di pianta nel sole,
come una cosa amata

FELINI*

La lunga tigre lucente, il leopardo fiorito
— la guardinga, la silenziosa grazia —
tuttora ci minacciano
ma della loro scomparsa

GABBIANI*

Gabbiani blu gridano ai pesci ingiurie
parolacce. Gridano in Gabbiano
ai pesci: ehi, voi! ehi, voi!
Ci si buttano sopra imprecando.
 Ultimamente i cieli
si erano fatti così muti che
perfino quest'ira dall'aria
sembra piacevole cosa se pure
atroce come la vita

*From Daria Menicanti, *Altri amici* (Forlì: Forum, 1986), translations from Blum and Trubowitz, *Contemporary Italian Women Poets*, 9.

— that yesterday I could no longer see —
now becomes flower and feast to me.
 Oh life, oh my dear happiness.
I again feel dark and warm
as a plant's sap in the sun,
as a thing loved

FELINES

The long lustrous tiger, the flowered leopard
— the wary, the silent grace —
still they threaten us
but with their disappearance

SEAGULLS

Blue seagulls yell insults
swearing at the fish. They yell in Seagulese
to the fish: hey, you! hey, you!
They dive at them cursing.
Lately the skies
had become so mute that
even this ire from the air
seems an agreeable thing though
atrocious as life

Translations by Cinzia Sartini Blum and Lara Trubowitz

TONINO GUERRA
(1920–)

Tonino Guerra was born in the small village of Santarcangelo di Romagna, near Rimini. During the Second World War his family took refuge in a nearby hut, and when his father sent him to feed their abandoned cat, Guerra was captured and taken prisoner by the Germans. While interred in the Troisdorf concentration camp, he began writing poetry in his native Romagnole dialect in order to entertain and comfort his fellow prisoners and countryfolk. These verses are collected in his first book, *I Scarabòcc* (Sketches). In the early 1950s he settled in Rome, where he met Lorenzo Vespignani, Elio Petri, Giuseppe De Santis, and Aglauco Casadio, and began work as a writer, principally of screenplays. Well known for his film work — especially his contributions to *Amarcord* — Guerra has collaborated with many directors, including Vittorio De Sica, Wim Wenders, Theo Angelopoulos, Andrei Tarkovsky, Francesco Rosi, and Federico Fellini. In much of his poetry Guerra explores with epigrammatic and playful language the relationships among the people, animals, and landscape of his homeland of Romagna, where he returned to live permanently in 1989. His many works include *I Bu* (Oxen), *Il Miele* (Honey), *La Capanna* (The hut), *Il Viaggio* (The journey), and *Il Libro delle chiese abbandonate* (The book of abandoned churches).

93

E' MI FIÓMM*

*Èulta e' mi fiómm
u i è tótt un mònd
ch'l'è fat ad cani, ad fraschi
e bagarózz chi dórma te su bòzal,
chi sòuna se ta i scróll
mo sa girài?*

*E u i è dal còunchi 'd réina
da stè cucléd dri l'aqua
in zirca d'ór
s'óna ad cal sdazi vèci da faréina.*

*Te zil
una culòmba a un téir ad s-ciòp.*

E' PARADÉIS L'È BRÓTT

*E' paradéis l'è brótt
s'u n gn'è un pó' d'animèli
s'u i mènca la girafa se còl lòngh
e al mièri di gazótt ch'i rèsta sòtta tèra
in vòula piò te zil pri cazadéur.*

*Mo cum faràl se u i capita e' mi ba
che pasa dò tre òuri dla su vciàia
s'una gatina biènca tla faldèda
e la mi ma ch'la pénsa d'artruvè una gata
ch'l'è andè a muréi dalòngh, d'fura da chèsa.*

*All poems in this section are from Tonino Guerra, *I bu* (Rimini: Maggioli, 1993). Versions of these translations by Patrick Barron first appeared in *ISLE: Interdisciplinary Studies in Literature and Environment* 7.2 (2000): 265–68.

94

MY RIVER

Along my river
moves a world of bushy canes,
worms who sleep in cocoons and
make sounds if you bump them;
who knows what they say?

There are troughs of sand
where you can hunker down
and search for gold
with an old flour sifter.

In the sky
flies a dove within gunshot.

HEAVEN IS UGLY

Heaven is ugly
if there are no animals
if there is not the long necked giraffe
if there are not the flocks of birds that rest on land,
and fly no more in the air for hunters.

But what will my dad do
who spends hours of his old age
with a white kitten on his knees
and what will my mom do
who thinks she'll find the other cat there
that went away to die far away, out of the house.

I BU

Andè a di acsè mi bu ch' i vaga véa,
che quèl chi à fat i à fat,
che adèss u s'èra préima se tratòur.

E' pianz e' cór ma tótt, ènca mu mè,
avdài ch'i à lavurè dal mièri d'an
e adès i à d'andè véa a tèsta basa
dri ma la córda lònga de mazèl.

LA MÓRTA

Mu me la mórta
la m fa una pavéura che mai
ch'u s lasa tròpa ròba ch'la n s vàid piò:
i améigh, la tu faméia,
al piènti de Pasègg ch'agli à cl'udòur,
la zénta te incuntrè una vólta snò.

A vrèa muréi d'invéran quant che pióv
ch'u s fa la sàira prèst,
e 'd fura u s spórca al schèrpi te pantèn
e u i è la zénta céusa ti cafè
datònda ma la stóva.

E' MÓND L'È BÈL

E' mònd l'è bèl: u n bsògna aviléis mai,
e' basta un furminènt a zènd e' fugh
o i t vén a déi che a qua sal nòsti spiàgi
u s'è arenè stanòta una baléna.

E' mònd l'è grand ch'u n s pò gnénca pensè:
un bastimént te mèr l'è un pizòun biènch
e' tèra e' tèra ch'u n i sta niséun
e u s vàid dal gran pidèdi d'animèli.

96

OXEN

Go and tell the oxen to go away
that you don't need their work anymore
that today it's quicker to plow with a tractor.

And then we're even moved to think
of the hard labor they've done for thousands of years
now that they're leaving with heads held low
behind the long rope of the butcher.

DEATH

To me death
is so frightening
because you must leave too much
that you will never see again:
friends, your family
the plants of the street with their smell,
people who you met only once.

I would like to die in the winter when it's raining
when evening falls quickly,
and outside shoes get full of mud in the road
and people close themselves up in cafés
huddled around stoves.

THE WORLD IS BEAUTIFUL

The world is beautiful, no need to ever grow disheartened,
one match is enough to start a fire
yet they say that on our shores
a whale beached itself last night.

The world is so huge that you can't even imagine:
a ship in the sea is like a white pigeon,
then there are lands where no one lives
and others with only the giant tracks of animals.

Translations by Patrick Barron

97

ANDREA ZANZOTTO
(1921–)

One of the most respected of contemporary Italian poets, Andrea Zanzotto was born in Pieve di Soligo, a small village in the hilly farm country of the Veneto. He studied literature in Padua, took part in the resistance, worked for two years in Switzerland and France, and then returned to Pieve di Soligo in the late 1940s, where he has remained and worked as a teacher ever since. In his verse, Zanzotto delves beneath the surfaces of nature, history and language, an activity alluded to in the title of his first collection *Dietro il paesaggio* (Behind the landscape). With a rare lifelong familiarity with place, his poetry explores the complex interweavings of culture and nature evident in his village, the surrounding countryside, and the nearby remnants of the ancient Montello forest. Other important themes in his work include the tragic divide between the soul and the psyche, linguistics (especially local dialects), and the mythic underpinnings of culture and society. His many works include: *IX Ecloghe* (IX Eclogues), *Sull'altopiano: racconti e prose 1942–1954* (On the upland plain: stories and other writings 1942–1954), *La beltà* (Beauty), *Pasque* (Easters), *Il Galateo in bosco* (A woodland book of manners), *Idioma* (Idiom), and *Sovrimpressioni* (Superimpressions).

UN LIBRO DI ECLOGHE*

Non di dèi non di prìncipi e non di cose somme,
non di te né d'alcuno, ipotesi leggente,
né certo di me stesso (chi crederebbe?) parlo.
Né indovino che voglia tanta menzogna, forte
come il vero ed il santo, questo canto che stona
ma commemora norme s'avvince a ritmi a stimoli:
questo che ad altro modo non sa ancora fidarsi.
Un diagramma dell'«anima»? Un paese che sempre
piumifica e vaneggia di verde e primavere?
Giocolieri ed astrologi all'evasione intenti,
a liberar farfalle tra le rote superne?
Trecentomila parti congiunte a fil di lama,
l'acre tricosa macchina che il futuro disquama?

Faticosa parentesi che questo isoli e reggi
come rovente ganglio che induri nell'uranico
vacuo soma, parentesi tra parentesi innumeri,
pronome che da sempre a farsi nome attende,
mozza scala di Jacob, «io»: l'ultimo reso unico:
e dunque dèi e prìncipi e cose somme in te,
in te potenze, cose d'ecloga degne chiudi;
in te rantolo e fimo si fanno umani studi.

ECLOGA I*

I lamenti dei poeti lirici

Persone: a, b

a – *Alberi, cespi, erbe, quasi*
veri, quasi all'orlo del vero,

---

*From Andrea Zanzotto, *IX Ecloghe* (Milano: Mondadori, 1962). Versions of the translations of "Un libro ecloghe," Per la finestra nuova," and "Ormai" by Patrick Barron first appeared in *ISLE: Interdisciplinary Studies in Literature and Environment* 7.2 (2000): 269–72.

A BOOK OF ECLOGUES

Not of gods not of princes and not of things sublime,[14]
not of you nor of anyone, readable hypothesis,
nor certainly of myself (who would believe it?) do I speak.
Nor can I guess why so much lying is needed, strong
as the true and the sacred, this song which is out of tune
but commemorates rules, draws itself towards rhythms and stimuli:
this which with another mode still knows not how to trust.
A diagram of the "soul"? A land that is always
sprouting feathers and raving of green and of springtimes?
Jugglers and astrologers intent on escape,
on freeing butterflies among ethereal wheels?[15]
Three hundred thousand parts joined along a knife blade,
the bitter jumbled machine which disrupts the future?

Exhausting parenthesis that isolates and supports this
like a burning ganglion that endures in the uranic[16]
vacuous burden, parenthesis within innumerable parentheses,
pronoun forever waiting to become noun,
Jacob's severed ladder, "I": the last made singular[17]:
and thus gods and princes and things sublime in you,
in you powers, things worthy of an eclogue you enclose;
in you death-rattle and filth become human studies.

ECLOGUE I

Lament of the lyrical poets

Personae: *a, b*

a – Trees, bushes, grasses, almost
real, almost on the edge of the real,

dal dominio del monte che la gran luce
   simula
sempre tornando, scendendo
a incristallirvi
in oniriche antologie:
mite selva un lamento
mite bisbigliate un accorato
ostinato non utile dire.
Significati allungano le dita,
sensi le antenne filiformi.
Sillabe labbra clausole
unisono con l'ima terra.
Perfettissimo pianto, perfittissimo.

. . . .

E tenta di valere, accenna, avvampa
l'altra mano dell'uomo.
Da lei protesa
rugge, accelera il razzo a dipanare
il metallo totale dei cieli.
Per lei fibrilla il silenzio, incellulisce.
Oh aquiloni orientati
più su dell'infanzia, più del punto che brilla,
mano da un fuoco a un altro, mano bisturi.
Mano dove gli strati serpeggiano nel coma,
dove il ventre della terra accampa
profili irriferibili,
funzioni insospettate, osceni segni,
foglie e corpi di sofismi, il libro
che non scrisse, la penna, non illustrò, il colore.
Autopsie, autopsie.
Mano da un fuoco a un altro, mano bisturi.

. . . .

Ma pure, ecco, «le mie labbra non freno»
insinui, selva,
tu molto umiliata,
tu quasi viva, più che viva, quasi viva

from the dominion of the mountain which the great light
    simulates
always returning, descending
to crystallize
in oneiric anthologies:
quiet forest you whisper
a quiet lament, an aggrieved
obstinate useless speaking.
Meanings elongate fingers,
senses stretch out their wiry antennae.
Syllables lips clauses
unite with the deep earth.
Most perfect lament, most perfect.
. . . .
Attempting to be of value,
man's other hand beckons, burns.
From it propelled
roaring, the rocket accelerates to unravel
the total metal of the skies.
Through it silence seeps, forms cells.
Oh kites steered[18]
higher than infancy, higher than the shining point,
hand from one fire to another, scalpel hand.
Hand where the layers creep in the coma,
where the earth's belly advances
inexplicable profiles,
unsuspected functions, obscene signs,
leaves and bodies of sophisms, the book
the pen didn't write, color didn't illustrate.
Autopsies, autopsies.
Hand from one fire to another, scalpel hand.
. . . .
And yet, look, "I do not curb my lips"[19]
you insinuate, forest,
you much humiliated,
you almost alive, more than alive, almost alive

— le tue foglie movendo
bagliori come d'insetto nel lago
albuminoso che fu notte fu giorno
occhio in gioia occhio in lutto...

. . . .

Chiedono, implorano, i poeti,
li nutre Lazzaro alla sua mensa,
come cigni biancheggiano.
Invocano l'amata
l'iddio la pia vittima le orme
che s'addentrano al simbolo
(morì quel simbolo, morì).
Nomi hanno, date con interrogativo,
schede, schemi,
cadaveri com'elitre
in oniriche antologie.
Perfettissimo pianto, perfettissimo.
I poeti tra cui
se tu volessi pormi
«cortese donna mia»
sidera feriam vertice.

b – Come per essi, basterà la tua
confessione, immodesta, amorosa,
e quasi vera e più che vera
come il canone detta:
a – «Ma io non sono nulla
nulla più che il tuo fragile annuire.
Chiuso in te vivrò come la goccia
che brilla nella rosa e si disperde
prima che l'ombra dei giardini sfiori,
troppo lungo, la terra.»

– your leaves moving
gleams as if from insects in the albuminous
lake that was night was day
eye in joy eye in grief…
. . . .
They ask, implore, the poets,
Lazarus feeds them at his table,[20]
like white swans they shine.
They invoke the loved one
the god the pious victim the tracks
which penetrate the symbol
(it died that symbol, it died).
They have names, dates with question marks,
filing cards, diagrams
cadavers like the wing-casings of insects
in oneiric anthologies.
Most perfect lament, most perfect.
The poets among whom
if you wished to place me
"cortese donna mia"
sidera feriam vertice.[21]

– As for them, your confession,
immodest, loving, is enough,
and almost true and more than true
as the canon dictates:
– "But I am nothing
nothing more than your fragile assent.
Closed in you I will live like a drop
that gleams in a rose and is scattered
before the gardens' shadow withers,
stretched too long upon the earth."

105

ECLOGA II*

La vita silenziosa

a M.

I

Sediamo insieme ancora
tra colli, nella domestica selva.
Tenere fronde dalle tempie scostiamo,
soli e cardi e vivaci prati scosto
da te, amica. O erbe che salite
verso il buio duraturo, verso
qui omnia vincit.
E venti estinguono e rinnovando
a ogni volgere d'ore e d'acque
le anime nostre.
Ma noi sediamo intenti
sempre a una muta fedele difesa.
Tenera sarà la mia voce e dimessa
ma non vile,
raggiante nella gola
— che mai l'ombra dovrebbe toccare —
raggiante sarà la tua voce
di sposalizio, di domenica.
Non saremo potenti, non lodati,
accosteremo i capelli e le fronti
a vivere
foglie, nuvole, nevi.
Altri vedrà e conoscerà: la forza
d'altri cieli, di pingui
reintegratrici
atmosfere, d'ebbri paradossi,
altri moverà storia
e sorte. A noi
le madri nella cucina fuochi

*From Zanzotto, *IX Ecloghe.*

ECLOGUE II

The silent life

to M.

I

Again we sit together
amidst hills, in the domestic wood.
We brush branches from our foreheads,
suns and thistles and vivacious meadows I brush away
from you, friend. Oh grasses that climb
towards enduring dark, towards
qui omnia vincit.[22]
And winds extinguish and renew
at every turn of hours and waters
our souls.
But we sit intent
always in a silent, faithful defense.
Kind will my voice be and restrained
but not cruel,
shining in the throat
— which never should the shadow touch —
shining will your voice be
of the wedding, of Sunday.
We will not be powerful, nor praised,
we will draw near hair and brows
to live
leaves, clouds, snows.
Others will see and know: the strength
of other skies, of rich
restorative
atmospheres, of intoxicated paradoxes,
others will shift history
and fate. For us
mothers in kitchens watch over

poveri vegliano, dolce
legna in cortili cui già cinge il nulla
colgono. Poco latte
ci nutrirà finché
stolti amorosi inutili
la vecchiezza ci toglierà, che nel prossimo
campo le mal fiorite aiole
prepara e del cuore
i battiti incerti, la pena
e l'irreversibile stasi.

II

Ma tu conoscerai del mio sorriso
l'implorazione ferma
nei millenni come una ferita,
io del tuo l'alba ad ogni alba.
Germoglio lieve ti conoscerò:
quanto aprirai, quanto ci appagherai
di lievi avvenimenti.
Droghe innocue, bufere di marzo;
orti d'iridi e cera, sinecure
per menti e mani molli d'allergie;
letture su pulviscolo d'estati,
letture su piogge, tra spine infinite di piogge.
Talvolta Urania il vero
come armato frutto ci spezzerà davanti:
massimi cieli,
voli che la notte
solstiziale riattizza,
gemme di remotissimi
odî e amori, d'idrogeno
sfolgorante fatica:
deposti qui nell'acqua di un pianeta
per profili di colchici e libellule.

Forse alzerò fino a te le mie ciglia

poor fires, gather mild
firewood in courtyards walled by
nothingness. A little milk
will nourish us until,
foolish useless loving,
old age carries us off, that in the next field
prepares the poorly blooming flowerbeds
and in the heart
uncertain beats, the pain
and the irreversible stasis.

    II

But you will know from my smile
the pleading, fixed
like a wound through the millennia,
I, from yours, the dawn at every dawn.
I will know you as a light bud:
how much you will unfold, how much you will please us
with light events.
Innocuous drugs, March storms;
gardens of rainbows and wax, sinecures
for minds and allergy-softened hands;
readings on the fine dust of summer,
readings on rains, amidst innumerable thorns of rain.
Sometimes Urania will split truth[23]
before us as if it were armored fruit:
maximum skies,
flights that the solstitial
night sets blazing again,
gems of the remotest
hates and loves, of hydrogen
raging travail:
laid down here in the water of a planet
through profiles of saffron and dragonflies.

Perhaps I will raise my eyes up until I see you,

fino a te la mia bocca cui l'attesa
alterò dire, esistere.
E anche nella terra,
domani, l'ultimo mio indizio
inazzurrirà di stellari entusiasmi,
di veloci convulse speranze.

Avremo lontananze capovolte
specchi che resero immagini rubate
fiori usciti da mura ad adorarti.
Saremo un solo affanno un solo oblio.

PER LA FINESTRA NUOVA*

Brilla la finestra del verde lungamente
lungamente composto, sogno a sogno,
orti o prati non so; ma quanta brina
prima ch'io mi convinca, quanta neve.

Verde del grano che alzi il capo e irridi
tra l'incerto oro e il vuoto:
tu, mia finestra, e tu, cielo, che porti
a me tra placidi astri gli squillanti satelliti

che il gioco umano ha lanciati, con lampi
di fantascienza, a vagheggiare in orbite
leggiere i colli, e li vede a piè fermo
il bue sul campo arato e la vite e la luna.

O mia finestra, purezza inestinguibile.
Per farti spesi tutto ciò che avevo.
Ora, non lieto, in povertà completa,
ancora tutti i tuoi doni non gusto.

Ma tra poco
tutto mi darai quel che anelavo.

*From Zanzotto, *IX Ecloghe*.

until to you my mouth reaches, that in waiting,
changed speech, existence.
And even in the earth,
tomorrow, my last sign
will turn blue with starred enthusiasms,
with swift convulsive hopes.

We will have distances reversed
mirrors that returned stolen images
flowers sprouting from walls to adore you.
We will be a single care, a single oblivion.

THROUGH THE NEW WINDOW

The window shines with lengthening green
long shaped, dream by dream,
orchards or meadows I don't know: but how much frost
before it convinces me, how much snow.

Green of the wheat that raises its head and laughs
between uncertain gold and emptiness:
you, my window, and you, sky, that carry
to me amidst quiet stars the blaring satellites

that the human game launched, with lights
of science-fiction, to gaze longingly in orbit
at the hills, that are seen in turn by the unmoving
ox in the ploughed field, vines and the moon.

Oh my window, inextinguishable purity.
To make you I spent all that I had.
Now, unhappy, in complete poverty,
still all of your gifts I do not enjoy.

But before long
you will give me all that I longed for.

ORMAI*

Ormai la primula e il calore
ai piedi e il verde acume del mondo

I tappeti scoperti
le logge vibrate dal vento ed il sole
tranquillo baco di spinosi boschi;
il mio male lontano, la sete distinta
come un'altra vita nel petto

Qui non resta che cingersi intorno il paesaggio
qui volgere le spalle.

---

*From Andrea Zanzotto, *Dietro il paesaggio* (Milano: Mondadori, 1951).

BY NOW

By now the primrose and the warmth
at your feet and the green insight of the world

The uncovered carpets
the loggias shaken by wind and sun
tranquil worm of the thorny woods;
my distant pain, distinct thirst
like another life in the breast

Here all that's left is to wrap the landscape around the self
and turn your back.

Translations by Patrick Barron

PIER PAOLO PASOLINI
(1922–1975)

Best known for his work as director of such films as *Il Decamerone (The Decameron)*, *Il Vangelo secondo Matteo (The Gospel according to Saint Matthew)*, *Medea*, *Teorema* (Theorem), and *Accattone*, Pier Paolo Pasolini was also a respected poet, novelist, critic, and scholar. One of the most complex and infamous figures of the arts in Italy after the Second World War, Pasolini was a passionate experimentalist and remained open to a variety of artistic and idealistic approaches — from neorealism to his own brand of largely heretical Marxism. He was dedicated to bringing the traditional and the contemporary back into a meaningful dialogue, and was convinced that the lowest underclasses of society held a crucial, uncorrupted vitality, despite problems of spiritual and environmental degradation. His interest in (experimental) linguistics and regionalism produced several anthologies of dialect poetry, and influenced his novels *Ragazzi di vita* (*The Ragazzi*) and *Una vita violenta* (*A Violent Life*), written in a mix of Roman dialect and Italian. His poetry, stretching from the early, Viareggio Prize-winning *Le ceneri di Gramsci* (The ashes of Gramsci) to *Poesia in forma di rosa* (Poetry in the form of a rose), is at once lyrical, narrative, and by turns hermetic. It combines the influences of the nineteenth-century poetic forms and meters of Pascoli and Carducci, with the innovations of Umberto Saba, Montale, and Ungaretti.

IL PIANTO DELLA SCAVATRICE (SEZIONE II) *

Povero come un gatto del Colosseo,
vivevo in una borgata tutta calce
e polverone, lontano dalla città

e dalla campagna, stretto ogni giorno
in un autobus rantolante:
e ogni andata, ogni ritorno

era un calvario di sudore e di ansie.
Lunghe camminate in una calda caligine,
lunghi crepuscoli davanti alle carte

ammucchiate sul tavolo, tra strade di fango,
muriccioli, casette bagnate di calce
e senza infissi, con tende per porte...

Passavano l'olivaio, lo straccivendolo,
venendo da qualche altra borgata,
con l'impolverata merce che pareva

frutto di furto, e una faccia crudele
di giovani invecchiati tra i vizi
di chi ha una madre dura e affamata.

Rinnovato dal mondo nuovo,
libero — una vampa, un fiato
che non so dire, alla realtà

che umile e sporca, confusa e immensa,
brulicava nella meridionale periferia,
dava un senso di serena pietà.

Un'anima in me, che non era solo mia,

*From Pier Paolo Pasolini, *Le ceneri di Gramsci* (Milano: Garzanti, 1976).

THE TEARS OF THE EXCAVATOR (SECTION II)

Poor as a cat in the Coliseum
I lived in a slum of limestone
and dust clouds, far from the city

and from the country, wedged each day
in a wheezing bus:
and every going, every return

was an ordeal of sweat and anxiety.
Long walks in the hot haze,
long dusks in front of my papers

piled on the table, amidst muddy streets,
low walls, small whitewashed shanties,
windowless, with curtains for doors…

The olive seller and ragman passed by,
coming from some other slum,
with dusty goods that seemed

the fruits of theft; and the cruel faces
of youths aged among the vices
of those with hardened and hungry mothers.

Renewed by the new world,
free — a blast of heat, an indescribable
breath, gave a sense of serene piety

to that humble and squalid,
confused and immense reality,
swarming in the southern slums.

A soul within me, not merely my own,

una piccola anima in quel mondo sconfinato,
cresceva, nutrita dall'allegria

di chi amava, anche se non riamato.
E tutto si illuminava, a questo amore,
forse ancora di ragazzo, eroicamente,

e però maturato dall'esperienza
che nasceva ai piedi della storia.
Ero al centro del mondo, in quel mondo

di borgate tristi, beduine,
di gialle praterie sfregate
da un vento sempre senza pace,

venisse dal caldo mare di Fiumicino,
o dall'agro, dove si perdeva
la città fra i tuguri; in quel mondo

che poteva soltanto dominare,
quadrato spettro giallognolo
nella giallognola foschia,

bucato da mille file uguali
di finestre sbarrate, il Penitenziario
tra vecchi campi e sopiti casali.

Le cartacce e la polvere che cieco
il venticello trascinava qua e là,
le povere voci senza eco

di donnette venute dai monti
Sabini, dall'Adriatico, e qua
accampate, ormai con torme

di deperiti e duri ragazzini
stridenti nelle canottiere a pezzi,
nei grigi, bruciati calzoncini,

i soli africani, le piogge agitate

a small soul in that boundless world,
grew, fed with the joy

of one who loved, though the love be unrequited.
And everything filled with the light of this love,
perhaps still the heroic love of a young boy,

yet matured by experience,
born at the foot of history.
It was the center of the world, in that world

of sad Bedouin slums,
of yellow prairies scoured
by a relentless, unquiet wind,

that came up from the warm sea of Fiumicino,[24]
or from the plains, where the city
disintegrated amidst the hovels; in that world

that could be dominated only
by the square sallow specter
in the sallow haze

of the Penitentiary, punched in by a thousand
identical rows of barred windows,
amidst old fields and sleepy farmhouses.

Trash and dust were blindly
tossed about by the breeze,
the poor echoless voices

of women come down from the Sabine
hills and the Adriatic, and here
encamped with swarms

of underfed, hardened and shrieking
children in tattered undershirts
and gray, sun-bleached shorts,

in the African sun, the restless rains

che rendevano torrenti di fango
le strade, gli autobus ai capolinea

affondati nel loro angolo
tra un'ultima striscia d'erba bianca
e qualche acido, ardente immondezzaio...

era il centro del mondo, com'era
al centro della storia il mio amore
per esso: e in questa

maturità che per essere nascente
era ancora amore, tutto era
per divenire chiaro — era,

chiaro! Quel borgo nudo al vento,
non romano, non meridionale,
non operaio, era la vita

nella sua luce più attuale:
vita, e luce della vita, piena
nel caos non ancora proletario,

come la vuole il rozzo giornale
della cellula, l'ultimo
sventolio del rotocalco: osso

dell'esistenza quotidiana,
pura, per essere fin troppo
prossima, assoluta per essere

fin troppo miseramente umana.

that turned the streets into muddy
torrents, the buses mired

at the end of the line in a corner
between a last strip of whitened grass
and some heap of rancid, fermenting garbage...

it was the center of the world,
as my love for it was at the center
of history: and in this

maturity, still growing, there was
love all the same, and everything was
on the verge of becoming clear — it was

clear! That slum, naked in the winds,
not Roman, not southern,
not working class, was life

in its clearest light:
life, and light of life, full
in the chaos not yet proletarian,

as the rough newspaper of the
cell or the latest waving
of magazines would have it: bone

of daily existence,
pure, because so
close, absolute because

all too miserably human.

Translation by Patrick Barron

JOLANDA INSANA
(1937–)

Jolanda Insana was born in Messina and lives in Rome, where she works as a teacher. Her poetry has appeared in numerous anthologies, including *Poesia femminista italiana, Poesia degli anni settanta, Poesia erotica italiana del novecento, Poesia italiana oggi, Contemporary Italian Women Poets, The Defiant Muse,* and *Italian Women Poets of the Twentieth Century.* She has received awards for *Fendenti fonici* (Mondello) and *Il collettame* (Rimini Poesia). Insana's scholarly interests include Sappho's poems and Plautus's and Euripides' plays. She has also edited Ahmad Shawqi's *La passione di Cleopatra* and Aleksandr Tvardovskij's *Per diritto di memoria.**

---

*Introductory note by Cinzia Sartini Blum and Lara Trubowitz from Blum and Trubowitz, *Contemporary Italian Women Poets,* 284.

EXCERPTS FROM IL RADICAMENTO *

. . . .

non sente nessun bisogno d'innalzare pergole
e si mette in ginocchio
per curare il seme buono che germoglia
perché riconosce le erbe tossiche e anche i fiori
e non farebbe mai una frittata di ranuncoli
ma prepara insalate di foglie di fragola tenerelle

e si stringe stretta al petto reggendosi in piedi
quando soffia malo vento e sturati rigurgitano
gli sfiatatoi delle anime bolle

alla moltiplicazione del pesco
più d'ogni altro conviene
l'innesto a occhio dormiente^{25}

volendo godere maggior frutto e di maggior durata
zappa la vigna tre volte l'anno
e la netta dagli erbaggi che tolgono alimento

e ariosamente ordina i rami

*From Jolanda Insana, *L'occhio dormiente: 1987–1994* (Venezia: Marsilio, 1997), translation from Blum and Trubowitz, *Contemporary Italian Women Poets*, 181.

124

EXCERPTS FROM THE ROOTING

. . . .

she doesn't feel the need to erect pergolas
and kneels down
to care for the good seed that sprouts
because she recognizes toxic herbs as well as flowers
and would never make an omelet with buttercups
instead she prepares salads with tender strawberry leaves

and hugs her chest tightly remaining on her feet
when bitter wind blows and unplugged vents
overflow with bubbling souls

most fitting
is the grafting of a dormant bud
for the multiplication of the peach tree

as she wants to enjoy more and more lasting fruit
she hoes the vineyard three times a year
and rids it of the greens that sap nutrition

and airily orders the branches

Translation by Cinzia Sartini Blum and Lara Trubowitz

MARIELLA BETTARINI
(1942–)

Mariella Bettarini was born and lives in Florence. She worked as an elementary school teacher for twenty-five years. In the 1960s she began writing literary analyses and cultural commentaries for national journals and newspapers. She is the founder and director of the journal *Salvo imprevisti* (1973–1992), which adopted the title *L'area di Broca* in 1993. Since 1984, she has been editor, with Gabriella Maleti, of the poetry and prose series Edizioni Gazebo. In addition to her editorial work, Bettarini has written articles on George Bataille, Ralph Waldo Emerson, Pier Paolo Pasolini, feminist poetics and nineteenth-century poetry. She translated the work of Simone Weil and, with Silvia Batisti, edited *Chi è il poeta?* — a collection of photos and interviews with thirty-three poets. Some of her poems have been translated into French, English, Greek, Rumanian, Russian, and Spanish. Her work is included in various anthologies of contemporary Italian poetry, including *Poesie d'amore, Contemporary Italian Women Poets, The Defiant Muse,* and *Donne in poesia: Incontri con le poetesse italiane.**

---

*Introductory note by Cinzia Sartini Blum and Lara Trubowitz from Blum and Trubowitz, *Contemporary Italian Women Poets,* 271.

IL LECCIO*

*Il geranio ha bisogno
d'acqua. Ma all'acqua non importa
se è un geranio o un lillà:
chi crederà di tenermi tra i denti
mentre ride e prepara cose
da contrappormi, non mi avrà
più; ecco io sono una pecora che possiede
altri foraggi, una
che non riesce ad intrupparsi,
che non si rassegna di come va
il mondo e che per questo parla
con la morte con mezzi medianici, le cadono
gli oggetti di mano, vaga con il sacco dei semi
che le è stato dato all'ingresso
e cerca il campo ed esamina che terra c'è
— se roccia o terra —, prova la concentrazione
in acqua dei minerali, il grado
di siccità o pioggia, misura il lavoro
e si pone all'opera senza séguiti
nè baldacchini,*
                   attacca il blocco,
*annaffia, sarchia, ara e semina e non teme
se il campo di fronte ha già la spiga
che si è fatta alta e un altro il fiore denso
perché può darsi che la sua semente non dia
grano né fiore, ma sparto o erba medica
o un unico leccio
in mezzo a una piana secca.*

23 giugno 1968

---

*All poems in this section are from Mariella Bettarini, *Tre lustri e oltre*
(*Antologia poetica 1963–81*) (Caltanissetta-Roma: Sciascia, 1986), translations
from Blum and Trubowitz, *Contemporary Italian Women Poets*, 197–205.

128

THE HOLM OAK

The geranium needs
water. But water does not care
if it is a geranium or a lilac:
they will not have me anymore, those
who believe they hold me in their teeth
laughing and preparing to counter
me; see, I am a sheep who possesses
other fodder, one
not able to join the ranks,
who does not resign herself to the ways of
the world and so speaks
with death through a medium's means, drops
objects from her hands, wanders with the sack of seeds
she was given at the entrance
and searches for the field examining what earth there is
— rock or dirt — tests the concentration
of the minerals in water, the degree
of draught or rain, measures the work
and sets in without entourage
or baldachins,[26]
                              attacks the block,
waters, hoes, plows, and sows, and does not worry
if the opposing field has ears
that have already grown tall or another dense blooms
because it may be that her seed does not give
either wheat or flower, but esparto or alfalfa
or a single holm oak
in the midst of a dry plain.

                                        23 June 1968

BIOGRAFIA

Poi firmo un armistizio, ascolto le voci
che dicono ‹‹zitto!›› al bambino; una cosa
è sicura: la giustizia non emana più
dal re, né da nessuno altro su questa Terra.
Ma poi questi sono discorsi
che vanno e vengono, discorsi che non entrano
nel vivo del tema: o ci si consola da sé
o non si può essere consolati;
ora la mia ‹‹consolazione›› è che sono
una terra vestita di ventisette strati, un tronco
con ventisette anelli, ventisette
vite e morti in capo e — se ho ancora voglia
di giocare con i numeri e rovescio le cifre (1942) —
ecco, scopro l'America.

E poi un boato e siamo sulla luna
— generazione che cresce ormai sui sassi
del Mare della Tranquillità, venuta su
da fuoco e fumo, apprendimento
della parola e sua perdita, presa d'aria
e presa di gas, vita che nasce dal nero
di bombe, oceani spalancati
e colombi morti — senza troppe speranze ma già
non più disperata.

Maggio 1969

SE LA NATURA PARLA A TUTTA GOLA

Se la natura parla a tutta gola
è chiaro che tremo; se mi guardo
nello specchio lungo della vecchiaia
è chiaro che penso; se chi chiama
è l'amore (ed esso chiama a festa, a morto,
con grida terribili, a tempo e del tutto

BIOGRAPHY

Then I sign an armistice, I listen to the voices
that yell "shut up!" to the child; one thing
is certain: justice no longer emanates
from the king, nor from anyone else on this Earth.
But then these are arguments
that come and go, arguments that don't go
to the heart of the issue: either you console yourself
or you cannot be consoled;
now my "consolation" is that I am
a land dressed in twenty-seven layers, a trunk
with twenty-seven rings, twenty-seven
lives and deaths in my head and — if I still feel like
playing with numbers and I reverse the figures (1942) —
voilà, I discover America.

And then a boom and we are on the moon
— generation that now grows on the rocks
of the Sea of Tranquillity, raised
on fire and smoke, acquisition
of the word and its loss, air intake
and gas intake, life born from the blackness
of bombs, gaping oceans
and dead pigeons — without many hopes but already
no longer despairing.

May 1969

IF NATURE BELLOWS

If nature bellows
of course I tremble; if I look at myself
in the long mirror of old age
of course I think; if it is love
that is calling (and it calls in celebration and mourning,
with terrible cries, in time and entirely

fuori tempo) sono terrificata.

Tirata per i capelli, c'è la faccia
dei girasoli che mi arringa,
c'è disavanzo
tra me e me, tra la mia carne e la carne
cumulativa e io sono ormai
quello che mangia e quello
che non ha più fame di nulla.

DICO CHE IL GRILLO LO SCORPIONE
LA CAVALLETTA

dico che il grillo lo scorpione la cavalletta
hanno più forze di me di cui non vale più
parlare né in questo modo né in altri
dato che del soggetto si è parlato anche troppo
e conviene parlare dell'oggetto
a chiare lettere chiare note a chiarissime
grida

poiché i boschi hanno già preso tutti fuoco
e la cenere che rimane sono fatti
da raccontarsi più crudamente con le mani
attorno ai ginocchi dando un calcio soave
a questo mondo perché si metta a camminare.

out of time) I am terrified.

I am dragged by the hair, there are faces
of sunflowers haranguing me,
there is deficit
between me and me, between my flesh and the cumulative
flesh and I am now
the one who eats and the one
no longer hungering.

I SAY THAT THE CRICKET THE SCORPION
THE GRASSHOPPER

I say that the cricket the scorpion the grasshopper
have more strength than me, and I'm no longer worth
talking about neither in this way nor others
since plenty has been said about the subject
and it is better to speak of the object
in clear letters clear notes in the clearest
                                        cries

because the woods have already caught fire
and the remaining ashes are facts
to be recounted more crudely with hands
around knees while giving a gentle kick
to this world so that it begins walking.

Translations by Cinzia Sartini Blum and Lara Trubowitz

LUCIANA NOTARI
(1944–)

Luciana Notari was born in Terni. She graduated from the University of Rome with a degree in Modern Literature. Since then she has taught literature in junior high school and has worked for the RAI radio series "I luoghi della cultura" (The places of culture). Selections of her poems have appeared in such anthologies as *Diapason di voci, L'altro Novecento,* and *Melodie della terra.* She was awarded the Felsina prize for *Animanimalis* and the Nuove Scrittrici prize for *Aiuole di città.* She is currently president of the Gutenberg Association of Terni and has organized festivals of contemporary Italian poetry. The anthology *Oltre il mare ghiacciato,* which Notari edited in 1996, came out of one such event. Her work has appeared in English in *Contemporary Italian Women Poets.* *

*Introductory note by Cinzia Sartini Blum and Lara Trubowitz from: Blum and Trubowitz, *Contemporary Italian Women Poets,* 293.

IL CORPO E L'ANIMA*

Quello che so
lo so con le mie membra,
fatica delle mani e fuoco agli occhi,
stretta allo stomaco di vuoto
e scudisciate rapide al respiro.
L'anima non è astrale, rarefatta,
percorre stretta al corpo la sua strada,
s'intriga forte dentro l'esperienza,
dilaga nelle cose, in confidenza;
batte nei cigli glabri di ogni rospo
e sale nella linfa verticale
dell'albero, germoglio sotto il cielo.

Ed ora che il dolore è oltre il dosso
l'anima sta a suo agio
e si rispecchia
in ogni coda nuda fino all'osso.

SCARTO*

Sullo scarto incolmabile
di voci e desideri
si stampano le orme
scendendo a tratti
al centro della strada
e gli occhi oltrepassano
la folla
attratti da una luce
di segreta origine ma forte.

---

*From Luciana Notari, *La vita è nella vita* (Venezia: Edizione del Leone, 1994), translations from Blum and Trubowitz, *Contemporary Italian Women Poets*, 209, 211.

BODY AND SOUL

What I know
I know with my limbs,
my toiling hands and burning eyes,
I know it from the sinking in my stomach
and the rapid lashing of my breath.
The soul is not astral, rarefied,
it travels close to the body
is tightly entangled in experience,
flows into things, on familiar terms;
beats in a toad's glabrous eyes
and rises in the vertical lymph
of a tree, budding under the sky.

And now that sorrow is beyond the hill
the soul, at ease,
mirrors itself
in every tail, stark-naked.

DISTANCE

Footprints tread
the unfathomed distance
between voices and desires
descending at intervals
onto the middle of the road
and the eyes move beyond
the crowd
drawn by a light
of secret yet forceful origin.

Quello scarto incolmabile
feroce
che rende me
pietosa madre
dell'albero e del seme
del pelo elettrico
di tutti gli animali
di piuma implume
che nasce già violata.

La parola nuota con fatica
trasporta a terra le scorie
le piccole tracce dall'oscuro
le annusa le riplasma ricompone
attenta stringe in mano per fissare
la forma quasi piena
carente di sublime.

ASPRA STAGIONE METROPOLITANA*

Aspra stagione metropolitana,
grigia, riarsa, incenerita;
ai bordi d'un'aiuola incatramata
tracima rinnegata la Natura, la Vita.

PAESAGGIO INVERNALE*

Sui bordi d'autostrada i passerotti
alle ruote s'immolano festosi.
La briciola si tinge un poco in rosso
come rubino di gracile allegria.

*From Luciana Notari, *Aiuole di città* (Pescara: Tracce, 1997), translations from Blum and Trubowitz, *Contemporary Italian Women Poets*, 213.

That unfathomed
fierce distance
which makes me
compassionate mother
of the tree and seed
of the electric hair
of all animals
of unfledged feather
born already violated.

With difficulty the word swims
bringing dross to the shore
small traces from darkness
it smells reshapes recomposes them
carefully holding them, fixed
on the almost full form
which lacks the sublime.

HARSH METROPOLITAN SEASON

Harsh metropolitan season,
gray, parched, burnt to ashes;
repudiated Nature, Life, overflows
at the borders of a tarred flower bed.

WINTER LANDSCAPE

On highway edges the sparrows
offer themselves to the wheels.
The crumb turns a bit red
like a ruby of frail joy.

Translations by Cinzia Sartini Blum and Lara Trubowitz

PROSE

CORRADO ALVARO
(1895–1956)

Born in southern Calabria, Corrado Alvaro at first studied at home with his father, then attended a Jesuit college (until being expelled for reading the "prohibited" writings of Giosuè Carducci, Gabriele D'Annunzio and Guy de Maupassant), and eventually finished his schooling in Umbria. Wounded in the First World War, he turned his full attention to journalism, working for *Il Restino del Carlino*, *Il Corriere della Sera*, and *Il Mondo*, eventually settling in Rome in 1929. Sought by the Germans in the Second World War, he hid in Abruzzo; after hostilities ended, he became director of public radio broadcasting, and then organized the restructuring of Naples. Alvaro's literary output is prodigious and includes poetry, travel writing, and novels. *Gente in Aspromonte* (People of Aspromonte[27]), his best known work, explores southern Italy's difficult web of long-entrenched relations stretching between landowner, peasant, and the landscape. It recounts the ruinous attempt of the Calabrian shepherd Argiro to give his son a religious education and thereby raise his family's standing. Argiro is soon dismissed by his employer, his son Antonello loses his job as a bricklayer, and his other son Benedetto, unable to pay his tuition at the seminary, must withdraw from his studies. In anger and frustration, Antonello becomes a brigand, killing the landowner's cattle and giving the meat to the villagers — until he is arrested. Alvaro's other works include *Itinerario italiano* (Italian travels), *I maestri del diluvio — Viaggio nella Russia sovietica* (Masters of the flood — a journey in Soviet Russia), *L'uomo è forte* (Man is strong), *Incontri d'amore* (Encounters of love), and *L'età breve* (The brief age).

FROM: PEOPLE OF ASPROMONTE[*]

The life of the shepherds in Aspromonte is not easy in winter-time, when the tumultuous torrents rush to the sea and the earth seems to float on water. The shepherds take shelter in their houses built of branches and mud, and sleep with their animals. They go about dressed in long cloaks fastened to tri-angular hoods that protect their shoulders, as might have been worn by a wandering Greek god of winter. The torrents make a deafening roar. In the snowy clearings over fires steam large black cauldrons in which milk curdles with a greenish, strengthening serum of wild herbs. Standing around them, the shepherds with their black cloaks and black clothing ani-mate the gloomy peaks and the scrawny trees, while the green oaks swell their acorns for the black pigs. Into the cauldrons they thrust long and carved wooden spoons, and throw in thick slices of bread. They pull them up through the mix, steaming and glistening with the purest white of bread soaked with milk. They often draw out their rough knives to work on wood. They engrave flowery hearts on whalebones for their sweethearts, carve figurines out of olive branches to put on distaffs, and with red-hot skewers make holes in reed syrinxes. Crouched down at the thresholds of their huts before the shin-ing white earth, they await the day of traveling down to the lowlands, where they can hang their jackets and flasks on the gentle trees of the plain. When the new moon has swept away the rain, they will descend to the village where the houses have walls and are thick with the chatting and sighing of women. The village is hotter and denser than a herd. On clear days the oxen ascend the steep, rough trails, as if in a crêche. So finely shaped and white, they seem larger than the trees, almost like giant, prehistoric animals. Every so often the news arrives that an ox has fallen into a ravine, and the village, like a pack of hounds, waits for the animal to be quartered and hung from the butcher's pole in the piazza, where the dogs sniff the blood and the women buy the meat at low prices.

*From Alvaro Corrado, *Gente in Aspromonte* [1955] (Milano: Garzanti, 2000).

Neither the sheep, nor the oxen, nor the black pigs belong to shepherds. They are the property of the lazy seigneur, who awaits the market day and the whiskered merchants who come up from the harbor. In the windy solitude of the mountain the shepherd smokes his charred pipe, watches his son leap about like a fawn, and listens to the far off songs of younger ones, which interweave with the sound of water falling in the rocky clefts, murmuring like old women out collecting wood. Someone sitting atop a knoll, as if on another earth, gives breath to a small bagpipe — and everyone begins to think of women, wine, and houses with walls. They think of Sundays in the village below when they fill the narrow lanes with their heavy sighs — and responding to them, breathing, are the mules in their stalls and pigs in their pens, the children suddenly shrieking like little sparrows, the old men who can't move anymore gazing at the last bit of light, the old women cooling their tired and swollen bellies in the air, and the young wives peaceful as doves. They think of the visit they will make to some well-off neighbor, where they will see a bottle of wine glimmer in the miserly hands of their host and watch the wine splash down into the glass — which they will gulp down all at once, and then violently shake the last few drops on the ground. Thought of during their long days on the mountain, where they are have nothing to drink but milk, that wine brings memories of a thirst-quenching fire.

It happens every so often that from the neighboring herds some lost, daft sheep or gelded bull stumbles by. Knowing animals as we do humans, the shepherds can tell where they are from, as we would recognize a stranger. They approach the unfamiliar animal and immediately hush their alarmed dogs. Silent and cautious, they grasp and roast it. One thrusts a spit into the body, another turns it over the fire, and another, solemn as a victim before a sacrifice, sprinkles the browning fat with a little bunch of wild herbs. They drink only water, yet feel drunk the same. But evenings such as this happen once a year, if that, and life is hard. At least in the spring their wives climb up to meet them. Then, with the first lambs leaping on the earth are heard the creatures of man wailing on the grass or swinging in cradles strung from branch to branch, where the reawakened dormice and squirrels scurry about. Everything turns green again, even the rocks, and people begin to climb the mountain with the summer wind. The pilgrims commence their journeys to the sanctuaries and are heard on their way across the slopes, singing and playing both day and night. The wine-seller builds his hut of branches next to a spring and at night sets fire to dry tree branches to light the road. Love-struck boys scramble through the crowds to catch a glimpse of their beloved, and there are throngs of mad dogs, seekers of revenge, devotees, fugitives, and drunkards, who all tumble about on the slopes like rocks. And thus the mountain comes alive, and all around the sky is sown with the lights of fireworks that rise up from the villages along the sea like signposts indicating where the houses are, and where the saints are with the faces of those peasants, who no longer need to work and now rest in the spacious silence of the churches.

Translated by Patrick Barron

GIANNA MANZINI
(1896–1974)

Gianna Manzini was born in Pistoia in 1896 and educated in Florence, where she collaborated with several influential journals of the 1920s and '30s. The critically acclaimed author of twenty-four volumes of novels and short stories, spanning six decades, produced four novels: *Tempo innamorato* (Time in love), *Lettera all'editore* (Letter to the publisher), *La Sparviera* (The sparrow hawk) and *Ritratto in piedi* (Standing portrait). Although Manzini eventually moved to Rome where she died in 1974, she retained vivid images of Tuscany in her imagination that continued to inform her fiction. The two pieces here about two typical trees of the Tuscan landscape demonstrate her innate anthropomorphic view of nature, artistically refined into fables. Manzini is known as a writer of "prosa d'arte" or "lyrical prose." With her hallmark of sometimes startling comparisons and contrasts and unusual images she has us take another look at the common things around us, and see them anew. In the last story she wrote, "Sulla soglia" (On the threshold), a young writer enumerates the subject matter of her art: "Birds, flowers, the seasons...smiles: the universe is full of them...sounds, voices."

THE FABLE OF THE OLIVE TREE[*]

The olive is a self-contained tree. On those circumspect limbs, because of the many rigid joints of the saintly plant, the leafy branches make no sound: at the most they discreetly rustle an invitation to silence. In the distance they look like unfocused eyes, with a light submerged in the iris — the eyes of one listening to distant voices. They love to hear singing, and you

---

* From Gianna Manzini, *Favola dell'ulivo e altre prose liriche* (Pistoia: Via del Vento, 1994), 19–23.

mustn't think they bend toward the sea just because they like its color or are flattered by the silver wave that fringes the green, breaks it, overturns it, and thus validates their leaves. They lean sideways toward the sea as though lending an ear: they listen and find a tired but determined courage that needs fables to rock the drowsiness that makes them so dreamy. Then they believe in a remote and erotic life: something fabulous that must be about to begin, perhaps a secret to share with the moon and the water, perhaps the sin of a happiness that earth had denied them, and then a sentence of mortifying exile so that bent arms must rise to face level: sad purgatorial gestures.

They grow old quickly because they contain too many echoes, present and past; or rather, they never seem young, unlike poplars that are so happy to rise, and, it might be said, are like partially clothed children growing up in a hurry.

■

But the tree I wish to tell about is a pitiful olive, bewildered and corrupted, so to speak. Corrupted (it seems impossible) by children singing in a school that has an absolutely white façade, harsher and more unequivocal than a command: a whiteness that must seem cruel to those leaves that veil with gray, almost keep in abeyance, their preference for blue. And yet it was the light from that abrasive whiteness that attracted the olive tree — more than the row after row of sociable vines behind him, too involved with their own company for a poor lonely tree to turn to. And here and there, the road running so straight and sure, unpleasant for an olive tree that is always a little untidy, in spite of all the cosmetics, and which has leaves that certainly hold a passionate memory of the sea. (This can be seen at dawn when the sea is everywhere so near you can smell it. The leaves feel visited, and damp, as though crying, while stirred by a glistening happiness.)

The tree kept moving closer to the school. Its branches bent toward it like elbows in search of support: it resembled an old man patiently prepared to listen for a long time; and it was easy to understand how the cadenced voices pleased it, and how it enjoyed the singsong of the recited lessons. But it was gladdened most of all by the choir that poured from those windows three or four times a day. Then a moving garland of fantasies could be seen on its foliage, a little cloud of resonance that revived the faded silver of the leaves.

In this way the tree grew lazy: it forgot its own legend. By now somewhat plain and unadorned, it wasn't excited by the full moons that once could stir up and engage the happiness of every leaf and free the light imprisoned in it, reviving the contemplative face forgotten by the earth. It didn't take into account the fables that aroused the longing and suffering that becomes a chaste olive flower, a yellow flower that seems like the memory of itself. It lost the aspect of its kind elsewhere. It nearly lay prone in its happiness—a happiness entirely in the present, as if the remote secret of its roots meant nothing. Weak with bliss, it almost never rustled.

∎

Toward the end of October, on one of those bright new mornings that seems like an invitation to activity, when there is a kind of urgency in the air, and one feels behind in his work, the shabby—but nonetheless satisfied—olive tree seemed like a mistake of autumn, an inconvenient disruption, a rent in the year's demanding industry.

They sent a farmer to cut it down, precisely between ten and eleven, the most energetic hour of the day.

A kinship between the man and olive tree was inevitable from first sight, in spite of the ax shining wickedly on the ground. It might be said that they both had similar expectations, grave with certainty, nourished by the faithful rotation of seasons. Time's equal, respectful love bestowed on both the same age; and it is understandable how the farmer, looking at the olive tree, might have felt pity and might have looked at it closely, touching it lovingly with his knuckles. Perhaps he would have liked to sit under it, and compare his wrinkles with those on the trunk, enjoying it as an affirmation; and it would really have been good; but a horse with bells and pink tassels came trotting by and immediately in the distance was the sound of cracking whips. A busy chicken boasted noisily about producing an egg, a gust of wind scattered the last leaves from four mulberry trees which, completely stripped, presented themselves as examples of care and virtue: naturally, then, the farmer began to wield his ax.

At first the tree took no notice, and its impassivity could even be taken for haughtiness and disregard for all that desire of a tired and loving cheek. Then it staggered and seemed about to fall backwards, toward the shriveled vines whose dry old leaves were still (ultimate vanity) distractingly gold and red; but with another blow it bent over and fell against the wall, extending two branches into the window.

As it crashed down, consoled by a brief rustling of leaves, a silence followed that suddenly revealed, almost forced into the open, a luminous gray that lies at the bottom of some extravagant yellows; an absorbent silence in which a child finally rebelled with a sudden burst of tears, and immediately, higher up, a thrush repeated a lament two or three times and then flew in an arc over the oblique crown of the tree that was no more.

A CYPRESS[*]

Cypresses are not particularly sociable as a rule. They stand in pairs, peaceful, neither anxious nor curious. They cannot be expansive, and they have no need to seek consensus by talking about or explaining themselves. One responds to the other, exactly, receives it totally, justifies it in itself; and we have confirmation of that fact because when we put ourselves in line with two cypress we see only one.

Naturally, the one I knew was standing alone, and in vain I looked for its companion on the horizon, the incognito twin. I saw two in the distance keeping watch over a white house, keeping it from being afraid of the nearby woods, which perhaps were moving slowly toward the clearing around it.

Not that the solitary tree told me about itself: effusiveness is something a cypress will not allow itself, and even the wind cannot get it to talk; I found its scar, the sign of a momentous

* From Manzini, *Favola dell'ulivo e altre prose liriche*, 6–10.

event, by myself (an unaccompanied cypress is less intimidating and one can examine it closely).

Once it was enveloped by a cloud. As long as the trunk and branches remained above the cloud it felt it was really in the sky, like an assumption: a lover's delirium; and it felt fulfilled, because it had always imagined its tapered height was made just for this reason: to sooner or later pierce a cloud and live above it. That moment of ecstasy left its tip slightly drunk and waving like a queen to her subjects. The part remaining below the cloud then realized it could no longer support the swaying of the top and, maternally, reached for it, sending up arm-like branches to hold it. The tree made this assiduous effort to feel and appear whole, to maintain the certainty of the earth along the trunk, to hide the scar: the cut made by light, visible, like that appearing on the face of women in love; an effort that made it so consistent and hard as to appear selfish.

■

I returned to greet the lonely tree at the end of a softy sighing September when we believe we are walking on the edge of summer, and in the country there is the sense of fulfillment and slow departure, pleasant delays and long farewells — a diligent laziness. Among the fields, undulating meadows, and soft hills that the eye caresses like a large warm, intimate hand; among those greens that have dissolved, melted and eased into gold, so that the summer seemed like a joyful and well-deserved adventure; among all that the lonely cypress looked old, downhearted, dispirited, dark, therefore more alone than ever. It seemed like a human being: it had the face of someone who has paid for an audacious act. Without a top, the tallest thick branches composed a small crown into which sweetly trickled a bit of blue.

It was like this.

In the faded blue of night, thick clouds lowered, seeking out and mingling with each other. Among the line of trees only one was curved like a penitent. All the others looked up. But in the top of this cypress there was anxiety and alarm, a restless questioning, a startling twisting, a frantic palpitation. With its flexible point it gingerly tested the voluble weight of the sky in all directions. Here a foggy heaviness like contrition and impending tears; there, to the east, a very clear, yielding space, in which it thought it could lightly rise; and right at its zenith, a fan-shaped opening that the tree deceived itself into thinking it had made, perhaps widened, with its unbearable swaying in the air; and the bedazzled top of the cypress made one bold zigzag into that opening. Then another and a third. Now the sky was broken; and in convulsive flashes appear new skies, naked, as at birth.

The tree felt surrounded by a cool cloud right at the level of its old scar; and since the cloud was vacillating, the tree was sure of slowly getting loose and rising. For a moment it was completely in the blue, really an assumption, and it saw through a cloud's flaming red wound the threshold of a compact, rainbow-colored, very fragile sky, certainly the last one.

It was struck: a plunge down through itself to its roots, and the sense of life in its veins just when they seemed to be drying up; then the certainty of having touched the earth in the vertical slide, reentering, of having touched it even with its highest branches and of being cured by its dampness.

The next morning the tree was wet and smelled of resin. On it clearly appeared the face of a devastated happiness: as when one is reluctantly pardoned after too much suffering, before one learns that such a pardon is a little like dying.

■

I didn't care much for cypresses. They had a weapon shape, lacked originality, were extremely standoffish, thick like a row of crows sitting on an embankment just moving their heads. They seemed too ceremonious in a landscape of olive trees and encircling walls, where naive bushes offer a childlike protection for the fields, and genteel adolescent reeds are so luminous and innocent that only water can be their companion, and wheat goes through its seasonal cycles — among all that they seemed like snobbish gentlemen always in evening clothes.

One day, to make my peace with them, I dared to think of them as a way to love God, in a monastic way: fasting and eyes skyward. Then I fancied myself a fugitive from an easily imagined convent on the horizon; and I understood better why they are almost always in pairs. But I was more impressed by the story about the cloud, which is really true. In fact, look at any cypress, and you'll see the mark of that cut made by light: maybe chest high on those cypresses that test the sky's weight with their tips in all directions; or maybe at eye level, like the eyes of a woman in love, on those trees whose tops have been sliced off by lightning.

Nevertheless, sparrows swarming from branch to branch at the onset of evening cover the scar. At night the tree is full of them, and it hides and protects them. Then you can imagine that a good shake of the trunk would make the cypress sway and screech like an enormous toy.

Translated by Martha King

IGNAZIO SILONE
(1900–1978)

Born in the small village of Pescina dei Marsi in the moun-
tainous region of Abruzzo, Ignazio Silone (pseudonym of
Secondino Tranquilli) never strayed far in his writing from
his homeland. He participated in the founding of the Italian
Communist Party, but left in 1930, disillusioned with
Stalinism. After many years spent exiled in Switzerland due
to his unpopular political activities, Silone returned to Italy
in 1945 after the liberation in order to take part in the Social-
ist Party. In 1948 he abandoned his political career. His first
book, *Fontamara*, was composed during his exile and is the
semi-autobiographical account of the slow death of a poor,
marginalized Abruzzese village caused when the local Fascist
ruler diverts its only source of meager irrigation, a mountain
stream. Silone's other works include *Pane e vino* (*Bread and
Wine*), *Il seme sotto la neve* (*The Seed beneath the Snow*), *Il segreto
di Luca* (*The Secret of Luca*), and *L'avventura d'un povero cristiano*
(*The Story of a Humble Christian*). The selection that follows
below is divided into two parts: the first is narrated by the
peasant woman Matalè and the second by her husband.

FROM: FONTAMARA *

A poor, thin spring rises from beneath a heap of stones at the
entrance to Fontamara and forms a puddle. A few paces away,
the water burrows into the stony soil and disappears, to reap-
pear later in the form of a more abundant stream at the bottom
of the hill. The stream makes a number of bends and then
flows in the direction of the Fucino. The *cafoni*[28] of Fontamara
have always drawn their water from it, to irrigate the few fields

---

*From Ignazio Silone, *The Abruzzo Trilogy: Fontamara, Bread and Wine, The Seed
beneath the Snow*, trans. by Eric Mosbacher and Darina Silone (South Royalton, VT:
Steerforth, 2000).

they possess down in the valley, which are the village's meager wealth. Furious quarrels about sharing the water break out every summer. In years of drought these sometimes end in stabbing frays, but the flow of water doesn't increase because of that.

The custom with us at that time of year is for the men to get up early in the morning, at half past three or four, when it's still dark. They drink a glass of wine, load their donkeys, and take the road down to the plain in silence. To avoid wasting time and to get there before the sun is high they eat their breakfast on the way. Breakfast? A crust of bread with an onion or a red pepper or a bit of cheese.

The last Fontamara *cafoni* to go down the hill on June 2 on their way to work met a gang of roadmen who had come from the local town with picks and shovels to divert the wretched stream (so they said) from its course between the fields and vegetable plots, which it had irrigated since time immemorial, and send it in the opposite direction so that it first skirted some vineyards, and then watered some land that did not belong to Fontamara at all, but to a wealthy landowner from the local town called Don Carlo Magna. He belongs to one of the oldest families in our part of the world, now through his own fault greatly in decline, and he got this nickname Magna because at whatever time of day anyone calls on him and says, "Is Don Carlo at home?" the maid always answers, "Don Carlo *magna*, he's at the table, but you can see madam if you like." And indeed it is the mistress who rules the roost in that household.

For a moment or two we thought the roadmen were getting a rise out of us, which the people of the local town (not all of them, of course, but the usual idlers and loafers) never miss an opportunity of doing. A whole day wouldn't be enough to describe all the tricks they have played on us in the last few years. The most disgraceful hoax of all, the famous story of the donkey and the priest, will give some idea of the kind of thing they did.

There has not been a priest at Fontamara for the past forty years; the parish revenue is not sufficient to support one. So the church is generally open only on great feast days, when a priest comes from the local town to say mass and preach the Gospel. Two years ago the people of Fontamara sent a last appeal to the bishop to send us a parish priest. A few days later, contrary to all our expectations, we learned that our prayer had been granted and that we were to prepare to celebrate the priest's arrival. Naturally we did our best to give him a proper reception. We may be poor, but we know how to behave. The church was given a thorough cleaning. The road leading to Fontamara was mended and in some places actually widened. A big triumphal arch was put up at the entrance to the village and decorated with flowers and drapery. The doors of the houses were decorated with green branches. When the great day arrived, the whole village turned out to meet the new priest. After walking for a quarter of an hour we saw a strange-looking crowd coming toward us. There were no priests or representatives of the authorities among them, nothing but strange types and many young hooligans. We went on to meet them in procession, carrying the banner of San Rocco, singing hymns, and reciting the rosary. In front walked the elders, among them General Baldissera, who was to make a short speech, and the women and children brought up the rear. When we were near the people from the town, we divided into two ranks along either side of the road to welcome our priest.

General Baldissera went ahead, waving his hat and shouting excitedly, "Blessed be Jesus! Blessed be the Virgin Mary! Blessed be the Church!"

At that moment the strange crowd of townspeople also divided, and the new priest, in the shape of an old donkey, adorned with colored paper to represent sacred vestments, advanced toward us, urged on by kicks and the throwing of stones.

Jokes of that kind are not easily forgotten, even if the town loafers constantly think up new ones. So our first thought was that the diversion of the stream was a practical joke, too. After all, it would be the end of everything if men started interfering with the elements created by God, and diverted the course of the sun, the course of the winds, and the course of the waters established by God. It would be like hearing that donkeys were learning to fly or that Prince Torlonia was no longer a prince, or that *cafoni* were no longer to suffer from hunger — in other words, that the eternal laws of God were no longer to be the laws of God.

But the roadmen without further ado put their hands to their picks and shovels to dig the new streambed. That seemed carrying the joke a little too far. A boy, Papasisto's son, rushed back to Fontamara, telling everyone he met on the way.

Hurry, hurry, we must tell the *carabinieri*, [29] we must tell the mayor, there's not a moment to lose," he shouted.

There were no idle men in the village. In June there's far too much work in the fields. So the women had to go. Well, you know what women are like. The sun was high before we even started. The whole village was in an uproar. Women repeated the news to each other from one alley to the next; even those who already knew had it repeated ten times by everyone who passed their door. But no one moved. As always at that time of day, I was in the house of poor Elvira, the dyer, whose mother had just died and whose father had been paralyzed since the accident at the quarry. I was helping Elvira look after the old man, who was grumbling and cursing and, as usual, to his daughter's great distress, kept saying he wanted to die. When I heard what the roadmen were doing I refused to believe it. In short, no one would budge. No one wanted to go. No one "could" go. Some had children who couldn't be left, others had chickens or a pig or a goat, or had to do the washing or prepare the sulfur for spraying the vines, or get the sacks ready for the threshing. As usual, nobody "could" go. Everyone wanted to mind her own business. But then Marietta volunteered to go, "because I know how to talk to the authorities," and she was joined by another woman, better not to mention her name, who, although her husband had been in America for ten years, was pregnant — it was hard to believe that her husband could have been responsible for that at such long range.

Michele's wife came to see me and said in a state of great agitation, "Can we allow Fontamara to be represented on a question affecting the whole village by two women who, with all due respect, are no better than whores?"

"Matalè, you go," Elvira said to me. "We can't allow such a disgrace to the village."

It would have been an affront to us all. So we hurried along to see Lisabetta Limona and Maria Grazia and persuaded them to come with us. Maria Grazia persuaded the Ciammaruga woman to join us, and she persuaded Cannarozzo's daughter, who in turn persuaded Filomena and the Quaterna woman.

We had all gathered outside the church and were ready to go when Ponzio Pilato's wife started making a frightful row — because we hadn't asked her.

"You want to go behind our backs, do you?" she screamed. "You want to put yourself forward at the expense of all the rest, do you? Do you suppose my husband's land doesn't need water?"

So we had to wait while she got dressed. But instead of hurrying, she went and fetched Filomena Castagna, Recchiuta, Giuditta Scarpone, and the Fornara woman, and persuaded them to come. Old Faustina, whose husband has been in prison for twenty years, wanted to come, too, but we said to her, "What do you want to come for? Your husband has no need of water."

"But supposing they release him?"

"You've been waiting for him for twenty years and still they don't release him. And even if they did, where would he raise the money to buy back the land?"

"What you really mean is that you don't want to be seen with me," the old woman flung at us, and shut herself up in her house so as not to be seen weeping.

At last about fifteen of us were ready to go, but there was another wait outside Baldissera's shop while Marietta tarted herself up. Eventually she appeared in her Sunday best, wearing a new apron, a coral necklace, and the dead hero's silver medal on her breast. So when at last we left the village, the sun was high and the heat was stifling. At that time of day not even dogs go places if they can help it. The dust was blinding.

When the roadmen saw us approaching, making a clamor and raising a cloud of dust, they were terrified and fled through the vineyards.

. . . .

In the days that followed, an escort of two armed guards was provided for the roadmen, who went on digging the channel that was to take part of our water to the land bought by the contractor. But exactly how much water?

"You worry about your own affairs and let others compromise themselves," every woman at Fontamara told her husband. "Don't get mixed up with the guards and bring ruin to your family."

Everyone waited for others to compromise themselves, and on the way to work in the morning and on the way home at night everyone passed by the guards in silence and in fact tried to look the other way. Thus no one compromised himself. But there was bitterness in our hearts, and in the evening, sitting on the threshold of our houses with our soup plates on our knees, we talked about nothing else. How could we possibly think about anything else?

"When misfortunes begin, who can stop them?" we said to one another. "Perhaps the worst is still to come."

We weren't educated enough to understand how the water could be divided into two parts of three quarters each. Even the women who had agreed to the arrangement disagreed about what it actually meant. Some said the water would be shared out equally, others that Fontamara would keep more than half, that is, three quarters, and Michele Zompa tried to persuade us that the three quarters referred to the phases of the moon, that is, that the stream would irrigate the land of the people of Fontamara for three phases of the moon and the Contractor's land for the following three phases, and so on indefinitely.

Not one of us was educated enough to solve the problem, because we had been taught little except how to write our names, and we were afraid of consulting some educated person, not wishing to add expense to injury. So every evening, while we ate our supper sitting on the threshold of our houses with our soup plates on our knees, from one end of the alley to the other there was no talk of anything but of this new swindle. The same old theories were trotted out over and over again. That it was a swindle was certain, but exactly what sort of swindle? As usual, one Saturday evening General Baldissera made one of his fiery and extravagant speeches about wickedness striking down the innocent but being overtaken in the end by the infallible sword of justice.

"I'll go myself," he started shouting. "I'll go myself and recall the truth to those who have forgotten it."

However, his ardor never went beyond words, not only because of his age but also because of his timidity. In his youth in Fossa, where he had practiced his cobbler's trade, he had learned manners from an old baron who had gone down in the world and on Sunday afternoons and holidays employed him in the ancient and dignified office of Sunday footman. The job was unpaid, but it was gratifying and not in the least tiring, since it consisted solely of following the baron at a respectful distance on his afternoon walk. The baron had been reduced to extreme poverty and often did not have enough money to buy food, let alone employ a servant; he lived in a corner of his old and dilapidated baronial mansion. His last creditors had long since sold all the furniture and movable objects, leaving him only a four-poster bed and an armchair. So he was reduced to the most complete solitude and was looked down on by everyone. But he would never give up his Sunday afternoon walk, which the honor of his house prevented him from taking unaccompanied. Many years had passed since then, but our Baldissera still remembered every detail of what the decayed nobleman had said and done on every occasion, and often he actually invented things and attributed them to him, and those were his best stories. But we let him tell them, because they were obviously a great comfort to him.

General Baldissera was poor enough himself; perhaps he was the poorest of all the inhabitants of Fontamara, but it hurt his pride that this should be known, and he resorted to a variety of little tricks to conceal the hunger from which he had suffered for many years. Among other things, he would seize on the most farfetched excuses to leave Fontamara on

Sundays, and in the evening he would come back, actually hungrier and more sober than ever, but with a toothpick between his teeth and reeling slightly, like someone who has been eating meat and drinking to the point of tipsiness, wanting to look like a man able to spend money and satisfy his whims.

In this state of simulated insobriety he would describe in detail the bold arguments and courageous encounters he had had with prominent personalities in the local town, most of them creditors of the dead baron.

"Oh, if only you could have seen me, if only you could have heard me," he would say, his features transformed by self satisfaction.

Two or three of his old friends knew that all this was complete invention, but we kept the secret to avoid hurting him and depriving him of the only pleasure he had in his wretched existence.

The row about the water also brought us the honor of a totally unexpected visit from Don Abbacchio, the priest. He arrived at Fontamara one evening, sweating and panting, in a trap drawn by a fine horse, and he sent for some of the elders among us, desiring to talk to us about a grave matter.

"You see what sacrifices I make for you?" he said. "I came here because I have more regard for you than for myself. For heaven's sake, don't take on the Contractor," he warned us in a voice as grim as when he talked to us about hell in his sermons. "He's a terrible man," he went on. "A demon such as he has never before been seen in our part of the world. Be patient, that is the best course you can adopt. All you can do is pray."

"If he's possessed by a devil, why don't you exorcise him?" old Zompa interrupted.

Don Abbacchio made a gesture of helpless resignation.

"Perhaps he's not just possessed by a devil, perhaps he's a real devil. The Church can do nothing about it. You are too ignorant to understand these mysteries."

"A real devil?" I said.

"Giovà," the priest replied, "perhaps he's Satan himself."

"Then why hasn't he got horns and cloven feet?" I objected.

"Oh, Giovà," the priest said, "that is no longer the practice. Satan is cunning."

The priest's words made a deep impression on us, and this was further increased when Baldovino told us that he had heard from the coachman that the horse and trap used by Don Abbacchio to come to Fontamara actually belonged to the Contractor. We had never before heard of a devil actually having a priest in his service, and we were too ignorant to understand how such a thing could be possible. So, instead of quarreling with the devil each one of us thought of grabbing for his own benefit and at the expense of everyone else in the village the biggest possible share of the little water that would be left. There were still some weeks to go before irrigation time, but arguments and rows began immediately.

At that time most of us were going to the Fucino[30] for the reaping. We had to get up before dawn and be in the market place in Fossa before sunrise and wait for someone to offer us work. I can't tell you how humiliating that was. At one time only the poorest *cafoni* were forced to offer themselves in the public square in that way, but bad times had come for everyone. The land we small landowners had was mortgaged up to the hilt and yielded hardly enough to pay the interest, so in order to survive we, too, had to go and offer ourselves as day laborers. The landlords and big tenant farmers immediately took advantage of the greater supply of labor in the market to reduce the wages, but, however low they were, there were always *cafoni* forced by hunger to accept them; and some actually got to the point of offering to work without the pay being fixed in advance; they were willing to accept anything at all. From the square at Fossa to the Fucino was another six to ten miles, depending on where the work was, and that was on top of the two and a half miles we had walked to Fossa; and the same distance had to be covered again to get home in the evening, so that every night I was completely exhausted and at the end of my tether.

"I'm not getting up tomorrow morning," I would say to my wife. "Matalè, I can't stand on my feet anymore, I want to die."

But at three o'clock next morning as soon as the cock crowed I woke my son, we drank a glass of wine and off we tramped again behind the donkey.

On the way to the Fucino and on the way back quarrels about the water grew more violent every day. Things began to look serious between me and Pilato, my brother-in-law, as neither of us was willing to sacrifice himself for the other, and both of us went to work accompanied by our sons. When we met, we no longer greeted each other, but the glances we exchanged made it obvious that a quarrel could not be avoided.

Going down to Fossa with my son one morning, we caught up with Pilato just when he was talking to the roadmen.

"Listen, what matters is that you leave enough water for my beans," he was saying. "The others can go to hell."

Whom could he have been referring to except me?

"You'll be in hell first," I shouted, going for him with my billhook.

Berardo Viola and the two guards rushed to intervene, and that day violence was avoided. But for the next few days Berardo came with me to the Fucino to prevent a repetition of the incident. He was able to act as peacemaker in this matter of the water for the simple reason that he no longer had any land, whether irrigated or not, and owned nothing that had to be shared with other *cafoni*. Several years before he had sold to Don Circostanza a good plot of land his father had left him to meet the expenses of a lawsuit and pay for a passage to America. At the time he was thinking of emigrating and, if things went well for him, never again returning to Fontamara. He was sickened by the treachery, as he called it, of a man from Fossa whom he had believed to be his friend. He had met the man during his military service and had subsequently shared bread with him on many occasions and struck up a close friendship with him. He went to his defense in a brawl that suddenly broke out one day near Fossa and hit several heads rather hard, after which he returned to Fontamara, feeling pleased at having done his friend a service without being identified. But his good friend got himself out of trouble by giving *his* name to the *carabinieri*. Berardo was deeply hurt, and for some days was uncertain how to retaliate.

But, as he basically liked the man, he decided never to see him again and leave for some faraway place. Neither his mother's appeals nor our advice made any difference. "If you have land, why go to America?" we said to him. "I'm not staying here," he replied. "It stinks here. I can't breathe here." The only one to encourage him to go was Don Circostanza. "If you stay here," he kept telling him, "you'll die in prison." So Berardo sold his land, paid hush money to the men who had been hurt at Fossa, and bought a passage to America with what remained. But before he left, a new law (that Don Circostanza perhaps already knew about) put a stop to emigration. And so Berardo had to stay at Fontamara like a dog freed from its chain that does not know what to do with its liberty and keeps circling desperately around its empty plate.

But no one blamed him for that. How can a peasant resign himself to the loss of his land? That land had belonged to Berardo's father, and Berardo himself had worked on it since the age of ten. In our part of the world, and perhaps elsewhere too, the relationship of a peasant to his land is a serious thing, like that between husband and wife. It's a kind of sacrament. It's not enough to buy land to make it yours. It becomes yours in the course of years, with toil and sweat, sighs and tears. If you own land, on stormy nights you don't sleep; even if you're dead tired, you don't sleep, because you don't know what is happening to your land; and next morning you rush to go and see. If someone takes your land, it's always rather as if he were taking away your wife, even if he pays hard cash for it, and even when a piece of land is sold, it keeps the name of the former owner for a long time.

Translated by Eric Mosbacher
Revised by Darina Silone

CARLO LEVI
(1902–1975)

Born in Turin, Carlo Levi was a doctor by training and a painter and writer by choice. His first and best known novel *Cristo si è fermato ad Eboli* (*Christ Stopped at Eboli*) depicts the isolated and downtrodden peasant culture of Italy's backcountry south — a world, with its witchcraft, magic, and the belief in animal-deities, largely forgotten by the rest of "civilized" Italy. The book records Levi's stay in the small isolated village of Gagliano in the region of Basilicata during the 1930s — a government-enforced "exile" brought on by his anti-Fascist political activities. Levi's progressive discovery of Gagliano reveals a malaria-infested, despoiled landscape, and a peasant culture oppressed for centuries by a seemingly unending series of exploitative governments. The people of Gagliano are close to their submerged, archaic civilization, whose beliefs are not so much Christian as pagan (the peasant saying that the title refers to states, "We're not Christians. Christ stopped short of here, at Eboli"). Levi's other works include *Le parole sono pietre* (*Words Are Stones*), *Il futuro ha un cuore antico* (The future has an ancient heart), and *Tutto il miele è finito* (All the honey is finished).

FROM: CHRIST STOPPED AT EBOLI*

I stayed three weeks in the widow's house, waiting to find other quarters. The summer was at its dreary pinnacle; the sun seemed to have come to a stop straight overhead and the clayey land was split by the burning heat. In its thirty crevices nested the deadly poisonous, stubby snakes that the peasants call *cortopassi*, "shortsteps": *Cortopassi, cortopassi, ove te trova là*

---

*From Carlo Levi, *Christ Stopped at Eboli: The Story of a Year*, trans. by Frances Frenaye (New York: Farrar, Straus and Giroux, 1989).

te lassi. Snake in the grass; let lie and pass. A continual wind dried up men's bodies, and the days went by monotonously under the pitiless light until sunset and the cool of the evening. I sat in the kitchen gazing at the random flight of the flies, the only token of life in the motionless silence of the dog days. My eyes focused lazily on the thousands of stationary, buzzing black dots that covered the greenish blue wooden shutters. Every now and then, one of the back dots suddenly disappeared in the whir of an abrupt and invisible flight, and its place was taken by a very bright white point, ringed with gold, like a tiny star, whose light gradually died away. Then another fly took off into the air and another star came out on the blue of the shutters. At last Barone, who lay asleep at my feet, was awakened by a dream; he jumped to his feet and caught a fly on the wing, breaking the silence with the violent snapping of his jaws.

Strings of figs hung from the balcony railing, black with flies that were busy sucking the last moisture from them before the blazing sun dried them out altogether. Out on the street, on wide-rimmed tables below the black pennants decorating the front doors, blood-red liquid masses of tomato conserve lay drying. Swarms of flies walked without wetting their feet over the portions already solidified, in numbers as vast as those of the children of Israel, while other swarms plunged into the watery Red Sea, where they were caught and drowned like Pharaoh's armies as they hotly pursued their prey. The pervading silence of the countryside hung heavily over the kitchen, and the monotonous buzzing of the flies marked the passing hours with an endless refrain.

All of a sudden the bell began to ring out from the church nearby, in honor of some unknown saint or as a summons to some unattended function, and its lament filled the whole room. The bell-ringer, a ragged, barefoot boy of about eighteen, with a hypocritical, thieving smile, rang the bell according to an interminable, mournful fancy all his own, in the rhythm of a funeral march. My dog, who was sensitive to the presence of spirits, could not bear this lugubrious sound and at the first note he began to howl in pain, as if death were brushing our shoulders. Or was there something of the devil in him that was ruffled by this sacred music? Anyhow I had to get up and take him outside in order to quiet him. Big, hungry fleas in search of a refuge jumped on the white paving-stones; ticks hung in ambush from blades of grass. The village seemed empty of men; the peasants were in the fields and the women were hidden behind half-closed doors. The street sloped down between the houses that bordered it and the ravines behind them all the way to the landslide without a fragment of shade. I climbed slowly in the opposite direction, toward the cemetery, in search of the slender olive trees and the cypresses.

An animal-like enchantment lay over the deserted village. In the midday silence a sudden noise revealed a sow rolling in a pile of garbage; then the echoes were awakened by the shattering outburst of a donkey's braying, more resonant than the church bell in its weird, phallic anguish. Roosters were crowing; their afternoon song had none of the glorious shrillness of their early morning call, but reflected rather the bottomless sadness of the desolate countryside. The sky was filled with black crows and, above them, circling hawks; their still, round eyes seemed to follow me. Invisible animal presences continued to make themselves felt in the air until finally a goat, the queen of the region, jumped with its bow legs from behind a house and stared at me with blank yellow eyes. Some half-naked, ragged children were chasing it; among them a four-year-old girl wearing the habit, wimple, and veil of a nun, and a five-year-old boy in the cowl and cord of a monk. It is a local custom for parents, in fulfillment of a vow, to dress them thus, in a miniature of religious garb or like the princelings painted by Velasquez. The children wanted to ride the goat; the little monk seized its beard and put his arms around its face, the nun tried to get up on its back, while the others held its horns and tail. For a moment they all managed to straddle it until the beast jumped abruptly, shook itself, tossed them into the dust, and stopped to look at them with an evil smile. The children picked themselves up, recaptured the goat, and mounted it again; the goat ran away, jumping wildly, until the whole lot of them disappeared around a curve.

The peasants say that there is something satanic about goats. This is true of all the animal world, and of the goat in particular. Not that it is wicked or has anything to do with the devils of the Christian religion, in spite of the fact that they often show themselves in its guise. It is demoniacal like every living thing, and even more so than the rest, because some strange power lurks behind its animal exterior. To the peasants the goat represents the ancient satyr, indeed a living satyr, lean and hungry, with curling horns, a crooked nose, and pendulous teats or male organ; a poor, hairy, brotherly, wild satyr, looking for grass on the edge of a precipice.

Under the gaze of these eyes, neither human nor divine, and accompanied by these mysterious powers, I climbed slowly toward the cemetery. But the olive trees gave no shade; the sun pierced their delicate foliage as if it were lacework. I decided to go through the broken-down gate into the enclosure of the cemetery proper; here was the only cool and private spot in the village, and perhaps the least melancholy as well. As I sat on the ground, the dazzling reflection of light from the clay disappeared behind the wall; the two cypresses swayed in the breeze and clusters of roses bloomed among the graves, a strange sight in this flowerless land. In the middle of the cemetery there was a ditch, a yard or two deep, neatly cut out of the dry earth in readiness for the next dead body. A ladder made it easy to get in and out of this open grave, and I had made it my custom on these hot days when I came up here to lower myself into it and lie down. The earth was smooth and dry, and the sun had not burned it. I could see nothing but a rectangle of clear sky, crossed occasionally by a wandering white cloud; not a single sound reached my ears. In this freedom and solitude I spent many hours. When my dog tired of chasing lizards on the sunny wall he peered questioningly into the ditch, then lowered himself down the ladder, curled up at my feet and soon fell asleep. I, too, listening to the cadence of his breathing, eventually let my book fall from my hand, and closed my eyes.

We were awakened by a strange voice, without sex, or tone, or age, mumbling incomprehensible words. An old man was leaning over the edge of the grave and talking to me through his toothless gums; I could see him against the sky, tall and a little bent, with long, thin arms like the vanes of a windmill. He was almost ninety, but his face gave an effect of timelessness; it was shapeless and wrinkled like a dried-up apple; two magnetic bright blue eyes shone out from among the folds of flesh. Not a single strand of beard grew or had ever grown on his chin, and this gave an odd effect to the texture of his skin. He spoke a dialect other than that of Gagliano, a mixture of tongues; he had lived in a number of places, with the idiom of Pisticci predominant, because there, in faraway times, he was born. This mixture, the toothlessness that garbled his words, and the terse and proverbial form of his speech at first made it hard for me to understand him, but as I gradually caught on, we held long conversations together.

I never knew whether he really listened to me or whether he simply followed the mysterious skein of his own thoughts, which seemed to issue forth from the shadowy, remote reaches of a primitive world. This indefinable being wore a torn, dirty shirt open over his hairless chest, which had a prominent breastbone like that of a bird. On his head he wore a reddish cap with a visor, perhaps the badge of one of his many public functions; he was now both gravedigger and town crier. At all hours of the day he went through the village street, blowing a trumpet, beating a drum, which he wore hung about his neck, and calling out in his unhuman voice the news of the day: the arrival of a peddler, the slaughter of a goat, an edict of the mayor, the hour set for a funeral. And it was he who carried the dead to the cemetery, dug their graves, and buried them.

These were his normal activities, but behind them lay another existence, filled with a dark, impenetrable power. The women teased him when be went by, because he had no beard, and rumor had it that he had never made love all his life long. "Coming to bed with me tonight?" they called from the doorways, laughing and hiding their faces in their hands. "Why do you leave me to sleep alone?" They teased him, but at the same time he inspired them with respect and something like fear. The old man had a secret talent: he was in touch with forces below the earth, he could call up spirits, and he had a power over animals. His original trade, before old age and vicissitude had brought him to Gagliano, was that of wolf-tamer. He could either make the wolves come down into the villages, or keep them away, as he wished; they simply could not resist him, but had to bend to his will.

People said that when he was young he wandered over the mountains followed by savage wolf-packs. This talent caused him to be held in high esteem, and when the winter was severe, various villages called upon him to keep away the woodland beasts that cold and hunger drove to invade them. Every kind of animal was susceptible to his power, although he could not wield it over women; and not only animals but the elements and the spirits that dwell in the air as well. In his youth he could mow as much wheat in a day as fifty men because an invisible presence worked for him. At the end of the day when the other peasants were covered with dirt and sweat, their backs aching from fatigue and their heads buzzing from exposure to the sun, the wolf-tamer was as fresh as he had been in the morning.

I climbed out of my ditch to speak to him and offered him a cigar, which he put into a blackened holder made from the right hindleg of a buck rabbit. As he leaned on his shovel — for he was always digging new graves — he bent over to pick up a human shoulder blade, which he held for a while in his hand while be talked and then tossed aside. The ground was littered with calcified bleached bones, flowering out of the graves and worn away by wind and sun. To the old man these bones, the dead, animals, and spirits were all familiar things, bound up, as indeed they were to everyone in these parts, with simple everyday life. "The village is built of the bones of the dead," he said to me in his thick jargon, gurgling like a subterranean rivulet suddenly emerging among the stones, and twisting the toothless hole that served him for a mouth into what might have been meant for a smile. Whenever I tried to make him explain what he meant he paid no attention, but laughed and repeated exactly what he had said before, with not a word added to it; "That's it; the village is built of the bones of the dead." The old man was quite right, whether he meant these words literally or symbolically, as a figure of speech.

170

A short time later, when the mayor ordered an excavation made not far from the widow's house for the foundations of a small building to house the Fascist Scout organization, thousands of bones were turned up instead of dirt, and for days wagons carried these ancestral remains through the tillage and dumped them down the Fossa del Bersagliere. The bones from the tombs that had lain under the pavement of the fallen church, the Madonna of the Angels, were of more recent vintage. Some of them still had vestiges of flesh or parchment-like skin attached to them, and the dogs fought over them whenever they dug them up; they ran up the village street barking madly in the pursuit of one of their number with a tibia in his mouth. Here where time has come to a stop, it seemed quite natural that bones of all ages, recent, less recent, and very ancient, should turn up all together at the traveler's feet. The dead of the Madonna of the Angels, in their ruined tombs, were the most unfortunate. Not only did birds and dogs disperse their remains, but other and more terrifying presences visited the dreadful, slimy hole under the ruins where they had come to rest.

One night some few months or few years before (he could not tell me exactly when, because his notions of time were vague) the wolf-tamer, on his way back from Gaglianello, had just reached a slight rise of ground across from the church, known as the Mound of the Madonna of the Angels, when he felt a strange weariness in his body and had to sit down on the steps of a small side-chapel. He could not get up again and go on his way; someone was holding him back. The night was black and the old man could not see through the darkness, but from the ravine a bestial voice called him by name. A devil, who had settled down there among the dead, forbade him to go farther. The old man made the sign of the cross and the devil began to gnash his teeth and to cry out in pain. Among the shadows the old man made out for a second the form of a hideous goat, which leaped with terror over the ruins and disappeared. The devil fled howling down the ravine. "Uuuuuhhhh!" he bayed as he vanished. All at once the old man felt free and strong again, and a few steps brought him into the village. He had had endless adventures of the sort and when I drew him out he told them to me without ascribing to them the least importance. He had lived so long that it was inevitable such meetings should have been numerous.

He was so old that in the days of the brigands he was already a full-grown young man. I could never find out for certain whether, as was most likely, he had been one of them, but he had known the famous Ninco Nanco and he described to me as if he had seen her only the day before this brigand's consort, Maria 'a Pastora, who was, like himself, from Pisticci. Maria 'a Pastora was a beautiful peasant woman who lived with her lover in the wooded mountains, fighting and robbing at his side, clad like a man, and always on horseback. Ninco Nanco's band was the cruelest and most daring of the region, and Maria 'a Pastora took part in the raids on farms and villages, the highway robberies, the division of spoils, and the murders for revenge. When Ninco Nanco tore out with his bare hands the heart of the bersagliere who had captured him, Maria 'a Pastora handed him his knife. The gravedigger remembered her distinctly, and there was pleasure in his strange voice when he told me how beautiful she was, with the pink and white coloring of a flower and black braids that hung down to her feet, as she sat straight, astride her horse. Ninco Nanco was killed, but the old man did not know what had been the end of Maria 'a Pastora, goddess of the peasant war. She neither died nor was captured, he told me; she was seen at Pisticci, swathed in black, then she disappeared on horseback into the woods and was never heard of again.

Translated by Frances Frenaye

GIUSEPPE DESSÌ
(1909–1977)

Giuseppe Dessì was born in Cagliari, Sardinia, the son of a general. After a childhood spent traveling to garrisons in both Sardinia and the Italian peninsula, he studied literature and philosophy and eventually became a teacher. He is best known as a prolific novelist whose books describe the intricate social and environmental realities of his beloved homeland Sardinia. Dessì's works include *Il disertore* (The deserter), *Racconti vecchi e nuovi* (Tales old and new), *Introduzione alla vita di Giacomo Scarbo* (Introduction to the life of Giacomo Scarbo), and *I passeri* (The sparrows). His Strega award-winning *Paese d'ombre* (*The Forests of Norbio*), here excerpted, takes place in the late nineteenth century in the fictional Sardinian town of Norbio (based loosely on Villalcidro, Dessì's hometown). At a time when the newly independent Italy was reorganizing the army and expanding the navy, its royal foundries' need for charcoal drove the search for wood to Sardinia and its forests. The main character in *Paese d'ombre*, Angelo Uras, comes of age in this climate. Once a young man, he is soon confronted by a government-sponsored plan to cut down the forests surrounding Norbio. In his attempt to protect them, he runs a nightmarish gauntlet of corrupt bureaucrats and businessmen.

FROM: THE FORESTS OF NORBIO *

After the rains, Zio Raimondo proposed to sow wheat on the land that Sofia had inherited from her husband near the mineral springs of Acquacotta, and Angelo was to go with him. Sofia told the old man to sow no more than three bushels; she was unwilling to venture more, especially as the land hadn't been prepared during the summer. One Monday morning Zio

---

*From Giuseppe Dessì, *The Forests of Norbio*, trans. by Frances Frenaye (New York: Harcourt Brace Jovanovich, 1975).

Raimondo came to fetch Angelo. He hitched Zurito to the cart, loaded two half bags of wheat, some fertilizer, the heavy iron plow, the lunch basket and a bottle of wine, and off they went. Their journey took them through the village of Leni where the road ran past the foundry. The foundry, which had lain idle, had been reactivated some time before and was spewing out into the autumn sky smoke and soot that drifted onto the vegetable gardens of Leni. When they came to Acquacotta, Angelo recognized the mineral spring at the foot of a low, bare hill, and pointed out the boundaries of his mother's terrain: the spring and a wild pear tree on the east, and on the west, two boundary stones of the kind commonly used at Norbio, which the boy himself had whitewashed the year before to make them visible from a distance.

The old man mentally calculated the measurements involved and picked out the area he would sow that day. Then he hung a canvas sack full of seeds around his neck and, walking with long, regular steps, threw them out with a broad, rotating motion of his arm. The assurance of his gesture lent him a misleading air of age-old wisdom and experience. The seeds bounced off the hard earth and disappeared among tufts of dried grass. Near the white horse, Zio Raimondo fancied he could see the angry ghost of Don Francesco, who would never have allowed him to sow in this old-fashioned and inefficient manner. But then Don Francesco had tried to change many ways in Norbio and now he was dead. Zio Raimondo was sure that the seed would take hold and sprout just as well this way as any other. When the sack was empty, he shrugged his shoulders and spat into the distance. Then he hitched the horse to the plow and stuck the plowshare into the ground to turn the earth over and cover the seeds. Zurito walked in a straight line, with no need of guidance or encouragement; obviously he was accustomed to this work.

Angelo sat by the cart, munching a piece of bread and looking on. Plowing looked fun, even easy, and he wanted to try his hand. But his head was no higher than the handles and he could only hang on and be carried along. Zio Raimondo laughed, displaying his strong, white teeth, and set him aside. At the edge of the field, he effortlessly lifted the heavy plow, pulled the gleaming plowshare from the dark earth, and put it in again to cut another parallel furrow. Every now and then, someone passed by on the road, stopped to look on, and asked: "Plowing, are you, Zio Raimondo? Go ahead and plow, and may God be with you!" To which he replied: "Plowing, yes. I'm plowing the land of Sofia Curreli and this one here." He pointed to Angelo, who turned away blushing, feeling embarrassed, although he did not know why. Perhaps he shouldn't allow the wheat to be sown in the old-fashioned way when Don Francesco had told him many times that the land must be readied long before the actual sowing. Or perhaps he was ashamed to sit there doing nothing, while an old man with the bowed legs wearied himself behind the plow. The sun shone wanly out of the gray sky and the few parched trees around the steaming spring cast no shadows, but the boy knew, all the same, when it was noon. He saw the old man stop, look at his watch, then detach the horse from the plow. At the same time, he heard the bells gaily ringing in Norbio, although the village was no more than a light patch at the foot of the bare mountains.

"You did well to light the fire," said Zio Raimondo as he drew near. He bent over to wash his hands in the hot water, which ran, steaming, among the reeds and ferns. "Eggs can cook in this water," he added, taking them out of the basket. He set one egg on a flat stone and twirled it between his fingers, then touched it lightly to stop it. But he had no sooner withdrawn his hand than the egg slowly described another half circle.

"There's a trick you didn't know, did you?" said the old man, laughing.

"No, I didn't," said Angelo, but he did not ask for an explanation. He had understood immediately that a raw egg keeps on turning, while a cooked one doesn't. He gave a knowing smile and winked at Zio Raimondo. The old man was disappointed; in his time, he hadn't caught on so quickly. While Angelo gave the horse his fodder, Zio Raimondo slipped the eggs into the steaming water and looked at the second hand of his watch.

"How do you want your eggs?" he asked.

"Medium," the boy answered.

They ate, and Zio Raimondo poured wine from the bottle directly into his mouth, without letting his lips touch it, then handed it to Angelo. It was then that the dog went by, running so close to the fire that its passage raised a small cloud of ashes. The dog was young, with tawny hair and black stripes that emphasized the thinness of the body. The head and tail were like those of a greyhound. It was running at desperate speed toward the road, but some fifteen yards away came to an abrupt stop and looked around at the two human figures behind it.

"Pup!" Angelo called out. The dog lowered its head, twisted its body, and wagged its tail furiously. It even bared its sharp slender teeth as if to smile. Angelo held out a piece of bread. Only then did the dog advance, cautiously. Angelo threw the bread and the dog caught it in mid-air and noisily devoured it, salivating and trembling all over. It was a female.

"Let her go! She's just a mutt," said the old man. "I know dogs, and this one makes too many faces to be any good."

Angelo looked at him apprehensively. One sudden move and she'd run away.

"She's trying too hard to please," said Zio Raimondo, looking intently at his companion. "She's untrustworthy, for sure, and probably a thief in the bargain."

But when he saw the look on Angelo's face, he cut another piece of bread from the loaf and tossed it to the dog, which once more caught and gobbled it.

"She's ashamed because she doesn't know us and because she's hungry."

"If you're honest, there's no shame in being hungry," said the old men sententiously. If he had bent over and pretended to pick up a stone that would have been the end of it. But he didn't move. It would be up to Sofia to say no and send the animal packing. Angelo was thinking the same thing. Who could tell why the dog had run in their direction and then stopped to look back at them? Had she smelled the bread or had she caught the smell of him, Angelo? In any case, the decision was hers; she had chosen him. He had long wanted a dog, and this was the way to get one. You find a dog on the street or in the fields, all alone and hungry; you call out: "Pup!" and that's it; you're friends for keeps. Perhaps the dog would be a friend to Zurito also.

Zio Raimondo went back to his plowing. In the late afternoon light, the field had taken on a darker hue; it was a large rectangle of brown earth, different from the land extending as far as the eye could see around it. Suddenly the old man shouted and waved his arms. A hare dashed by, leaping through the air so fast that Angelo had hardly time to see its long ears, arched back, and white belly. Zurito shied, pricked up his ears, and turned to look. Zio Raimondo muttered to himself, as if he were repeating his outcry of a moment before when the hare had escaped from between the horse's legs. He stepped back and aimed the long whip, like a gun, at the hare, which, after its high jump, had squatted in a furrow and stared at him out of eyes as round and dark as the seeds of black grapes. With an unexpected but characteristic lightning-swift gesture, he shot the thong of the whip at the hare. But he missed his aim, and the hare, leaping again into the air, escaped westward, to safety. Once more Angelo saw its small dark body outlined against the sky like a bird about to land.

"If only I'd brought my gun!" the old man exclaimed. He clapped his hand on his thigh and bore down on the plow as a signal to Zurito to move ahead. When the dog heard his first shout, she instinctively froze, her tail sticking straight out in line with her back, the corners of her ears upraised, and her muzzle quivering. And when the hare escaped the stroke of the whip and took flight, she, too, went into lightning motion. She circled the old man and the plow, sniffing the furrow where the hare had squatted, picked up the scent, and followed.

"Tomorrow?" the old man shouted mockingly after her. At intervals, the dog barked in the distance and the white tip of the hare's tail could be spotted in the tall grass as it pursued its zigzag flight through the fields.

"It's late," said Angelo, silently overtaking Zio Raimondo. The old man pointed to a black cloud, as dense as the smoke thrown off by a charcoal pit, which seemed to be coming out of the summit of Mount Homo.

"Tomorrow there'll be rain again, and there's no telling how long it will go on raining. I've no more than a strip left to plow, and I'd better get it done."

Two or three times man and horse traveled the length of the field. Then Zio Raimondo detached the plow, loaded it onto the cart, and took a sip of wine from the bottle. Angelo was fitting the shafts of the cart into Zurito's harness when he saw the dog come back. First he heard her panting, and a minute later she was at his feet. He hadn't dare to hope that she would perform so well. "Carignosa" (this was the name he had already decided to give her) had brought back the hare, and Zio Raimondo proceeded at once to cut it open.

"You're better than I thought," he said to the dog, as he threw the entrails into the bushes. And he added, to Angelo, "There's a real hunting dog for you! Even if she's half-starved, she doesn't touch the guts. I'd never have believed it."

Angelo leaned over to pat the dog and to press her slender head to his chest. When he got up, he waved his hand and she jumped gracefully onto the cart, Zurito needed no encouragement to start for home. The harness bells tinkled like far-away chimes in the twilight.

. . . .

Angelo would have been happy with his work had he not felt guilty about collaborating with the Mining Consortium's destruction of the forests. At the beginning, when he accepted the job, he had thought that, with the engineer's support, he could prevent the rape of what remained of the forests of Escolca and Mazzanni — some two thousand acres on which the inhabitants of Norbio exercised their age-old rights of pasturage and wood-gathering. At Norbio there was no such extreme poverty as in other villages of Parte d'Ispi; even the poorest man had at least a pig, which could be fed on nuts and prickly pears, and if he had more than one, he took the lot of them to feed in the forest, where he had also a right to gather dry twigs and branches and dead or fallen tree trunks. On winter nights, in even the crudest mud hut, there were always a fire and a bowl of hot soup with bacon in it. Now, as the ovens of the Royal Foundry of Leni devoured the trees, springs had dried up, and there was an ever-greater danger that flood water would pour down from the bare mountains. Antonio Ferraris had persuaded Angelo to take a job as his assistant by holding out the prospect that in the future the foundry would burn pit coal and lignite from the mines of Iglesiente instead of wood and charcoal from the forests. But this project had been turned down, or at least postponed, because of transportation costs and the necessity of remodeling the ovens. With apologies and the promise that he would try again, the engineer had explained things to Angelo and made arrangements for a Tuscan contractor, Giuseppe Antola, to supply the foundry with wood or charcoal at the current price. Antola and his men were to cut the forest of Mazzanni, with the obligation to take precautions that would ensure the forest's renewal. Angelo had no choice but to accede, and he accepted the job of supervising the logging, to make sure that the least possible damage was done. He was reassured by the engineer's promise that this cutting would be the last.

One morning, from the courtyard, Sofia pointed out a column of black smoke rising behind the summit of Mount Homo. She and all the other inhabitants of Norbio knew that it was smoke from a charcoal pit and that the wood was from the forest of Escolca. Angelo read a mute reproach in their eyes, as if the fault were his, since he was a paid employee of the Consortium. He saddled his horse and took with him not only his lunch basket, but a gun and a hunting pouch as well. He rode first through the Piazza Frontera, with the gun slung over his shoulder. Fortunately he had obtained a permit to carry firearms only a few days before. Zurito arched his tail, shook his mane, and proceeded at a trot; Carignosa went ahead, with her tail erect, heedless of the other dogs that came to run along beside her. Men in black capes leaning against the wall next to the tavern smiled under their thick mustaches and waved their hands when Angelo raised two fingers to his cap to greet them. As he turned Zurito down the Via delle Tre Marie, he wondered where Ferraris might be at this hour. Perhaps he had already gone to the forest, and he could talk to him there.

As he posted to the horse's gait, he thought about the forest of Escolca and Mount Homo. Now they were cutting not only the age-old trees, but also the arbutuses, the mastics, the willows, and even the olives. And this slaughter was taking place against the wishes of the people of Norbio, contrary to the law, and in violation of the explicit promise made by the Mining Consortium through the engineer. The column of smoke was still rising from behind the Punta del Vischio, the highest peak of Mount Homo. Angelo was sure that if he could find and talk to the engineer the slaughter would cease. He could not get this idea out of his mind.

Carignosa had come to a halt a couple of hundred feet ahead, among the bushes. She had caught the scent of game. Angelo reined in Zurito, leaned the butt of his gun against his left foot, held it upright with his knee, and loaded it. The dog froze, her narrow head with its long, flapping ears thrust out, one forepaw upraised, and her tail sticking straight out in line with her head and body. She quivered all over as she waited to lunge forward in pursuit of the prey. Angelo slipped out of the saddle and stood near her, preparing to shoot. The dog turned her head to look at her master and make sure that he was ready, then she took off. At almost the same moment the woodcock rose out of the bushes and flew in a zigzag diagonal up over the treetops. Angelo took aim and fired. The woodcock, struck by a hail of shot, rolled and plummeted to the ground. Carignosa knew exactly where to retrieve the bird, and soon came back with the body. Angelo held it for a moment by the legs, then put it into his pouch. He took the blackened cartridge out of the gunbarrel and remounted his horse. Although he was not particularly tall, he had grown in recent months, as he was aware because of the ease with which he could slip his left foot into the stirrup and swing himself into the saddle. The most insignificant things often make a man happy. To have shot down a woodcock on the wing, with an old-fashioned, breech-loading shotgun was a feat whose accomplishment drove all the worries out of his mind. For the moment, he was self-confident and in high spirits. His heart was pounding and his ears still rang from the shot's detonation. He urged Zurito forward, keeping his eyes on the dog, which paused at intervals with upraised paw to look questioningly at him.

"You're the one that should know if there's other game in the vicinity," Angelo said aloud, as if the dog could understand.

Nearby he could hear the sharp blows of the axes and the voices of the men who were cutting down the trees. But the woodcock in his hunting pouch was a talisman against anger or melancholy. Soon he would be face to face with the woodcutters, and perhaps with Ferraris or Giuseppe Antola. The ax blows, louder and louder, acquired a feverishly rapid rhythm. Every now and then this rhythm was interrupted by a sort of roar, a sound of crackling branches and voices shouting in unfamiliar accents as an ancient tree, its base chipped away, hit the ground.

To Angelo, every sound evoked a picture. Soon enough he saw through the bushes the fallen trees and the great stumps that gave out the unmistakable odor of freshly cut wood. The woodcutters wore Tuscan-style black cotton shirts and bright-colored sashes around their waists. They worked individually or in groups, hacking away with billhooks and pruning knives at the young shoots that grew around the stumps, and leaving them no chance to grow up and replace the felled trees. Angelo stopped in a clearing and called out: "Hello there!"

"Salud!"

Some of the men returned his greeting without pausing in their work, others made no reply. Angelo dismounted, removed the bit from the horse's mouth, and led him over to the edge of the clearing where green grass was growing. Carignosa sniffed at the bundles containing food that the woodcutters had left on the ground and under the bushes. A tall, gaunt man was wielding an ax alone at the base of a big holm oak. With every stroke he let out a throaty Achhh! and the tree trembled from top to bottom.

"Who's in charge here?" Angelo asked.

The man scrutinized him at length, then spit into his calloused hands and once more raised the ax above his head.

"When Signer Antola's not about, I am."

He came out with another Achhh! and white chips flew around him.

"We're making charcoal, too," he said in a laconic but calm manner.

"So I see.... But there are rules and regulations. You're supposed to cut only one tree out of ten, and none that isn't full-grown.... What's your name?"

"Renato...Renato Graneri. I'm the foreman. And who are you? The mayor?"

"I'm Angelo Uras, and I'm supervising the logging operation on behalf of the Consortium. Is Ferraris, the engineer, anywhere around?"

"I work for Signer Antola. I don't know about any engineer."

"I'll have to register a complaint. The way you're doing things the forest will never come back. It's a great loss, and against the law, besides."

"The forest should never have been sold in the first place," said the foreman. "I see your point, but it's no use lodging a complaint with me. You'd better talk to Signer Antola.... Meanwhile, just step aside; the tree's about to fall."

The tree, with its base very nearly cut through, was leaning to one side, and a push was enough to tumble it over. Angelo leaped aside, while the woodcutters, all together, emitted a long, tuneful cry. There was a rustling and tearing sound and finally a crash. Then the men threw themselves at the trunk with axes, billhooks and pruning knives, as if they enjoyed the destruction. A bevy of wild pigeons passed, with rustling wings, over their heads, skimming the treetops. Before Renato's watchful and somewhat incredulous eyes, Angelo loaded his gun.

"Don't tell me you can shoot a pigeon on the wing," Renato said, laughing.

"I can always try," said Angelo, unafraid of the other's mocking look.

They were at the edge of the wood, and there was an expanse of level ground between them and the moor where Carignosa was running and jumping, now visible, now invisible, among the tobacco-colored rock-rose bushes. Her concern, however, was not with the doves but with a hare. The hare leaped out of the bushes, almost in the direction of the two men, then veered to the left. Angelo calmly loaded his long gun, ran his thumb over the sight, took aim, following the progress of the hare, and fired. The hare seemed to stumble, was catapulted into the air, then fell down and disappeared in the grass.

"Good shot!" the Tuscan exclaimed, spitting out the blade of grass that he had been holding between his lips. Carignosa ran after the hare, retrieved it, and ran to lay it at Angelo's feet and receive his caresses.

"Lucky fellow!" the Tuscan added.

Angelo waved his hand in farewell and started to ride downhill. The pouch weighed agreeably on his hip. Perhaps the foreman was right. He was a lucky fellow, and aware of his luck. He was trotting along beside the railway track when he heard a roar behind him. He reined Zurito to one side, and a minute later, with a clanking of iron and the sound of loud voices, the train passed close by, loaded with wood, sacks of charcoal, mules, and men. The mules, in the last car, held their ears erect, stiff with terror. From the head of the train, the loggers waved their caps and shouted a greeting. The train snaked its way up and down the steep terrain, now appearing and now disappearing from view, and was soon out of sight, leaving the countryside more silent and deserted than before. In the silence, the rustling of the trees seemed to Angelo as deep-toned and complex as the anxious bustling of a crowd.

Translated by Frances Frenaye

ANNA MARIA ORTESE
(1914–1998)

Anna Maria Ortese was born in Rome and grew up in southern Italy and in Tripoli. She was twenty-three when her first book, *Angelici dolori* (Angelic sorrows), appeared in 1937. In 1950 her second novel, *L'infanta sepolta* (The buried child), was published, and three years later the successful collection of short stories, *Il mare non bagna Napoli* (The sea doesn't wash Naples), which won the Viareggio Prize. In the years to come, Ortese's stories, novels, and articles received many awards, including the Strega and the Fiuggi. She lived for many years in Naples following the Second World War and also resided in Milan and Rome. For much of the last twenty years of her life, she lived a reclusive life in Rapallo, continuing to publish her visionary works in realistic settings. Among her works available in English are two volumes of her short stories, *A Music Behind the Wall I* and *II*, and her most famous novel, *The Iguana*.

THE TREE*

Last Saturday, as the first snow began to fall, which was just towards five in the afternoon, I found myself at the Central Station, having accompanied a person to a train. At first, I didn't even realize it was snowing, but it struck me, once again in the open, that something in the tone and color of the great, broad square before the station had slightly changed. It was the very same square that all of us can see at any hour of the day or night, to the right the large hotel surmounted by a flattened dome, and the tramway tracks on the left, leading

---

* From Anna Maria Ortese, *I giorni del cielo* (Milano: Mondadori, 1958), translation by Henry Martin from Martha King, ed., *New Italian Women: A Collection of Short Fiction* (New York: Italica Press, 1989).

towards the center of town past a variety of cafés where brightly lit windows open back through a whitish haze to a glimpse of the reds and yellows of bottles of liqueurs. But the cafés, and I grasped it only after a moment or so, were all dark and empty, though open, and no trams were running, not so much as the most distant clanging of their bells. I thought there must have been a power failure in this part of the city, perhaps elsewhere as well, and I made up my mind to go back to my hotel on foot. After all, it was not very far away, and the weather wasn't cold.

As I looked about, a little bewildered, in search of the street to take (at least ten streets run out from this square) that indistinct sensation of just a few moments before came back to me, but now with the weight of a real disturbance: the sensation that something abnormal had taken place. Where I found myself was not Milan, no more than Hamlet and Ophelia are citizens of England. The plain looking houses that rise up in the many streets around the square had an evanescence, and a heart-rending pallor. Their walls seemed to shine from some interior source and were no longer lit by starlight, nor by any ray of brightness belonging to the world of our own. "It must always be like this, at certain hours of the year, and for me to realize it now is to be explained by a particular fragility of my nerves."

I started down Via P., from which I would then cross Piazza Grande and reach my hotel. And I once again, skirting close to the walls, felt strangely intent, like a person who had just received an important piece of news, something concerning one's own personal life, only shortly before. But, to tell the truth, I couldn't remember what that news might have been; so my calm began little by little to creak and give way like a sheet of ice over a stream of warm, black water murmuring and fleeing beneath it.

"Let's see," I said to myself. "The hotel. Everything there okay. The bill paid up. Work to do for tomorrow…quite fine. Let's see what else." And then, suddenly, I grasped the reason for that sense of dismay I had felt at the exit from the station. My dismay lay in a fact that was quite entirely banal, yet alarming: I no longer had any idea of whom I had accompanied to the station.

"But nothing could be more normal," I remarked to myself after a moment of reflection. "When we're especially fatigued, even the name of what month it is, or of the season, can slip our minds. Maybe it wasn't even an important name. At any rate, I'll recall it again in a moment."

I wanted to give myself a rational explanation for what had occurred, but as soon as I had put my finger on it, I ceased to be at peace, and I might have said that a mouse had slipped inside my dress and found its way up close to my heart, where at first it nibbled tenderly and then with greater zeal, striking deeper. Finally it bit to the pulse and the seat of life itself, and I felt a lacerating pain.

The mouse fled. I saw it run away directly from in front of me and then across the street to hide at the curb, from where it watched me with a strange, flashing brightness in the tiny pupils of its eyes. But even though the pain was still horrid and the beast right there, I refused to own up to it. "The weather is really changing," I remarked to myself. "This twinge is a warning. I'll drink a small cup of hot rum as soon as I'm back in my room."

I began to feel cold, but paid it no attention as I trained my eyes upwards here and there onto those buildings that looked so dead while yet suffused with a vague spark of dawn, an uncertain reflection, those facades where not a single door or window stood unshuttered to allow the glimpse of a face, a light, and where not a single voice resounded, not a sound, not even the lightest sound, of passing footsteps. "At this hour, in Milan, everyone is asleep," I continued to spin out to myself. "It's a city of workers. They go to bed early, by nine o'clock."

At that point, a clock from a distant church, a clock, seemingly, that wasn't quite sure of this world and the clapper of which resounded with a clear, grave music, struck five hours and two quarters.

"There's one of those clocks that gets stuck," I mumbled after a moment.

I reached the park, and here I realized that it was really snowing, quite heavily. The snow fell from the sky like a whirlpool of light, and when looked at steadily, it gave the impression of swirling back upwards. It rose and fell. How beautiful it was! It didn't touch the ground, and its large, transparent flakes just barely caressed the branches of certain trees and then melted away. It seemed a hand that wants to write out something immense and portentous, or to stroke a forehead, and that continually repents, trembles, and vanishes. One felt a vague, profound desire to be ravished into that raiment of light, to hover upwards from the black earth and flee into a place made only of serenity, music, and joy. And why was that not to happen?

There was a bench, and I approached it. I sat down, and remained there quietly to look around me as I held the upturned collar of my coat tight against my face. In the spinnings and reversals of that eddying of white, inside that magnificent calm, as though a mantle of white velvet were rushing to fold itself around the world, I reheard a remote and harmonious echo of that clock, a song of hours. Any number of memories unwound through my mind, but without fever. I saw my mother and my father, early mornings in the sunlit garden, I listened to the ceaseless sound of the March wind on the hill. Then, at a certain point, all these images and sounds of light disappeared, and I saw myself again in this city, in my hotel room as I prepared to go out and turned off all the lights.... Yes, all the lights suddenly went out, and my mind lapsed back into its great confusion, and again that sensation of a brutal pain at my heart. Something must surely have happened, there was no longer room for doubt.

I would have given anything at all to have been left unreminded of it, and to let everything remain exactly as it was, with neither form nor name. I got up from the bench, and, vacillating, fixing my eyes as best I could in front of me, I set out to where I thought I would find the exit.

But the exit was no longer there, or at least it couldn't be seen because of the snow that had fallen. However, there was a great number of trees: their black, twisted roots came almost up from out of the ground, and some of them seemed to be human beings — human beings deprived of everything and at the end of their lives, and who huddled now against a wall and cried. In pure and absolute silence, the snow continued

187

to fall on these creatures. I walked in the midst of them, and would have said that they silently stepped aside to allow me through. Never before, here in the park, had I realized that there were so many trees, and all so sensitive. The sight of them began to feel oppressive, and to frighten me. Why were they suffering? I felt quite fine, entirely fine. No, it wasn't because of me.

"The hotel should be somewhere close by," I began again to repeat to myself with absurd intensity. "The windows will all of course be dark, but the entrance will be bright and full of people. There's Corrado, Daniele, the lovely Iris, the others."

A sign, quite large and just like the ones that parade one after the other along the highways, hung at the top of a pole fixed into the earth, and gigantic letters, in a sharp, bright green, spelled out these words before my eyes:

"SILENCE. DISAPPEARED. TRANQUILITY."

"Disappeared" was the word I stared at most, entranced, much more than at the others. It awakened my heart to such a depth of echoes and suspicions as to arouse a true terror that sucked all the heat from my forehead, and for an instant I was embraced with immobility itself.

"So even now," I continued, while breathing a sigh that released me from this horror, "they insist on putting up signs on the grass, as though that hadn't been proved already to be so entirely useless...." As I said this, my eyes, which were full of tears for which there was absolutely no reason, ranged off into the distance to a large open space where, once, a small monument to Cavour had stood. The small monument was no longer there, and in its place was a dazzling tree, rising up to a great height.

This time I said nothing; but as I shook myself together, pushing away the anxiety that like a crazed bird dashed against the walls of my skull, I looked at this solitary, towering tree of ice that stood before me and I attempted to see it as no more than an artificious and puerile Christmas tree. But those branches were decorated with nothing but ice, even the trunk was covered with ice, and the peak burned with no light that wasn't a light of ice. Here and there from out of the whiteness hung sharp, pointed daggers of that muted blue that ice can take on, and they gleamed.

A supreme need to ignore the meaning of what was happening drew me to the base of that tree, gazing upwards, just like any other citizen, to admire its wintry transformation; and that was where I stood, smiling though both cold and full of pain, when the tree first moved: laden and sparkling with its burden of frost, it bent down and touched my forehead. I retreated, and the creature moved again.

Its roots had drawn out of the earth, like paws, and they weakly advanced within the light of the snow. They advanced to follow me. This, naturally enough, was a dream, though a horrid dream. So while hurrying my steps as best I could towards where I imagined the gates of the park to be, I set to repeating my eternal, monotonous, refrains: "Work, okay; tomorrow, Sunday...; phone Corrado...; let's see what else." As I ran these statements through my weakened, submerging mind, the apparition of ice and branches slithered up beside me on its pitiful roots and emitted a sound that I'm sure you could hardly have listened to without crying. It was just that various, profound, and finally similar to the story of a human life.

"These branches really do creak," I remarked from out of my obstinate compulsion to lie to myself, "but I would never have imagined that snow could be so much like metal. And, yes, it's of course that this tree has grown so light that the wind can carry it along like a leaf while making its boughs resound with such an enchanted noise...."

I began to run, while thinking these phrases, towards the gates, which stood there, I could see them, facing onto Via Boschetti. I came out into the street and then halted, though still with the sense that this supernatural creature of ice was just behind my shoulder, because my heart was about to explode. I was to see, however, that the tree was no longer there.

At that point, finally safe, I felt a faint desire to see and hear it once again, as though that conjunction of light and pain had held the hidden secret, the name, the thing, everything the nature of which I could not understand, that had made my heart that night go mad.

But I didn't see the tree again. Instead, here I was at Porta Venezia, and then Viale Vittorio Veneto, and the high embankment at the edge of the park, and my hotel.

This large, modern building, eighteen storeys tall, its walls wounded by over a thousand windows, stood before me, and I stopped. I exclaimed, "At last!" but with a voice that was broken by regret and by a longing for a truth from which I had subtracted myself, fearing to look it in the face; and simultaneously I was struck by something extraordinary.

To the front of the hotel atrium, where a little elevator ordinarily runs and where friends are always coming and going, to the front of this atrium now brightly lit but totally empty, two goldfinches of precisely the size of a human form were roosted on a branch covered with snow, a branch that issued from the wall above the glass door, almost as though the wall itself were earth and the hotel a forgotten garden.

Their small, round eyes, round and black, were fixed, bright, and melancholic; and a song both acute and I couldn't say if more sweet or full of desperation, a song that spoke of tenderness and farewell, of the hope of regaining the woods, and the doubt, and of a joy besieged by cold and nothingness, issued from their unmoving beaks. These birds were dead. With their fiery foreheads and black and yellow wings, and perched on delicate legs of a material that seemed to be gold, they were dead and already cold beneath their silken plumage. Their song, a memory. Faced with their gracefulness and their death, I then suddenly understood why the city was dark, why the mouse had gnawed at my heart, why the tree laden with ice had pulled itself up from the ground to come and offer me company, singing songs about the past. I understood who I had accompanied to the station, and who these two marvelous shadows of birds had to be. I understood as well that my youth, which I had attempted to forget with all my phrases saying "fine...let's see...the bills...fine...tomorrow,..." I understood that my youth, and everything else that you too will have lost, had everywhere, that night, returned; frightened and full of sobs, it had run like a girl along this pitiful earth.

Translated by Henry Martin

CARLO CASSOLA
(1917–1987)

Carlo Cassola was born in Rome, where he lived until 1939 when he took an active part in the resistance in the area surrounding Volterra — the homeland of his mother and the setting of much of his subsequent work. Concerned primarily with poetic renditions of day-to-day life and humble people, Cassola's work often confronts the difficulties of growing up through the Second World War and the discomfort of being part of the "middle" generation caught in the aftershock of fascism. His many books include *La ragazza di Bube* (*Bébo's Girl*), *Un cuore arido* (*An Arid Heart*), *Fausto e Anna* (*Fausto and Anna*), *Il taglio del bosco: racconti lunghi e romanzi brevi* (The cutting of the woods: long stories and short novels), *La morale del branco* (The morale of the herd), and *Il cacciatore* (The hunter), which depicts his boyhood and life in the countryside.

SEA, SKY AND LAND*

This morning the sea is of three colors: yellow near the shore, green midway out, and blue in the distance. Of course, it's also white where the waves break (and they begin to break far offshore, because the surf is rather rough).

A strong wind is gusting, and no one is on the beach. I too, won't last long. The sea with no one along the shore gives an impression of solitude, of uselessness: as if the sea itself were aware of speaking to the void. For what purpose serves this diagonal running of the waves, pushed by the wind, if there is no one to see it? In the summer, when the beaches are crowded, the sea seems less lonesome. It puts on a show for the bathers, who in truth, pay little attention. It's a show that is always

*Translated from Carlo Cassola, *La morale del branco* (Milano: Rizzoli, 1980).

the same, and yet also changes just enough to avoid being wearisome.

A certain monotony, a certain repetition, is also necessary in art, which attempts to portray the spectacle of life: and in life there is a mix of that which repeats itself and that which continually changes. "A book must be boring," Romano Bilenchi told me. A piece of music, too, must be boring. I liked the Byzantine mosaics in Ravenna exactly because the same pattern is repeated many times. As regards boring writers, my mind runs at once to D. H. Lawrence, who is a great writer in part because of this.

Returning to the colors of this morning's sea: the yellow I now realize is rather more a brown, and the blue a dark turquoise. The green in the middle (a narrow strip, with uncertain boundaries) is difficult to define precisely. The white is a dirty white, given that welling up from below is a water that seems muddy (in fact, more than brown, the stretch along the shore is the color of mud). I follow a wave from when it rises up in the distance to when it unravels upon the shore: I see a ridge of foam build up; the wave smooths out; it becomes large again; it arches over for the last time, majestically, and collapses. The broken up water scatters in all directions. Only a thin veil of water is able to climb back up the slope. Tapering off, it darkens: because it reflects the darkness of the soft sand.

The mutable colors of the sea are easily explained by atmospheric phenomena. If I were to decide to observe it, I would easily understand why the sea is of one color, rather than of another. But to know why isn't important to me. I watch the sea only because it is a mirror of myself, and of my life.

The sea. The land (more varied, but it too has an unmistakable physiognomy). What a boundless richness of colors, of lights, of forms, of perspectives: almost all of it destined to vanish without anyone taking notice.

The poets and painters have captured only a very small portion of it. To give only one example: the hedges. There are many species of them. But no painter, of whom I am aware, has dedicated himself to depicting them. I remember a hedge in a landscape by Monet, but it is only a detail in a winter scene. And the writers? Even Pascoli gave them little attention — he who was so attentive to particulars.

And the sky? In the past I used to think that it wasn't worth the bother of watching: for the fact that it lies above, rather than around us. For its immateriality, its inconsistency. It didn't seem as real as the land and the sea. The sky alludes, winks; it presents passages, fissures; it opens and it closes; it comes near and draws away; it is no more or less unchanging and mutable than the land and the sea.

The land, in bad weather, shows a face of uniformity. The sky instead is more mutable.

The sea too, is more mutable when it is rough.

Art demonstrates its ineptness at presenting us with the variety, as well as the uniformity, of the real. And it is uniformity that hides the secret of existence.

The proponents of classicism take issue with modern art, claiming that it is scattered: the classics are thus focused on the essentials, whereas the moderns are lost in the details.

But it is necessary to see if what is essential is actually as it is expressed, or if it is born out of convention. Leopardi certainly admired the essentials: to the point at which he needed only a few poems to express himself thoroughly. A comparison between Leopardi and Pascoli perhaps ends up with the former having an advantage.

Dante seems to me even greater than Leopardi: he was equally anchored in the essentials and knew how to give them variety with the richness of details.

I believe that only we moderns have understood Dante, because only we moderns are spurred on by the need to reproduce the essential together with the accidental.

This morning's sea, with its uniform motion and its variety of aspects, suggests to me a path to follow in portraying the world.

I return there in the afternoon. It's still windy, and the beach is as deserted as it was this morning.

The nearby water has the same brown color; the distant band is still blue. The green strip in the middle has vanished.

Here and there the horizon cannot be seen. A ship seems suspended in the air.

I remember the mortification I felt as a child when my peers argued about the ships that used to pass by in the distance. They could recognize them even if they were little more than small dots. "That's a schooner." "No, it's a brig."

Some of them were helped by what they gathered of the shipping routes: they knew that certain sailing ships shuttled between the port of Livorno and the mines of Elba. I ignored all of it: the names of the ships, their shapes, the routes, and the maritime traffic. I was able to watch it too, the distant little dot, but as a detail in a picture. Like the seagulls that would fly low to the sea: when they were nearby, you could hear their harsh cries.

I also remember the comments of my companions: "The seagulls are always starving. That's why they follow the boats." Here there was a difference of opinion: between those who maintained that they ate the leftovers thrown into the sea by the sailors and those who held that they ate the fish who followed the ships in schools.

They would speak with a knowledge of the facts, or would speak haphazardly: those boys gave only practical explanations. The glances they shot around were directed at gathering information.

I never took the trouble to gather information, or to find explanations. If now I turn my back on the sea and interrogate the sky, it's not to know if it's going to rain.

The sky is black overhead, while lower down it's almost clear. I am attracted to the fraying shreds of the clouds. They dangle in the void, similar to black rags.

The clouds are often frayed. But I don't remember ever seeing such a huge cloud so unraveled along its edges.

Frayings, unravelings and shreds, all constantly changing: low clouds that pass by quickly, swelling, contracting, overturning.

It's the wind that pushes the clouds and swells the sea. And it's the cloudy sky that makes the sea what it is, here brown, in the distance the color of lead....

I don't want to know these explanations. I get angry with myself for having lost time.

The brown and lead-gray of the sea, the black of the clouds and the clearness of the distant sky, the swollen waves and the pressing wind: they have no relation to one another. They have only relation to me. The black slate of the nearby sky and the lead-gray of the distant sea are the colors of a palette that I have carried in my soul from the time I was a child and ignored all the habits of the seagulls and the routes of the ships.

The sea is the only view to the west that in the evening doesn't sadden or distress me. On land, the hills that darken when the sun is on the verge of disappearing, fill me with unease.

Already, they are no longer recognizable. Against the light, only their profiles are visible. And it is those profiles that have nothing familiar and assuring; on the contrary, they have something unknown and threatening.

To the west there's a need for space, of an expanse like that of the sea, which allows the sun to be seen until the very last moment. To the east there's a need for hills, and above, of clouds, which save a glimmer of light until night has completely fallen.

Translated by Patrick Barron

NUTO REVELLI
(1919–)

Nuto Revelli was born in Cuneo in the northern Italian region of Piemonte. He was an official in the Italian Alpine forces during the Russian campaign, and later a commander for the partisans. Many of his books recount his experiences of these years, and include *La guerra dei poveri* (The war of the poor), *L'ultimo fronte* (The last front), and *L'anello forte* (The strong ring). His book *Il mondo dei vinti: Testimonianze di vita contadina* (The world of the vanquished: testimonies of rural life) is one of his best received works and gathers together 270 interviews with rural inhabitants who lived before and through the World Wars — many of whom were forced to leave their native regions or suffer through the war's aftereffects, which included disfigured landscapes, extreme poverty, and devastated communities.

POLENTA THREE HUNDRED AND SIXTY-FIVE TIMES A YEAR *

Margherita Lovera (known as Nota 'd Batistin 'd Drea, born in Borgo San Dalmazzo, 1895, farmer and weaver)

(February 12, 1974 — Dalmazzo Giraudo, Michele Calandri).

Sun na burgarina [I was born in Borgo San Dalmazzo]. We lived in an ex-monastery along the road to Demonte, on the plain, in Tetti Deo. Fourteen in the family: nine boys and five girls. But five died when they were little, no one knew of what sickness; in two or three days they died. I was the youngest of the ones who lived. We had four days' worth of land[31]; two were my father's and two were the dowry of my mother.

---

*Selections in this section from Nuto Revelli, *Il mondo dei vinti: Testimonianze di vita contadina* (Torino: Einaudi, 1997).

196

When I was nine I began to go to work, collecting chestnuts. Do you know how much they paid me? Four cents every day. I went to work for an old man, Centu 'd Barbàno. They called him Barbàno because he had a long white beard. He was blind and used to scare me witless...he used to come looking for us. "Bastistin, would you send one of your daughters to collect chestnuts for me?" he asked my father. And my father told him, "Sure, I'll send one, how about this one." And then when I went, Barbàno used to search for me with his arm sticking out in front of him. "But where is she? where is she?" he would say. I was so small that he couldn't find me: I was one hand's breadth shorter than his outstretched arm. I used to go up into the woods, alone, full of fear, and kept thinking of Barbàno's words, "get all of them, even the rotten ones, good or bad." Every evening Barbàno would come to the woods to check on me, guided by a goat that he held on to. He would then always tell me, "you haven't gathered them up very well today, my goat keeps munching them." I used to collect half a sack of chestnuts a day. I would leave home at the crack of dawn and get back when it got dark. At noon my father would bring me a slice of *pulenta mitunà*[32] — and how good it was!

Little by little, as our family got bigger, my father rented other land. At first, we had one cow, then two, then three. He bought the cows on credit, and if we were lucky, they were already expecting; that way when the calf was born, we sold it as soon as possible and could get milk to drink. At the age of seven, my brothers went to work tending cattle. The money they got never made it to the house. As soon as they earned it, my father took it to where it needed to go.

Oh my, what a life my mother had!... At noon we always ate polenta — if there wasn't polenta, there wasn't lunch. Polenta three hundred and sixty-five times a year. In the evening it was tagliatelle al latte or minestrone. We had meat two times a year, at Easter and Christmas. We were all fat as could be, were always in good health, and dressed decently. *Suma sempre steit bin pulit ma tacunà* [We were always clean, but a little ragged].

When I was thirteen, I went to Cuneo to serve as a maid in a place where they never gave me anything to eat — it was the family of a captain. The lady of the house, who was from Naples, was tight-fisted. I earned eighteen lire a month. After fifteen days, my mother came to see me — I was so skinny that when she set eyes on me she could only say, "Oh what a state you're in! Oh what a state!" They would only give me the leftovers in that house — when there were any. I was dying of hunger, but I didn't want to go home — out of shame. It would have been a disgrace to give up the job, a true disgrace in front of all the others. When one gave up a job, people would say, "*Oh, ha purtà le siule*" ["Oh, [s]he's brought home onions."]. I would have preferred to die rather than have to hear this sort of thing. By the time I was fifteen, I started to catch on and began to buy mushrooms — it was a good trade, and I earned well....

I also had the idea of becoming a nun, having seen the mess my mother had to go through — I didn't want to end up like her. "If I become a nun, I'll have it much easier," I used to think. When I was still going to school, the nuns used to always try to convince me.... I got married in 1926. As soon as I saw Battista I liked him — it was fate. But Battista lived in the mountains, in San Maurizio, and my father and mother cried, saying "We're down here, but he lives so high up — you'll have a life up there...." Battista told me, "I make cloth and you'll help me — I won't leave you to go into the fields." I still have my wedding dress, made of black silk and beautifully embroidered. The woman would buy the wardrobe and bring the wedding shawl. Battista brought me to the jewelers and told me, "get whatever you want." I chose in a normal way, without exaggerating, thinking of tomorrow and thinking that we would need to have our resources in common. We bought a beautiful gold chain, with a silver pocket watch, and this ring, that's now so thin because it's been worn away by work.

It was a beautiful wedding. We went there in a small carriage pulled by two horses, followed by four other carriages, all paid for by Battista. We stopped in Vignolo for drinks, and then went on by foot to San Maurizio, followed by our relatives. Up there the lunch was already prepared. Whole tomatoes and peppers, anchovies, boiled eggs, and salami. This was followed by boiled meat and roasted chicken with potatoes. For desert, we had fruit, cheese, sweet pastries, and coffee. They played a joke on me during lunch — putting a few hot coals under my seat, covered by a handful of chamomile flowers.

At home we had two looms, one ours and the other my father-in-law's. They had studied and built the looms by them-selves — without boasting too much, they were intelligent. Everything went very smoothly in the family. Working and earning well, it was a good trade, and we were successful. God rest his soul, the father of Dalmasin[33] was our neighbor and would always tell us, "In the winter when we have some money saved up, we spend it. You, on the other hand, eat and save, even in the winter." Our clients were sharecroppers from the plain and ordered wedding shawls and cloth for the family from us. They brought us skeins of hemp and cotton spun by hand by their wives. We bought the colored thread only for designs, and for embroidery. It was exhausting work, done by the light of little gas lanterns.... My husband is the one who did the most difficult part — he made the loom work by ped-aling, and pulled up the cloth. It required strength — you needed to be on your toes, and skilled. My husband had learned the trade from his father. The bolts of cloth were ninety centimeters wide and nineteen meters long. We would make half a bolt in one day. Each bolt would be worth twelve lire, and we would earn six lire each day. We worked pure hemp, as well as normal hemp and cotton. The sheets of pure hemp were stronger and healthier. The ones of cotton are weaker and stay wetter longer.

I liked working as a weaver very much. The sharecroppers were satisfied and praised our cloth. And it also paid well — it was a secure occupation. My husband never had to work the fields for wheat, and we were never forced to raise silk-worms. We wove until 1960. By that point we already had electricity and so working at night no longer hurt our eyes. In 1960 we still had many clients.

Translated by Patrick Barron

IT DIDN'T SEEM LIKE IT,
BUT THE WOMEN WERE IN CHARGE

Bartolomes Spada (known as Tumé 'd Rübatin, born in Vignolo, 1878, cattle dealer)

(October 22, 1972 — Dalmazzo Giraudo)

In the last century people lived like pigs — a little polenta, rice, and beans — and many went hungry. There was only the countryside to live off of, and if it was a good year you ate, otherwise *"tiravu le müsole"* [Belts were tightened]. In the spring the first money always came from silkworms. We would buy the cocoon and then carry it to the priest. We would then give the priest *'l ramaset,* a bundle of heather with all the best silk-worm cocoons on top. This way, the priest's lot was always the best of the whole village. That priest was an important character, on his toes. People would say, "priests are only able to take — they pray for me and for the others, if there are any." In many houses meat was never seen. Coffee made from rye or barley was already a luxury. Wine was drunk only at the tavern in Vignolo. When trading if I had a little to drink, the words would come more smoothly.

Many in Vignolo led a miserable life, even if the people then were more lively than now. Every evening we would go in a festive group to see girls. We would leave in groups of eight or ten and go as far as Piano Quinto. During carnival they would give *le paghe*[34] to those who had spent the most evenings in the stables. The ones from the stables were the ones who would thank us. It was an honor to have, say, twenty young boys who regularly visited a stable — it would bring honor to the girl. We would go in search of *le paghe* from one stable to another. One time in Santa Croce di Cervasca, I struck gold and collected eight dozen eggs, walnuts, apples, and sweets. For at least twenty years in these parts they've stopped this custom — when television arrived, people stopped going out in the evenings.

In our family there were five sons. We had ten days' of land, all in the country, all good land — and three cows. We were among the richest. Half of the village had only goats. Many of the houses in Vignolo still had thatched roofs — poor houses. There were many people. I went to an elementary school that had one hundred students and one teacher, Teppati di Caraglio, who was strict but taught well.

My father was born in 1847. When he married he didn't have a cent, but when he died, he had twenty days' of his own land. He was mayor and councilor for Vignolo for fifty or more years. There were two or three parties. My father was for Galimberti. When Galimberti came to the piazza to give a speech, half the village came to listen. On the day of the election the candidates would offer food and drink to the voters, and every candidate had his tavern. For lunch there was a pot of tripe and *la carnëtta* — boiled goat or sheep meat. Either Galimberti paid, or those who wanted to become councilors. The voters would come all the way from France. The candidates would offer to pay for the expense of their journey. One time when Galimberti lost the election, he made a speech, saying that *"Ades che la pianta l'é veia völi campela giü"* [Now that the plant is old, they want to knock it down].

The countryside served only for our livelihood. Even today there are people here in Vignolo who live solely on the earth, but they live as they live. Many emigrated to France and America. Me, I already have America here — I was a dealer. The ones who made a bit of money did it by doing business. We were five in our cattle dealing business — my father and us, his four sons. Our area was the Valle Stura, from Gaiola to Argentera. The poorest part of the valley was *l'ubec*,[35] from Festiona and above. In Demonte there were people who had seven or eight cows, but most had two or three. We would climb up through the valley dealing and buying. Descending, we would collect the animals, all on foot. It was necessary to know your trade well, know how to master it. We counted a bit on *'d cüche*....[36] First we looked for a man who was held in high esteem. We paid him well for his animal — we treated him well and threw in a few extras. Then he would convince the others to sell. But the deal was still far from over. If the women decided to sell, we bought at a good price. If the women told their husbands not to sell, there was nothing we could do. It didn't seem like it, but the women were in charge. One time, on a single trip, we bought seventy-seven animals. On the day of the fair in the piazza of Demonte there were three or four thousand beautiful animals. People came as far as Alessandria to buy.

Translated by Patrick Barron

MARIO RIGONI STERN
(1921–)

Mario Rigoni Stern was born and currently lives in the northern Italian village of Asiago. He is best known for his 1953 book *Il sergente nella neve* (*The Sergeant in the Snow*), one of the most famous literary testimonies of the Second World War. Much of his later work examines the interrelationships of human and animal life, particularly those concerning the history of his native village and the surrounding countryside. His other books include *Storia di Tonle* (*The Story of Tonle*), *Uomini, boschi e api* (Men, woods and bees), *Il libro degli animali* (The book of animals), and *Inverni lontani* (Distant winters), which through a series of emotional remembrances, powerfully evokes the relationships between humanity and nature.

THE CROWS *

While I write, rooks are flying around my house and passing in front of the window. They come here from scattered areas among the meadows and from woodpiles stacked by farmers, still covered with snow. Before going to roost in the firs, they salute the evening in its rise from the darkest places with their *craa-craa-craa*. Their voice, even if familiar and deep, has a peculiar character. It is very different from that of the dawn, or when they are alarmed or regrouping. Before settling down for good they gather together, skimming along the tree-tops, following for a last time the path of air with their rustling wings. Even if you don't look in their direction you can follow them in flight with the sound that their feathers make in the evening sky, banking, rising, falling. Like a gust of wind they lower themselves onto branches that rock under their weight, and silence returns. But if before retiring to sleep it

*All selections in this section are from Mario Rigoni Stern, *Uomini, boschi e api* (Torino: Giulio Einaudi, 1980).

comes to me to take a couple of steps towards the woods, I hear them fly up in the deep of night with sudden noise and at once return to land as if they had recognized me.

It seems to me that members of the crow family have been repopulating these mountains and villages for about a decade. They inhabit the landscape as they do in many beautiful canvases by Pieter Bruegel. Perched on branches or power poles they wait by day for a passerby to leave or for someone to go back inside and then descend to the edges of the road or into yards to peck amidst cast out things.

Without a doubt they are among the keenest-minded and best seeing of birds. An old hunter once told me that from the summit of Mount Moor they could see a grain in the village square a mile distant and could smell gunpowder even from the well-cleaned barrels of a rifle. Apart from these exaggerations, it is known that crows represent the highest evolutionary stage of the entire class of birds. Reasons include their temperament, which allows them to easily adapt to the most disparate activities, their oftentimes very elaborate social organization (Konrad Lorenz's studies on jackdaws are of particular note), and also their extraordinary mental development, held by some experts to be superior to the best endowed mammals.

Three years ago in June at dawn I heard a rapping at the window and supposed that it was a friend passing by to say hello. But by the third time, I got out of bed and was surprised to see a young rook. She had not yet gone through her first molt of feathers and was perched there on the windowsill as if she were waiting for something. I understood what it was when she insistently kept her beak open after a soft *craa*. I sopped up a little milk with some bread, opened the window, and began feeding her. When full she emitted another *craa*, beat her wings, and took off towards the woods fluttering a little, walking a little.

She punctually returned other mornings, and with the bread I alternated cookie crumbs, little pieces of meat, and apple slices. Eventually she learned how to look after herself, and one morning she no longer came. This made me curious, and speaking with some children from the area, found out that towards the end of May a fledgling rook had fallen out of its nest and been picked up by a boy. But then, because she dirtied the house

204

and, in a particular manner defiled the bedding hung out to dry on the wire, which she loved to perch upon, the mother forced the boy to bring her back to the woods. Habituated as she was to await food from human hands, she had thus come to ask for it from me. I don't know now what became of her because I never thought of marking her in some particular way. However, I suspect that it was she who brought thieves to my chicken coop.

The rooks hid out, motionless within the trees, awaiting the clucking of the hens. If no one was near the house they swiftly flew down towards the nests, impaled eggs with their beaks and flew away into the depths of the woods to gobble them up. At first I believed that it had been squirrels or the weasel, because within the woods I had found the empty shells. But one day when I decided to patiently wait for the mail, I surprised them at the door of the chicken coop with their beaks in eggs.

There would have been a way to make them stop: kill one with a rifle and then hang it from a pole over the chicken coop. With a scarecrow like that no rook would come near. But forget it. The next spring, however, when they plant potatoes, one of our farmers will have to make a show of a dead rook if he doesn't want the fruit of his labor destroyed.

Taking crows from the nest and domesticating them is an ancient practice in our parts. Perhaps it is a tradition that came from the myths of Odin because, as Snorii in the *Edda* has written, "Huginn and Mininn / fly every day / above the vast earth, /…" and then relate to god what they have seen and heard. A crow used to do something similar with a bricklayer neighbor of mine: every time he returned home from work, the crow flew to meet him, perched on one of his shoulders, and quietly cawed in his ear. When this crow heard the bell tower sound noon, he flew to a rooftop and waited there, scrutinizing the village. When he saw his friend emerge from around a corner he went to meet him; he did the same in the evening. But one day he almost caused a disaster when he nipped a cigarette out of the bricklayer's lips and flew off towards a hayloft. It took a lot of patience to make him come back down, for he had found a taste for swaggering about with the lit cigarette in his beak. Another time he carried the house keys to the gutter.

But one Sunday afternoon the crow was on a garden fence, hopping from post to post as if he wanted to count them all. A sports car passed by, slowed down, and from the window emerged a *flobert*, a compressed-air gun. The crow, hit in the head, fell amongst the cabbages, beating his wings.

But those that I personally love are the ravens. They stand out from others in their family by their greater size, massive beak, burly claws, wedge-shaped tail, and beautiful, completely black plumage with bluish highlights.

Up until a few years ago in our region they were relatively rare. But now I come across them more often. They say that once mated, pairs stay together for life. In fact, they always fly in twos, high up, powerful, and in a straight line. It is their voice that announces them: the *pruc-pruc-pruc* that accompanies them in flight is perceptible from far away. When I hear it I look up into the sky. Now, in the high and bare mountains they have already made their nests among rocks free of snow. The male watches over but does not stray far; the female broods. We will see them again towards summer, when the young are independent. To find them up there where noise doesn't reach will be like seeing friends once again.

Translated by Patrick Barron

THE SHEPHERD *

Snow is falling on the woods and the houses. The rooks are flying in groups, calling to one another. In the village center people crowd about in shops and boutiques to buy last-minute presents. Multicolored lines of skiers plod along, step by step, towards the seats and bars of the lifts. On the slopes instructors patiently teach how to turn, stop, begin again, gradually increase speed, and to slow down with style.

In half an hour when evening falls, the young people will bunch together and dance around jukeboxes to wait for dinner and the big evening dance. Tonight there is an orchestra.

---

*This translation of "Il pastore" by Patrick Barron first appeared in: *ISLE: Interdisciplinary Studies in Literature and Environment* 7.2 (2000): 235–38.

But before evening ends I will see, as I have for many years now, Bepi dei Püne descend from the mountain on his way home along a narrow lane running through the deep snow, the wind carrying the scent of the oven fire and polenta to him.

He is eighty years old and has not yet resigned himself to looking at the fire in the hearth. Up in Valgiardini, in a little stable isolated from the rest of the world, he still wants to maintain the reason for his work: a few sheep, a dog, and a donkey.

At the age of seven he began taking his father's sheep to the pastures of the village common. At nine, he was sent to graze the mayor's sheep in the mountains of Verena. After four months of isolation he received four gold coins, which he gave to his mother. In exchange, his parents bought him a pair of wooden-soled shoes at the fair of San Matteo. He didn't finish fourth grade because he was needed as soon as possible to look after the sixty sheep that belonged to his father, who in the warm seasons crossed the boundaries, just like many other *eisenponnar*[37] who went to work building the railroad for the Hapsburg Empire.

It went like this for him until the Great War, when in the spring of 1916 our mountains were invaded and the villages destroyed. During the war he, along with his ten-year-old brother Toni and an old man of ninety, had to save a herd of one hundred and twenty sheep that shepherds called to war had left in their care. That spring, for the first time in history, instead of climbing up to the high altitude pastures on the mountain, the herds descended to the winter ones on the plain. And all this happened in the middle of bombardments and fires.

They did not have donkeys to carry their most important gear, and so were helped by children and old people who left their homes. They also hid many ewes, because it was their time to deliver. The regimental commanders who were climbing to the upland plains in order to meet the offensive hunted the sheep down because they hampered the movements of the troops. Once down in the plain, no one wanted to give up any pastures to the starving sheep, and no one wanted to buy them.

At long last they were able to find their father, who led the "white widows" and children through the falling bombs, away

207

from the area. Eventually he was able to sell the herd to suppliers at a cut rate for meat for the troops. Bepi, at the age of sixteen, was called into military service with workers who were digging shelters and trenches for the line of *extreme resistance* along the edges of the mountains facing the plain, an area much coveted by the Austrians. His ten-year-old brother served as a water-bearer to quench the thirst of the diggers. They earned 33 centimes an hour.

When the war ended people came back to find only houses torn to the ground and mountains ripped apart, unrecognizable. There were no longer meadows for sheep, alpine pastures for herds, woods for birds and deer, or houses for people. They reclaimed the area and the fields, around tangles of barbed wire, unexploded bombs, abandoned weapons, and the corpses of soldiers. Bepi worked with others in the stone quarries to gather material to rebuild the bomb- and fire-destroyed houses. He then felled trees in the woods, dead from the effects of gas and grapeshot.

His father began once again to be a shepherd with only a few sheep, about ten. Bepi was drafted into the military, and when he returned, he and his brother worked salvaging and secretly selling war materials, which they carried on their shoulders down from the Ortigara and Zebio Mountains. This went on for years, first here on our upland plains, and later in Carnia, Cadore, Pasubio, and Grappa. It was demanding work, difficult and risky. Many lost their lives, or, if luckier, a hand or an eye.

Eventually he was able to save up a little money, enough to get married, build a house, and buy a little herd of sheep. Afterwards he went with the other shepherds, his oldest friends, up into our mountains in the good season and then to the plains between Mincio and Isonzo from October to March.

The years of the Second World War weren't easy either. His sheep often fed the partisans, among whom were many of his nephews, cousins, and godchildren. From the Germans, in exchange for requisitioned lambs, he was able to get salt, which was invaluable for making cheese and polenta, and for preserving meats and lard.

208

But now, for about ten years, he no longer climbs up the mountain with his sheep and wise donkey. His wife and children won't let him, due to his age, but every summer he goes along with others to visit his shepherd friends. Or sometimes he goes on his own in order to catch his donkey that he has let escape, to take the ancient road of the pastures to reach the herd, up high.

Each day he knows where the mother sheep are grazing with their lambs and where the non-mating ewes and rams are and who it is that watches over the herd. The other shepherds ask him advice on how to cure sicknesses and deal with other mishaps that happen to animals, on the qualities of a dog, on the condition of the pastures, or on how the season is going. For him animals and nature are in harmony, because to his way of thinking, he has never seen mistrust in dogs or horses, sheep or donkeys, birds or deer or other wild animals. From them he has learned to recognize instinct, and to them he has taught the behavior of men.

Early in the morning when many are still asleep, and in the late afternoon, in all types of weather, he climbs up to the stable in Valgiardini to check on his animals' food and water. It is the practice he maintains to stay "in life" with the world.

One day when a boy from the city asked him how far away his house was, he responded, "once it was fifteen minutes away on foot, now it is thirty." The boy looked at him blankly, without understanding, and he explained, "when I was young I walked more swiftly and my house was closer, now I walk more slowly and my house has gotten farther away. If I get to be a hundred years old, it'll be an hour away."

It is snowing. On the balconies of the villas and in the halls of the hotels Christmas trees are brightly lit. In the stores of the center it is no longer possible to find a bottle of champagne. At the ice rink a hockey match is going strong. Bepi dei Püne is walking down the narrow lane running through the deep snow. He waves his hands in the air, shakes his head: he is following distant thoughts and memories while amidst the falling snow groups of rooks fly about, cawing.

Translated by Patrick Barron

209

ITALO CALVINO
(1923–1985)

Italo Calvino is one of the foremost Italian postwar writers, well known throughout the world. His many works include: *Il sentiero dei nidi di ragno* (*The Path to the Nest of Spiders*), *Il visconte dimezzato* (*The Cloven Viscount*), *Il barone rampante* (*The Baron in the Trees*), *Il cavaliere inesistente* (*The Non-Existent Knight*), *Le cosmicomiche* (*Cosmicomics*) and *Le città invisibili* (*Invisible Cities*). In *Marcovaldo, ovvero, Le stagioni in città* (*Marcovaldo, or, The Seasons in the City*),[38] one of his many works that contain strong environmental themes, Calvino recounts the comic misadventures of the buffoonish and melancholic Marcovaldo in his search for nature in the city. The book includes twenty short stories, each dedicated to a season.

SPRING: MUSHROOMS IN THE CITY*

The wind, coming to the city from far away, brings its unusual gifts, noticed by only a few sensitive souls, such as hay-fever victims, who sneeze at the pollen from flowers of other lands. One day, to the narrow strip of ground flanking a city avenue came a gust of spores from God knows where; and some mushrooms germinated. Nobody noticed them except Marcovaldo, the worker who caught his tram just there every morning.

This Marcovaldo possessed an eye ill-suited to city life: billboards, traffic-lights, shop-windows, neon signs, posters, no matter how carefully devised to catch the attention, never arrested his gaze, which might have been running over the desert sands. Instead, he would never miss a leaf yellowing on a branch, a feather trapped by a roof-tile; there was no horsefly on a horse's back, no worm-hole in a plank, or fig-peel

---

*All selections in this section are from Italo Calvino, *Marcovaldo, or, The Seasons in the City*, trans. by William Weaver (San Diego: Harcourt Brace Jovanovich, 1983).

squashed on the sidewalk that Marcovaldo didn't remark and ponder over, discovering the changes of season, the yearnings of his heart, and the woes of his existence.

Thus, one morning, as he was waiting for the tram that would take him to Sbav and Co., where he was employed as an unskilled laborer, he noticed something unusual near the stop, in the sterile, encrusted strip of earth beneath the avenue's line of trees; at certain points, near the tree trunks, some bumps seemed to rise and, here and there, they had opened, allowing roundish subterranean bodies to peep out.

Bending to tie his shoes, he took a better look: they were mushrooms, real mushrooms, sprouting right in the heart of the city! To Marcovaldo the gray and wretched world surrounding him seemed suddenly generous with hidden riches; something could still be expected of life, beyond the hourly wage of his stipulated salary, with inflation index, family grant, and cost-of-living allowance.

On the job he was more absent-minded than usual; he kept thinking that while he was there unloading cases and boxes, in the darkness of the earth the slow, silent mushrooms, known only to him, were ripening their porous flesh, were assimilating underground humors, breaking the crust of clods. "One night's rain would be enough," he said to himself, "then they would be ready to pick." And he couldn't wait to share his discovery with his wife and his six children.

"I'm telling you!" he announced during their scant supper. "In a week's time we'll be eating mushrooms! A great fry! That's a promise!"

And to the smaller children, who did not know what mushrooms were, he explained ecstatically the beauty of the numerous species, the delicacy of their flavor, the way they should be cooked; and so he also drew into the discussion his wife, Domitilla, who until then had appeared rather incredulous and abstracted.

"Where are these mushrooms?" the children asked. "Tell us where they grow!"

At this question Marcovaldo's enthusiasm was curbed by a suspicious thought: Now if I tell them the place, they'll go and hunt for them with the usual gang of kids, word will spread through the neighborhood, and the mushrooms will end up in somebody else's pan! And so that discovery, which had promptly filled his heart with universal love, now made him wildly possessive, surrounded him with jealous and distrusting fear.

"I know where the mushrooms are, and I'm the only one who knows," he said to his children, "and God help you if you breathe a word to anybody."

The next morning, as he approached the tram stop, Marcovaldo was filled with apprehension. He bent to look at the ground and, to his relief, saw that the mushrooms had grown a little, but not much, and were still almost completely hidden by the earth.

He was bent in this position when he realized there was someone behind him. He straightened up at once and tried to act indifferent. It was the street-cleaner, leaning on his broom and looking at him.

This street-cleaner, whose jurisdiction included the place where the mushrooms grew, was a lanky youth with eyeglasses. His name was Amadigi, and Marcovaldo had long harbored a dislike of him, perhaps because of those eyeglasses that examined the pavement of the streets, seeking any trace of nature, to be eradicated by his broom.

It was Saturday; and Marcovaldo spent his free half-day circling the bed of dirt with an absent air, keeping an eye on the street-cleaner in the distance and on the mushrooms, and calculating how much time they needed to ripen.

That night it rained: like peasants who, after months of drought, wake up and leap with joy at the sound of the first drops, so Marcovaldo, alone in all the city, sat up in bed and called to his family: "It's raining! It's raining!" and breathed in the smell of moistened dust and fresh mold that came from outside.

At dawn — it was Sunday — with the children and a borrowed basket, he ran immediately to the patch. There were the mushrooms, erect on their stems, their caps high over the still-soaked earth. "Hurrah!" and they fell to gathering them.

"Papà! Look how many that man over there has found," Michelino said, and his father, raising his eyes, saw Amadigi

212

standing beside them, also with a basket full of mushrooms under his arm.

"Ah, you're gathering them, too?" the street-cleaner said. "Then they're edible? I picked a few, but I wasn't sure.... Farther down the avenue some others have sprouted, even bigger ones.... Well, now that I know, I'll tell my relatives; they're down there arguing whether it's a good idea to pick them or not...." And he walked off in a hurry.

Marcovaldo was speechless: even bigger mushrooms, which he hadn't noticed, an unhoped-for harvest, being taken from him like this, before his very eyes. For a moment he was almost frozen with anger, fury, then — as sometimes happens — the collapse of individual passion led to a generous impulse. At that hour, many people were waiting for the tram, umbrellas over their arms, because the weather was still damp and uncertain. "Hey, you! Do you want to eat fried mushrooms tonight?" Marcovaldo shouted to the crowd of people at the stop. "Mushrooms are growing here by the street! Come along! There's plenty for all!" And he walked off after Amadigi, with a string of people behind him.

They all found plenty of mushrooms, and lacking baskets, they used their open umbrellas. Somebody said: "It would be nice to have a big feast, all of us together!" But, instead, each took his own share and went home.

They saw one another again soon, however; that very evening, in fact, in the same ward of the hospital, after the stomach-pump had saved them all from poisoning. It was not serious, because the number of mushrooms eaten by each person was quite small.

Marcovaldo and Amadigi had adjacent beds; they glared at each other.

Translated by William Weaver

SPRING: THE GOOD AIR

"These children," the Public Health doctor said, "need to breathe some good air, at a certain altitude; they should run through meadows...."

He was between the beds of the half-basement where the family lived, and was pressing his stethoscope against little Teresa's back, between her shoulder-blades, frail as the wings of a tiny featherless bird. The beds were two, and the four children, all ill, peeked out at the head and foot of each bed, with flushed cheeks and glistening eyes.

"On meadows like the flower-bed in the square?" Michelino asked.

"The altitude of a skyscraper?" asked Filippetto.

"Air that's good to eat?" asked Pietruccio.

Marcovaldo, tall and skinny, and his wife, Domitilla, short and squat, were leaning on one elbow on either side of a rickety chest of drawers. Without moving the elbow, each raised the other arm and then dropped it, grumbling together: "Where are we supposed to find those things, six mouths to feed, loaded with debts? How are we supposed to manage?"

"The most beautiful place we can send them," Marcovaldo declared, "is into the streets."

"We'll find good air," Domitilla concluded, "when we're evicted and have to sleep under the stars."

One Saturday afternoon, as soon as they were well again, Marcovaldo took the children and led them off on a walk in the hills. The part of the city where they lived is the farthest from the hills. To reach the slopes they made a long journey on a crowded tram and the children saw only the legs of passengers around them. Little by little the tram emptied; at the windows, finally freed, an avenue appeared, climbing up. And so they reached the end of the line and set forth. It was early spring; the trees were just budding in a tepid sun. The children looked around, slightly disoriented. Marcovaldo led them up a little path of steps, rising among the green.

"Why is there a stairway without a house over it?" Michelino asked.

"It's not a house stairway; it's like a street,"

"A street.... And how can the cars manage the steps?"

Around them there were garden walls, with trees inside.

"Walls without a roof.... Did they bomb them?"

"They're gardens...like courtyards..." the father explained. "The house is farther back, beyond those trees."

Michelino shook his head, unconvinced. "But courtyards are inside houses, not outside."

Teresina asked: "Do the trees live in these houses?"

As they climbed up, it seemed to Marcovaldo that he was gradually shedding the moldy smell of the warehouse in which he shifted packages for eight hours a day and the damp stains on the walls of his house and the dust that settled, gilded, in the cone of light from the little window, and the fits of coughing in the darkness. His children now seemed to him less sallow and frail, already somehow part of that light and that green.

"You like it here, don't you?"

"Yes."

"Why?"

"There aren't any police. You can pull up the flowers, throw stones."

"What about breathing? Are you breathing?"

"No."

"The air's good here."

They chewed it. "What are you talking about? It doesn't have any taste at all."

They climbed almost to the top of the hill. At one turn, the city appeared, way down below, spread flat on the gray cobweb of the streets. The children rolled around on a meadow as if they had never done anything else in their life. A little breeze sprang up; it was already evening. In the city a few lights came on, in a confused sparkle. Marcovaldo felt again a rush of the feeling he had had as a young man, arriving in the city, when those streets, those lights attracted him as if he expected something unknown from them. The swallows plunged headlong through the air onto the city.

Then he was seized by the sadness of having to go back down there, and in the clotted landscape he figured out the shadow of his neighborhood: it seemed to him a leaden wasteland, stagnant, covered by the thick scales of the roofs and the shreds of smoke flapping on the stick-like chimney-pots.

It had turned cool: perhaps he should call the children, But seeing them swinging peacefully on the lower limbs of a tree, he dismissed that thought. Michelino came over to him and asked: "Papa, why don't we come and live here?"

"Stupid, there aren't any houses; nobody lives up here!" Marcovaldo said, with irritation, because he had actually been daydreaming of being able to live up there.

And Michelino said: "Nobody? What about those gentlemen? Look!"

The air was turning gray and down from the meadows came a troop of men, of various ages, all dressed in heavy gray suits, buttoned up like pyjamas, all with cap and cane. They came in bunches, some talking in loud voices or laughing, sticking those canes into the grass or carrying them, hung by the curved handle, over their arm.

"Who are they? Where are they going?" Michelino asked his father, but Marcovaldo was looking at them, silent.

One passed nearby; he was a heavy man of about forty. "Good evening!" he said. "Well, what news do you bring us, from down in the city?"

"Good evening," Marcovaldo said. "What do you mean by news?"

"Nothing. I was just talking," the man said, and stopped; he had a broad, white face, with only a splotch of pink, or red, like a shadow, over his cheekbones. "I always say that, to anybody from the city. I've been up here for three months, you understand."

"And you never go down?"

"Hmph, when the doctors decide to let me!" And he laughed briefly. "And this!" And he tapped his fingers on his chest, with some more brief laughter, a bit breathless. "They've already discharged me twice, as cured, but as soon as I went back to the factory, wham, all over again. And they ship me back up here. Some fun!"

"Them too?" Marcovaldo asked, nodding at the other men, who had scattered over the grass; and at the same time, his eyes sought Filippetto and Teresa and Pietruccio, whom he had lost sight of.

"All comrades on the same holiday," the man said, and winked. "We're let out on a pass, before taps.... We go to bed early.... Obviously, can't go beyond the grounds...."

"What grounds?"

"This is part of the sanatorium. Didn't you know?"

Marcovaldo took the hand of Michelino, who had stood there listening, a bit scared. Evening was climbing up the slopes; there below, their neighborhood was no longer discernible, and it seemed not so much to have been swallowed by the shadows, but to have spread its own shadow everywhere. It was time to go back. "Teresa! Filippetto!" Marcovaldo called and started to look for them. "Sorry," he said to the man, "I don't see the other children anywhere."

The man stepped to a parapet. "They're down there," he said, "they're picking cherries."

In a ditch, Marcovaldo saw a cherry tree and around it were the men dressed in gray, pulling down the branches with their curved sticks, and picking the fruit. And Teresa and the two boys, all delighted, were also picking cherries and taking them from the men's hands and laughing with them.

"It's late," Marcovaldo said. "It's cold. Let's go home...."

The heavy man pointed the tip of his cane towards the rows of lights that were coming on, down below.

"In the evening," he said, "with this stick I take my walk in the city. I choose a street, a row of lamps, and I follow it, like this.... I stop at the windows, I meet people, I say hello to them.... When you walk in the city, think of it sometimes: my cane is following you...."

The children came back crowned with leaves, made by the inmates.

"This is a wonderful place, Papà!" Teresa said. "We'll come and play here again, won't we?"

"Papa!" Michelino blurted. "Why don't we come and live here, too, with these gentlemen?"

"It's late. Say good-bye to the gentlemen! Say thanks for the cherries. Come on! We're going!"

They headed home. They were tired. Marcovaldo didn't answer any questions, Filippetto wanted to be carried, Pietruccio wanted to ride piggy-back, Teresa made him drag her by the hand, and Michelino, the oldest, went ahead by himself, kicking stones.

Translated by William Weaver

SPRING: WHERE THE RIVER IS MORE BLUE?

It was a time when the simplest foods contained threats, traps, and frauds. Not a day went by without some newspaper telling of ghastly discoveries in the housewife's shopping: cheese was made of plastic, butter from tallow candles; in fruit and vegetables the arsenic of insecticides was concentrated in percentages higher than the vitamin content; to fatten chickens they stuffed them with synthetic pills that could transform the man who ate a drumstick into a chicken himself. Fresh fish had been caught the previous year in Iceland and they put make-up on the eyes to make it seem yesterday's catch. Mice had been found in several milk bottles, whether dead or alive was not made clear. From the tins of oil it was no longer the golden juice of the olive that flowed, but the fat of old mules, cleverly distilled.

At work or in the cafe Marcovaldo heard them discussing these things, and every time he felt something like a mule's kick in his stomach, or a mouse running down his esophagus. At home, when his wife, Domitilla, came back from the market, the sight of her shopping-bag, which once had given him such joy with its celery and eggplant, the rough, absorbent paper of the packages from the grocer or the delicatessen, now filled him with fear, as if hostile presences had infiltrated the walls of his house.

"I must bend all my efforts," he vowed to himself, "towards providing my family with food that hasn't passed through the treacherous hands of speculators." In the morning, going to work, he sometimes encountered men with fishing-poles and rubber boots, heading for the river. "That's the way," Marcovaldo said to himself. But the river, there in the city, which collected garbage and waste and the emptying of sewers, filled him with deep repugnance. "I have to look for a place," he said to himself, "where the water is really water, and fish are really fish. There I'll drop my line."

The days were growing longer: with his motorbike, after work, Marcovaldo set to exploring the river along its course before the city, and the little streams, its tributaries. He was especially interested in the stretches where the water flowed farthest from the paved road. He proceeded along paths, among the clumps of willows, riding his motorbike as far as he could go then, after leaving it in a bush, on foot until he reached the stream. Once he got lost: he roamed among steep, overgrown slopes, and could find no trail, nor did he know in which direction the river lay. Then, all of a sudden, pushing some branches aside, he saw the silent water a few feet below him — it was a widening of the river, practically a calm little pool of such a blue that it seemed a mountain lake.

His emotion didn't prevent him from peering down among the little ripples of the stream. And there, his stubbornness was rewarded! A flicker, the unmistakable flash of a fin at the surface, and then another, another still: such happiness, he could hardly believe his eyes. This was the place where the fish of the whole river assembled, the fisherman's paradise, perhaps still unknown to everyone but him. On his way home (it was already growing dark) he stopped and cut signs on the bark of the elms, and made piles of stones at certain spots, to be able to find the way again.

Now he had only to equip himself. Actually, he had already thought about it: among the neighbors and the personnel of his firm he had already identified about ten dedicated fishermen. With hints and allusions, promising each to inform him the moment he was really sure of a place full of tench that only he knew about, he managed to borrow, a bit from one, a bit from another, the most complete fisherman's outfit ever seen.

Now he lacked nothing: pole, line, hooks, bait, net, boots, creel. One fine morning, in a couple of hours from six to eight, before going to work, at the river with the tench — could he fail to catch some? And in fact, he had only to drop his line and he caught them; the tench bit, without any suspicion. Since it was so easy with hook and line, he tried with the net; the tench were so good-natured that they rushed headlong into the net, too.

When it was time to leave, his creel was already full. He looked for a path, moving up the river.

"Hey, you!" At a curve in the shore, among the poplars, there was a character wearing a guard's cap and giving him an ugly stare.

"Me? What is it?" Marcovaldo asked, sensing an unknown threat to his tench.

"Where did you catch those fish there?" the guard asked.

"Eh? Why?" And Marcovaldo's heart was already in his mouth.

"If you caught them down below, throw them back right now: didn't you see the factory up there?" And the man pointed out a long, low building that now, having come around the bend of the river, Marcovaldo could discern, beyond the willows, throwing smoke into the air and, into the water, a dense cloud of an incredible color somewhere between turquoise and violet. "You must at least have seen the color of the water! A paint factory: the river's poisoned because of that blue, and the fish are poisoned, as well. Throw them back right now, or I'll confiscate them!"

Marcovaldo would have liked to fling them far away as fast as possible, get rid of them, as if the mere smell were enough to poison him. But in front of the guard, he didn't want to humble himself. "What if I caught them farther up?"

"Then that's another story. I'll confiscate them and fine you, too. Above the factory there's a fishing preserve. Can't you see the sign?"

"Actually," Marcovaldo hastened to say, "I carry a fishing pole just for looks, to fool my friends. I really bought the fish at the village shop nearby."

"Then everything's all right. You only have to pay the tax, to take them into the city: we're beyond the city limits here."

Marcovaldo had already opened the creel and was emptying it into the river. Some of the tench must have been still alive, because they darted off with great joy.

Translated by William Weaver

GIUSEPPE BONAVIRI
(1924–)

Giuseppe Bonaviri was born in Mineo, Sicily, situated on the crest of a hill in the ranges that rise from the plain of Catania. His father was a tailor, who also secretly wrote poetry, and his mother was a baker, whose stories and fables made a deep impression on her son. The power of Mineo for Bonaviri is immense: it is the setting of all his books, whether the story is said to take place in India or the plain of Troy or in outer space. Bonaviri began to write poems, stories, and novels when he was ten and continued throughout his later schooling and training as a doctor. His first published novel, *Il sarto della stradalunga* (The tailor of Main Street) is the story of his childhood and was published in 1954. Many of his works, in contrast to the neo-realism dominant in postwar Italy, are characterized by fantasy and a powerful imagination, verging on science fiction and magic realism. His works include *La divina foresta* (The divine forest), the story of a molecule tossed through the winds of space, which finally finds, in the vicinity of Mineo, the propitious place for its later adventures, first as a plant, and later as a hawk, and *La Beffària* (The big joke), in which peasant wisdom views the chaos and narrow materialism of our time sarcastically. *Dolcissimo* is an account of the physician Ariete's return to his Sicilian birthplace (Zebulonia) to investigate the inexplicable disappearance of its villagers. He and Mario Sinus, the psychoethnologist sent to accompany him, discover a world of archaic gods, rituals, and beliefs that may provide redemption from the destructive forces of modern life. The central figure in this Eden is Dolcissimo, whose very name suggests a concentration of its sweetness and whose presence in the remembered time of the work contrasts with his virtual absence in its present time. A simple man who lives in poverty, Dolcissimo is also a mediator between nature and human beings.*

FROM: DOLCISSIMO[†]

"This way they go who would go into peace,"[39] the ethnopsychiatrist Mario Sinus quoted, smiling, as we advanced on foot (our car having broken down) through broom and thyme. Around us, from height to height, rugged spurs closed ranks in the direction of Zebulonia, over which the luminous sunset flared, splendid against dark spaces.

The investigation had been entrusted to us by one Ida Melange, any of whose features of appearance or character were hard to imagine. She was known to us through a little treatise, *De amore mutatis mutandis*,[40] in which, with an eye to keeping vice and corruption at bay, she discusses the incorporeal things that reflect the soul of the world.

Far ahead of us a falcon, winging the hot updraft, grew smaller and smaller, way up there, to our narrowed eyes. Far away, below, beyond the dusty green of the orange groves, among pockets of vapor, rose the exploratory rigs of the Exxon Company. Except for those dying groves, you saw only bare fields, which up until thirty years ago produced from ten to fifteen million kilos of wheat and fava beans, measured in *tumoli*. These were cylindrical containers, made of carob or walnut wood, followed in decreasing order by similar smaller containers, the *mondello* and the *carozzo*. The local noble families studded the borders of these cylinders with polished silver and precious stones. They were measures of Norman origin.

Grains were cultivated at that time at Violo, Ruccuvè, Sparagogna, on the banks of Ferro Creek, at Cameni, among the rocks of the Coste, on the estate of Castelluccio, around Lake Naftía, and, if you raised your eyes as I was asking Mario Sinus to do, you could see fava beans, barley, wheat at the Pietre Nere, on the slopes of Mount Catalfaro, in the valley of

---

*Introductory note adapted from Umberto Mariani's introduction to his translation of Giuseppe Bonaviri, *Dolcissimo* (New York: Italica Press, 1990).
[†]From Mariani's translation.

222

Donna Ragusa, and also, in the same direction, at Albano Bianco, at Malati, and proceeding downward, at Nicchiara as well, and further up, on the Càllari Plateau, or, coming back, among the crags of the Trezzito, at Camúti, Gianforte, at Vattàno, at Fiumecaldo, along ravines and ditches, and in so many localities that my friend asked, "How many localities around Zebulonia have names?"

The fields of Indian corn, spelt, hard wheat and soft, mingled in waves of yellow with the blooming mustard and the fava beans that condensed the rising dew, gathering the obliging moonlight under their leaves.

"This must have been a sea," exclaimed Mario Sinus. "Eating the tiny seeds of mustard," he added, "helps one to meditate on the physical world."

We continued to climb the mountain rapidly, while my friend said, "In a field of wheat one's hearing grows sharper, Ariete, and one's voice, like a vibrating body, becomes visible as it harmoniously bends the ear of grain." He added that the wheat kernel, with its floury substance and milky fluid, makes for a restorative bread that mellows the senses. In Zebulonia, in fact, in spite of the semiarid climate due to the scarcity of rainfall, between the pebbles and the fossil-rich sand there is a humusy soil that forms an aggregate with ferrous concretions when storms swell the creeks; their alluvial waters carry clays and auriferous nuggets downstream, causing the bedrock of the sea floor to emerge.

Because of its rather stony soil, Zebulonia did not have many groves. Nevertheless, it produced walnuts, almonds, apricots, blackberries and mulberries, cherries, figs, and in the fall capers, peaches, apples, medlars, onions, garlic, mushrooms. Some people even owned the tuttifrutti tree we have mentioned, or cultivated red peppers in open patches and, if they watched out carefully for the early frost, the reddish bunches of seven-flavor grapes. Food was obtained from roots, saplings, leaves, dandelions, chicories. The smells, colors, and sounds of these fruits were carried to the brain by the thin blood.

All this time I was urging Mario Sinus to look back at the great arc of the eastern mountains.

"Ariete," he said, "in the appendix to the *De amore mutatis mutandis* Ida Melange has studied the relationship between plowed fields and the winds. According to her, the north wind, by freezing the vapors of caves, sweeps away the rotten effluvia of the fields. The east wind makes the rising sun look asymmetrical, dissolving its rays into motes. The tumultuous west wind greatly enhances the aromas of thyme, catmint, and oregano."

"It may be true," I answered. "The air of Zebulonia, in fact, used to be good for sores, head wounds, and the weak constitution of the old. According to common belief, garlic, onions, and olive oil were good for worms. Lettuce and wild fennel increased the flow of milk in women. Canicular fevers were alleviated with infusions of wormwood and holy-thistle."

The great mountainside we were climbing was covered with wormwood and thistle. You could see their white corymbs and red flower-heads around dead tree trunks, on the flinty patches where we were already beginning to encounter boys and old men. As I climbed I began to realize that as a consequence of massive emigration the land had been radically changed: there were no more olive trees, no agave, no birds to drink the rain.

"Come on," Sinus tried to console me, "think of the new things we're going to encounter. You'll see, we'll do a good piece of research. You can be sure of it."

I did not answer. The earth had taken on a different physical shape, extruding clays, roots, geodes, schists.

"Listen," Sinus observed, "the different aspect of the countryside creates different feelings in those of your countrymen that have remained."

We saw kidney-shaped burls of dried-up wild olives full of dead earthworms. The surface of the soil exhibited purplish ferrous deposits and peculiar, indefinable nodules.

"The sun's refraction," the psychiatrist went on, "is different in these places."

In my opinion the greatest damage occurs in October and March, pivotal months, so to speak, since in October the light has diminished so much that the saline spirits of the fields, in which our eyes are mirrored, increase; in March, as in April, the humors melt at the foot of the almond trees and in the soil and correspondingly mortal flesh is weaker.

The rainfall did not exceed four hundred millimeters a year and was quickly dried up by the north wind that had destroyed the carob trees of the slopes, leaving them mere wood flattened to the ground. The filtering water and the telluric gases themselves had allowed the inferior terrestrial forces to gain the upper hand. Because light and the eye are one, after all, the fields looked as if they were strewn with decaying snakes and spiders.

. . . .

Dolcissimo, following the instructions of the travellers who were put up between the mules and the hay in the shop of my paternal grandfather, had made himself two guitars, perhaps to gratify his soul. One was made of wild rosewood, the other of eucalyptus. Gradually the custom arose for him to meet with the old and the blind. The latter came from the Centímolo quarter, one behind the other, finding their way with the bamboo canes in their hands. And you know, my brother Timor, that patches of bamboo abound in our region, on steep slopes, in ravines, and around houses. They are useful as material for hampers, breadbaskets, roofing lath, trays on which figs and split tomatoes are dried during the summer. They have singing leaves and hollow conduits through which one can hear the breath of the wind gurgling, if they have been carefully cut.

"Oh Dolcissimo," the blind men would call. "Are you in front of Don Papè's shop?"

They surrounded him trying to discern his shape with the feeble light of their corneas.

"We are here," one would say. "Will you talk to us about olive trees this morning?"

"Talking" for them meant playing, Yaluna continued. Dolcissimo plucked his rosewood guitar, drawing from it a folk tune that seemed gradually to fade into sleep over the waters of the trickling brooks.

"Oh," the blind men would say, "don't you hear the olive trees rustling?"

Another would ask, "Tell us about fava beans."

They were a substitute for bread. The peasants ate them fresh, fried with eggs in omelettes, as well as dried, cooked whole

225

and eaten using onion leaves as spoons. They were also consumed skinned and mashed, in a coarse mixture with olive oil and flour.

The guitar was gentle now, as if to give sensory properties to the imagined fava beans. The old people could feel its mild rhythm on their lashes.

"Now tell us about Fiumecaldo," another blind man begged.

"All right," Dolcissimo would say.

He would take the eucalyptus guitar and rouse its voice with his fingers and a tin pick in studied measures, even, odd, and odd-even. One heard a kind of flowing of waters, a mournful melody that brightened when Dolcissimo plucked the rosewood guitar again to combine the vibrations of the two. The old men compensated for their lack of the visual with the aural, their memory swollen and ailing. They did not know that the sterility of the soil of Zebulonia was absolute, now that, among other things, the olive trees had been destroyed by hypocrisy, deceit, and bad weather. If women went by with their black shawls over their heads, they walked quickly, not to be troubled by that sound.

Since it was daytime and the advancing sun flashed on the eaves and its refraction touched the eyeballs of the old men, they would ask: "Oh, is the sun rising? Is it light already? Is it burning?" Or: "Is it going to be hot? Can you see it on top of the Collegiate Church? If we move will we feel it better on our hands?"

To Sinus the sunlight is the sense of touch itself, which allows us to feel it in oscillating photons that spread through the air from the heavenly circles and reach us thanks to the receptive properties of our retina. Lacking the use of the latter, those Zebulonians felt the sunlight in what ocular membranes they had left and in the crossroads of their hearts. They would ask Dolcissimo to translate the light for them so they could again appreciate its points, its shapes, its cheerfulness.

Thus sound became a complex relationship of tiny intervals: the rosewood sound was sloth of memory or remorse alternating with lust; the eucalyptus sound produced spherical musical particles more rounded at their ends, recalling waters, chasms, and discordant whistling.

226

Hearing this story, Mario Sinus explained that Dolcissimo, sharpening the senses of the old men, had turned them into forces of the original chaos, in which small things expand to occupy immensity, and fava bean flowers in their cycle become one with the universe.

In the fall Don Mariddu the puppeteer came to Zebulonia from the coastal towns, since it was the season of the olive harvest. For his stories, which he altered at times, adding new parts, he followed *The French Paladins* by Lodico and the book by Pietro Manzaneres published in 1510 in Palermo by Pedone Lauriel. The puppeteer owned the *Guerin Meschino* in the 1473 Paduan edition by the publisher Valdezochio, the *Cantar de mi Cid,* and the *Chanson de Roland.* It seems that Dolcissimo played the guitar on those evenings, and my uncle Pino the violin, at the foot of the stage on which Don Mariddu, manipulating arms and strings, told the spectators of the ten thousand rivers that flow downstream into the black earth where death is a maiden garlanded with ivy. The sound of the instruments and the flashing of swords favored the rising of the wind abroad in Zebulonia that darkened the empty streets.

Don Mariddu owned seven hundred and twenty scenes painted on cardboard and the paper in which sugar was wrapped, that on Sundays, with the help of his children and us boys, he displayed on street corners, in the square, on the arches of the Adinolfo Gate, on patrician balconies. The town was red with autumnal forests, paladins, sendals, ladies' white shoulders, tents adorned with the horns of the crescent.

If it was raining very hard, the vendors would remain seated on the straw in my grandfather's shop listening to Dolcissimo read *The Arabian Nights.* Or they looked at the marionettes that my Uncle Carmelo, called Tutú, had made in the carpenter shop of Don Gisimo Leone. There were twelve of them, carved out of carob wood (later he gave them to me, and I kept them hidden in the lean-to next to Rondello, our donkey): Charlemagne with a purple mantle, Roland with a copper Durendal, Roger riding the Hippogryph, Bradamant with her head weighed down by bellicose thoughts, the pensive Oliver, Ganelon de Mayence with a horn on the nape of his neck, the giant Sacripant, a slaughtered Saracen, Medoro with his head

227

carved in the shape of a desert rose, Angelica whose hair gleamed with mercury sulphide.

The guests soaked up rain, memories, and the marionettes' speeches with their eyes, while my grandmother Cecè to cheer them up sent out dried sausages, homemade salami, slices of pork, that she kept hanging from big nails and pegs in a back room. If the cartdrivers' hands were full of melancholy because of the rain that fell in a million filaments outside in the square, my aunt Ignazina would prepare *angels' hair*, a Spanish sweet she had been taught to make by the nuns. She took one hundred egg yolks, beat them with the left hand to allow the heart's emanations to flow into them, and after having gently greased the bottom of a pan with olive oil, she poured in a very thin layer, tossing it very rapidly over a low flame, then laying it, paper thin, on a slab of pink marble. She rolled them up, cut them with an alabaster knife, and immediately glazed them with cinnamon-flavored honey or chocolate or infusions of rose petals. In the shop the guests ate them silently, listening to Dolcissimo, or following the movements of the marionettes of my young Uncle Tutú.

"Dolcissimo helped us," Yaluna told us, "when there was malaria around."

It came up from the plains in the rainy season, up through the valleys where the wild goats searched for plants to increase their milk. The children felt its arrival through a certain motion of the air that darkened the moon just then taking shape over the rooftops.

"It's coming, it's coming," they shouted.

We tried to escape it by wrapping ourselves in sheets, or by catching as much of the lunar ocean as possible in our hands. The women, my mother Algazèlia among them, even tried to ward it off with the fumes of tiny heads of hornets and cinnamon bark. The peasants fired their old muzzle-loading guns and their thunder dissolved the evil vapors for a time. But it was all useless. The fever, preceded by terrible shivering, disrupted the daily work of the farms. The malaria institute in Càtana, directed by a former student of Grassi, never failed to register between three and six thousand cases of malaria in my town every year. As evening approached all were seized by a dark dread of the sickness, which emerged from caves and ravines like a distant fear. With lamps lit the women went to the homes of their sick neighbors, encouraging them with propitiatory words and channeling the glimmer of the stars into their hovels.

Dolcissimo, still young then (we were listening to Yaluna in silence) used to go to the Trezzito district, where the last patch of oaks stretched in the direction of the plateau of Timucah. There were two cinchona trees there, the red kind known as succirubra. They had been imported by Michelangelo Buglio, brother of the Lodovico who had disseminated Thomism and Copernican heliocentrism in China. The adventurous Michelangelo left his brother in Chinese territory and reached the Peruvian coast in a galleon. Ibn Zafèr informs us: "There, with an almanac in enoplian verses,[41] he gained the sympathy of Countess Cin-Chon, wife of the viceroy, who was very knowledgeable about the anti-malarial virtues of quinine. Michelangelo was the first to import that tree into Europe, by hiding it with potatoes and prickly pears in the hold of a huge boat with which he attempted the return voyage, haunted by the memory of Zebulonia and the faculties of its ancient trees. The Zebulonians cultivated the cinchona so extensively that they supplied the entire island with the bark.

"Sinus," I said, "these trees were neglected when the government brought quinine here."

But the Zebulonians, secretly, so as not to incur penalties for unlawfully cultivating the cinchona, left some of them on the higher reaches of the valley of the Trezzito. The bark infusion, which the old women continued to make secretly in their lean-tos, was more highly valued. Dolcissimo was the liaison between those women and the healing trees, which through the strength of their chemical components burned the plasmodia that reproduced in the blood. The Zebulonian poets who had been cured of malaria usually came to those trees looking for inspiration. Through their feverish thirst and the obstruction of their spleen they had experienced wonderful visions and, shivering and sweating, had sharpened the geometry of their words.

Thus Dolcissimo got into the habit of frequenting country lanes, olive groves, blanched river banks where the egg sacks of the dragonflies were developing. To earn a living he collected fennel, chicory, dandelion, which he sold in town. The peasants who had remained, after the emigration of the younger ones, did not care much for the aromatic plants, but gradually, with Dolcissimo's help, they learned to appreciate them. Between 'Alqama's father and those aromatic herbs a loving relationship existed, due to the tiny shade they cast in the heat of noon or to their warm nature that he assimilated through his fingers from the very gravel where they grew, and a practical relationship as well, because gradually the demand for them grew in the nearby towns. He came to know the places where the squills grew, their flowers rising on straight stems from the thirsty ground. The same was true for oregano, mandrake, cinnamon, which he helped to spread, because they were already becoming rare.

When 'Alqama was a little older she followed her father on these excursions.

"He took her along at the break of day," Yaluna told us, "with Polieno."

"Who was Polieno?" the psychiatrist asked.

"Oh you don't know about him? He was a wise rooster who had taken to warning Dolcissimo with his crowing if something strange was in sight."

From what we could gather, Polieno, by sensing low radioactive currents, was able to distinguish the exact places, the soils and sands that contained the seeds, fibers, and roots of unusual trees. Eventually, Dolcissimo experienced every thought in relation to the soil and the subsoil; he had become attuned, that is, to the stony element from below. He was an earthy temperament, in that he loved to sink his hands in the hot soil and to stretch out in ditches to feel surrounded by tendrils and roots. His daughter, on the other hand, was attracted by things that grow upward, like, for example, the fragrant flower of the almond tree, the branches of the quince, the sunflower, whole fields of which they found (cultivated for their edible seeds), through which she walked to gather the images that flow to the pupil from above.

Translated by Umberto Mariani

CARLO SGORLON
(1930–)

Carlo Sgorlon was born in the small village of Cassacco near Udine in the region of Fruili, near Austria and Yugoslavia. He spent much of his childhood with his maternal grandparents in the countryside, where he attended primary school only rarely but came into daily contact with Friulian peasant life. He taught history and Italian in a technical institute in Udine until 1980, when the success of his publications made it possible for him to devote himself entirely to writing. He has written a number of books in the dialect of Friuli, as well as twelve novels and numerous short stories in Italian. His literary scholarship, aside from translations from German, includes two major critical works, one on Kafka and the other on Elsa Morante. Sgorlon is a sensitive and reflective observer of the boundaries between the worlds of fiction and reality, and of how modern industrial-consumer society is destroying the sense of the sacred that once bound all people to the earth and that expressed itself in myth and archetype. *Il trono di legno* (*The Wooden Throne*) tells the story of a young man's choice between the worlds of creative imagination and physical experience. Growing up in Fruili early in the twentieth century, Giuliano leaves his native village in pursuit of his beautiful young mistress and of his own past. So begins a series of adventures in which the mountain landscapes, the tiny village he finds, and the people he meets belong to a strange world of fable. As Giuliano slowly unravels the identity of his new lover, her myth-weaving grandfather, and their mysterious community, the reader senses them all as remote and archaic, nowhere and everywhere, evanescent and eternal at the same time. *Il trono di legno* was awarded the prestigious Premio Campiello and has been translated into French, Spanish, Slavic, and English.*

THE ENCHANTED VOYAGER[†]

I realized that Cretis was a dying village, a village of old folks who didn't dare leave only because of age and who considered it an antechamber of death, and of children who stayed only because they had not yet awakened to the possibility of going away.

But the youth went away. They needed novelty, excitement, life. They dreamed of working in a factory, of putting on caps and goggles to drive the automobiles or trucks they probably knew only from drawings they had seen once or twice in newspapers. Many of them began to busy themselves in the fields or stables or to learn to use woodcarvers' or blacksmiths' tools in dark rooms or smoky sheds, but their thoughts were far away, and as soon as they had put aside enough money for the trip they went off to seek their fortunes.

Even though I wasn't an attentive observer I still felt that something in the village was weakening, diminishing, dying out. Departures occurred almost surreptitiously; often the one who was leaving didn't even say good-bye to his friends, as if at the last minute he were inexplicably reticent about letting people know what he was doing or as if there were something shameful about it, like abandoning one's post on a ship or a firing line.

Still, every departure confirmed my notion of a steady day to day disappearance. A similar thing was also happening in Ontàns and although one village was on the plain and the other in the mountains both appeared to be linked to the same destiny. I derived from my observations a definite and increasing awareness, but since it was for the moment only a personal conviction I began to study Pietro, without asking him directly, to see if he shared my opinion. It might even be

*Introductory note adapted from Jessie Bright's introduction to her translation of Carlo Sgorlon, *The Wooden Throne* (New York: Italica Press, 1988).
†From Bright's translation.

that this same feeling formed the basis of his melancholy, of his bewildered slowness. He had a much more profound intuition than I did, and I was only beginning to notice things (since age had matured and sharpened my insight), that he had sensed long ago and already weighed in the balance of his existence.

If the same thing was occurring in Ontàns and Cretis that meant peasant civilization was coming to an end, and Pietro and I belonged to something that was slowly sinking out of sight. I had read about places progressively sinking because of diastrophism, like the islands on which Venice was built, for example. Perhaps it was as if I, the old man, Lia, and the others were living in an area that was slowly settling until one day it would disappear without a trace....

I had always lived either in the country or in the mountains, far from factories, smokestacks or busy streets; therefore I hadn't had many opportunities to notice that peasant-artisan society was vanishing and being replaced by a civilization based on manufacturing and motors. Nonetheless it was easy even for me to imagine that automobiles would become more and more numerous until they took the place of carriages and that trucks would likewise supplant wagons pulled by horses or cows. The world I loved would vanish and in its place would appear one to which I was indifferent. Who could say whether I might not have been drawn to Cretis by a profound instinct, like the one which guided Pietro or Lia, and while I was ostensibly searching for Flora or the Dane I was really trying to avoid detaching myself from those places where one could yet live in close contact with nature and it was still possible to believe in stories. By now I had intuited the close link between Pietro's stories and the fact that he worked with knives and chisels carving wood. Artisan or peasant culture and the telling of stories seemed meant for each other.

If I had understood these things, that meant I had acquired Pietro's mentality. If I were beginning to believe my steps were guided by something powerful and infallible, then I had gone completely over to his side and my youth was over. This thought aroused an annoying and strident anxiety, and I felt I had descended into a shadowy area, into a mysterious eclipse. When the old man ended his narrative, when we came out of the "story room," I felt a need to open the shutters and the iron gates that centuries before had been kept closed for days and weeks during invasions, to keep off hunger, fear and death. Perhaps as Pietro talked other undefined monsters were put to flight by his words: the fear of death, of time passing, the weary wait for what never came, the thought of what was disappearing; because the word was magic and potent. Or was it life that was exiled, and were Pietro's words lifting us into an enchanted stagecoach to take us to a place where reality no longer mattered?

In flinging open doors and windows I seemed to be escaping from a powerful fascination as if I were in danger of turning into a statue of salt, of being bewitched into entering a treacherous cloister where the gray monastery walls would close me inside rules as frigid as ice. I felt the risk I was running, from which no one was trying to save me. I knew that Pietro would never urge me and Lia to leave Cretis, even though we were young and had the possibility of beginning life again in a place that had a destiny, because basically he did not believe in the future or the past and maintained that history itself was a sequence of muddled dreams, which acquired form only in the telling.

Everybody and everything led me to pursue these paths to the end. My heart was clogged with opaque fears. My entire environment took on a sphinx-like quality which, like the Pied Piper's flute, drew me further away from reality toward perdition. Lia's gentle beauty, ready to satisfy my every desire; old Namu, who looked at the world as an immense amulet in which to search for the face of God; Pietro, who saw no difference between dream and reality — all seemed organized to lull to sleep whatever rebellious or turbulent vitality I might still have. So what could be done? If I continued to stay here longer the trap would snap closed and I'd be caught forever. I was a man teetering between two equally attractive versions of reality rendered equally unstable by my suspicion that they might both be mirages. Deciding between them terrified me. And yet I knew I had to choose because Cretis was not the result of any decision I had made but rather of destiny. Perhaps the real game was between me and the Great Gambler who had filled my life with his fascinating appointments. I had to decide quickly because otherwise my hesitation itself would be a decision.

When the balance tipped toward Pietro's world it seemed to me that Lia's grandfather continued to be a frontiersman even in Cretis, that he was still carrying out his mission. He had to guard the threatened world of storytelling and bring myth back into a world in which the soot from smokestacks and the noise of automobiles were putting it to flight, and people were beginning to believe only in machines and factories. I was sure that in many of the Jàsnaja Poljànas of this world, in the Russian steppes or the deserts of Arabia, on American plantations or in the Danish lowlands, numerous Tolstoys, be they illustrious or obscure, famous writers or unknown storytellers like Pietro, were in their own particular way defending a dying civilization.

Tolstoy (I happened to read it in a newspaper) had died a few months before and Pietro would die before long. Nonetheless he continued to hang on, to obey an order that no one had given him, an order to behave with unfaltering dignity as the exiled king of stories.

I wondered sometimes if the Dane had been merely an adventurer and a hedonist who, like a capricious god, loved only the present, or whether he too was given to storytelling, like an obscure Tolstoy of ships and the sea. I instinctively preferred the second hypothesis, hoping at the same time that something of him had passed into my veins....

After the evening when I had noticed that Pietro's voice was strangely tired I became aware that he was dying. He walked more slowly, the trembling of his legs increased, and he didn't take a single step without his cane. Sometimes he no longer had the strength to turn the lathe and entrusted the work to me. His gestures appeared more and more to belong to an archaic civilization, which had mysteriously surfaced in the present like a relic, to bear witness to a vast ruin.

One evening I found him in the armchair tracing circles with his cane in the cooled ashes of the hearth. I asked him what he was doing. "What do you expect me to be doing? I'm dying," he smiled.

"Well then so am I and so is Lia and everybody else. Everybody who's alive is dying," I replied.

He left off stirring the ashes. "For me it's different. I always used to move around in the world. Now I've put down roots. I've come to a complete stop. But for me stopping means dying," he added mysteriously.

I now also did his share of our work, which a wagon-driver came up from the plain every now and then to pick up. The less Pietro worked the more he seemed to reflect. His stories became ever more halting and fanciful. I asked him when and how he thought them up. "Mostly when I dream," he said. According to him we ourselves didn't think or invent but an unknown force thought and invented through us; we were only instruments by which it revealed itself. I almost never asked myself any more if what he recounted belonged to the territory of his experiences or his fantasies. I had known for quite a while that for Pietro life was simply an immense reservoir of appearances into which anyone could dip at will. I knew everything was illusory for him; everything was enchanted appearance like an iridescent bubble, or the tail of a kite drifting in infinity; joy and sorrow, love and death, were nothing but shadows projected on a mysterious screen. But nobody understood the nature of the screen or the magic lantern or the source of the light; nobody knew which was spirit and which material, whether they were one entity or two, or how they flowed into one another. For Pietro material was merely spirit that had dozed off and was waiting to be awakened and spirit was material that had climbed out of sleep and become activity. Life was only a disjointed fable, which someone recounted in our ear and we kept on listening to because we couldn't resist its attraction; it was an illusory tunnel of marvels, which Pietro had passed through like an enchanted voyager, allowing himself to be drawn to everything but bound to nothing.

Translated by Jessie Bright

236

GIANNI CELATI
(1937–)

Gianni Celati was born in Sondrio, northern Lombardy, and first became known for writing associated with the neo-avant-garde of the late 1960s. This early work, in books noted for their disjointed, experimental language, focused on unstable identities and the socially marginalized. Later, from this exuberant, playful writing, his work moved towards minimalism and demonstrated a distrust of large social (and literary) institutions. *Narratori delle pianure* (Storytellers of the plains[42]) is a collection of tales told along the length of the Po River from its initial stretches near Milan, to its mouth that feeds into the Adriatic Sea. As the river valley widens and moves east, the plains open up and are dotted with small villages, often built on what were islands set amidst marshes. Now, most of the former wetlands have been drained, and a seemingly dreary and monotonous landscape extends in all directions. Set in this area, Celati's tales and tellers are wildly varied, and range from two children vainly searching for kind adults, who eventually give up and become lost in a fog-covered, endless mass of identical housing developments, to a young couple who for months listens on short-wave radio to the detailed descriptions a secretive man gives of a small island he lives on off the coast of Scotland, to a photographer attempting to understand what the old women in a small village and the dead say when they speak together in the cemetery. Celati is a masterful storyteller, able to depict the very strange and often disturbing, inner characteristics of what appears at first glance to be the epitome of the ordinary: the landscape of the Po River and its surrounding plains. His works include *Le avventure di Guizzardi* (The adventures of Guizzardi), *La banda dei sospiri* (The gang of sighs), *Quattro novelle sulle apparenze* (*Appearances*), *Verso la foce* (Journey to the mouth of the Po), *Cinema Naturale* (Natural Cinema), and *Avventure in Africa* (*Adventures in Africa*).

237

HOW A PHOTOGRAPHER DISEMBARKED
IN THE NEW WORLD*

Ca' Venier, much less an actual village, is rather an area of houses dispersed along the river Po di Venezia before it splits into two large branches — the Po di Pila and the Po di Gnocca — on its way to the small coves of lagoons and then the sea. In that place you can look out in all directions and see only long stretches of cultivated fields, mainly of wheat. Further on, in the direction of Ca' Zullian, marshes break through on the horizon but everywhere roads, which are straight as far as the eye can see, traverse plots of unchanging flat lands that are old lagoons now filled in.

Nothing could be less photogenic than this landscape, which extends in unbroken flatness and uniformity up to the very fringes of earth, which jut into the sea. And in the middle of the sea, small islands break through here and there and often have the form of tongues of sand. Some emerge only at low tide, while others, colonized by grasses that hold mud carried to the sea by the large river, show in the distance tufts of rushes and other plants adapted to the wet, brackish environment, and are called "barene."

A photographer one day was sent to take pictures of these places as a correspondent to a popular weekly magazine. His photographs were to illustrate a story that a celebrated author was to write on the subject of "the humble folk of the mouth of the Po."

After having photographed the river channels at sunset, a few bundled up women collecting grass along the road, a few old women doubled over carrying bundles of marsh cane on their backs, seagulls on a lagoon, and a large boat on the water, the photographer ran out of ideas and readied himself to return home. And it was exactly then that he heard it said that in those parts the women went to the cemetery to talk with the dead, holding actual conversations with the deceased members of their families in front of their tombstones.

---

*All selections in this section are from Gianni Celati, *Narratori delle pianure* (Milano: Feltrinelli, 1985).

He therefore decided to photograph a few women intent on conversing with the dead. Lying in ambush in the cemetery of Ca' Venier one afternoon with an extremely long telephoto lens, he secretly took a few photos. Afterwards he sent the negatives to his magazine and then went to Venice for the weekend.

The photos taken in the Ca' Venier cemetery in reality showed next to nothing, apart from a woman dressed in black making a gesture with her lips parted in front of a tombstone. The editorial board of the magazine asked the photographer to return to the area, make contact with someone, get them to explain exactly what the dead say, and ideally take a few photos of more dramatic poses, in order to give their readers a more precise idea of what went on in those cemeteries.

The photographer therefore returned to the area and found himself in another cemetery, where he attempted to approach (and to secretly interview, with a tiny microphone incorporated into a button of his jacket) a woman dressed in black who was kneeling in front of a tombstone. She not only refused to respond but would not even look him in the face, and immediately abandoned the place along with all the other women who had been resting among the tombs.

Finding himself alone and without knowing what to do, the photographer noticed that he was being observed from a distance by a very thin man. He was, as the photographer soon learned, the caretaker of the cemetery.

Unlike his fellow villagers, the very thin man stopped to talk with him. He informed him that there the dead confided only with the women. And, after having smoked a cigarette offered by the photographer, he recounted his entire life story and then invited him to his house.

He was born on one of the lagoons now filled in, and for many years had been a hunting guide, living in a straw hut where coot hunters went to find him to take them across the marshes and lagoons. He had then been hired by an oilman from Ravenna who owned a boat at the mouth of the Po on which he served as a sailor and fisherman when the oilman wished to go to the open sea. Selling the boat, the oilman also sold the thin man together with all the fishing gear, to buyers who never used to come to those parts. In this way the man still carried on his job of tending for the boat, but was also able to do other things, such as going fishing on his own boat and watching over the cemetery.

The man's face was very wrinkled, furrowed everywhere with creases. On his head he wore a sort of busby and under his jacket, a checked cowboy shirt.

Only when they had sat down at a table in the man's house, which consisted of a single room of new and shiny furniture, did the photographer realize that the old fisherman was missing three fingers from his right hand. After having recounted his life story, the very thin man then also wanted to tell how he had lost the missing fingers.

Immediately after the war for a time near Chioggia there were many German bunkers where you could find shells, cartridges and grenades everywhere. Children emptied the cartridges and grenades and for fun made the gunpowder explode. In this way the man had lost his fingers: wanting to help a child close up a grenade in order to save a little of the gunpowder, he had caused the percussion cap to fire, and then watched one finger fly up into the air, another dangling from his hand, and the thumb, which was no more.

Continuing to speak almost entirely in dialect, the very thin man confided to the photographer that on the hand where once there had been the index finger (with the other index finger he pointed at the empty space) at times he felt pain, a creeping sensation or throbbing as if from arthritis.

The missing index finger had a current passing through it. He understood very well how the needle of a compass worked, for the current passing through the finger always pointed off in some direction like a compass. This ability of his finger to point in a particular direction had enabled him to find many lost items, because at times, if he was searching for something, the finger would begin "to point."

The man said that once the finger had even played a joke on him. It had indicated all the winning scores for the soccer matches and he had written them down on a betting slip, ready to become a millionaire. Then, however, he had lost the slip before bringing it to a bookie, and the finger had managed to find it only the next Sunday, after he had found out the results of the game on television.

The thin man spoke very gravely. The photographer listened to him, amused by his seriousness. Yet, it being already late, he wanted to bring the discussion back to the subject of the dead who speak at the cemetery only with women.

The fisherman confirmed that that was the way it was. Yet, if the photographer was curious to know what the dead say, perhaps asking his missing index finger about it might help.

He thus lifted his mutilated hand into the air and began beating in empty space the missing finger with the other hand. Meanwhile, he explained that there exist points on some tiny islands or sandbars in the middle of the sea where you can hear what the dead say. A few times he had found them while heading out to hunt or fish, but always by chance and without ever being able to track them down again afterwards.

If now he succeeded in awakening the missing index finger by slapping it, perhaps it would point in a direction, and then the following day they would be able to head that way.

The photographer, amused by the explanations, let the thin man talk right up to when it was time to go to bed. At about midnight he turned in, sleeping on a cot offered by the fisherman.

Early the next morning the fisherman woke him up, saying that his index finger was "pointing," and that they had to move quickly in order to follow the direction in which the finger indicated.

They left in the photographer's car and went to a spit outside the village of Pila where a channel couched between two marshy areas led to the open sea. Here the two jumped into a boat the thin man kept amidst the swamp grass and began rowing out towards the sea.

The rest of that journey became an increasingly strange adventure for the photographer. Rowing towards small distant islands and sandbars, some full of birds the photographer had never before seen, the fisherman spoke of the bizarre names given to those islands in the middle of the sea: Barea, Zoaglia, Ca' Morta, Morosina, Pegaso, Bacucca.

When they steered towards a small sandbar in the water full of birds that fled upon their arrival—which his guide called the New World — the photographer understood that they had reached their destination.

Here, after asking the photographer to quickly get out and listen to the dead, the fisherman spun the boat around and abandoned him to the mud and rushes of that square meter of earth, yet not without explaining — with his back already turned, rowing and getting farther away — that the missing finger had taken him to the New World, and the same finger had ordered that he remain.

Translated by Patrick Barron

THE RETURN OF THE TRAVELER*

In the train at dawn, traveling towards Polesella, I began the search for the village my mother was born in, without knowing exactly where I was going. I knew only the approximate area of where the village was and had not found it on any roadmap. I was counting on buying a larger scale map along the road in order to locate it.

Before getting on the train in Ferrara I saw a character standing half asleep who wearily lifted up his eyelids every time someone entered the station. Then his eyelids fell shut and his head collapsed forward with a sudden, light wag. Afterwards, getting off the train in Polesella, I found myself in the middle of people with the same air of unsteadiness, people who like me had awoken at dawn with the impression that they were in an unfamiliar place, who had left their homes semiconscious of repeated gestures and habits ingrained in their bodies, and who found themselves ready to go anywhere. In the station bar a few men were waking up, lighting the first cigarettes of the day.

When I asked where the center of Polesella was, some teenagers sitting on chairs outside the bar answered, guffawing

*This translation of "Il ritorno del viaggiatore" by Patrick Barron first appeared in: *ISLE: Interdisciplinary Studies in Literature and Environment* 7.2 (2000): 171–77.

that the center was there. The teenagers had long hair and denim jackets, were smoking, laughing, making a racket, and eating popcorn at eight in the morning.

The city center was made up of two boulevards divided by a meridian without vegetation. On the sides there were not very tall houses with bland, uniform fronts in postwar style. And that place still seemed to be postwar, after a disaster which no one would speak of. The entire length of the street was dedicated to essential services: an electrical appliances shop, a tobacconist's, a commercial agency, a pharmacy, a women's hat shop, and at the end of the boulevard, a gray box without a roof that was simply called "CINEMA." It was showing a porno film.

Later I was in another part of the town looking for road maps. There was a yellow merry-go-round, cars from an accident covered in plastic, and everything around so overlaid with asphalt, as if men should forget forever what the surface of the earth is like.

In Polesella I caught a bus, and heading towards Guarda Veneta was afraid to speak and hear my own voice, just as when I was on another continent. I avoided looking at the other passengers so that they would not talk to me.

After Crespino and Villanova other road signs read "CORBOLA," "PAPOZZE." In fields with almost no grass, gray sheep grazed up to the edge of a canal. On the other side of the canal stood old houses with chimneys, which jutted out from external walls, narrowed at the height of the first floor, and had daring, tower-shaped caps that pointed at the sky.

Truck after truck passed. It was raining, and with the dark sky you could barely make out distant objects. The bus stopped in front of a long, deteriorating farm building all covered by ivy, which even grew over the closed shutters. At the door a woman appeared holding a basin in which she was rinsing her hair. At the moment the woman realized that I was watching her, she stiffened her neck, holding it bent over the basin. I would have liked to get off the bus and speak to her, to understand what sort of words people might use in a place like that. A little later a sign on a curve in the road announced Adria.

In the early afternoon in Adria I entered a bar that was covered with the postings of soccer betting winnings, where a television dominated the small space from up above and acted as a sort of background to a discussion men at the bar were having in dialect. The men were speaking of an incident, which involved someone or other, and spoke of whether it was the case to go around armed. Someone suggested that it was dangerous because "those guys don't look anyone in the eye." I wasn't able to understand what exactly they were talking about. In front of the bar a line of boys sat taking shelter from the rain, observing the asphalt. No cars drove by on the road. As I left, for a long moment, I could hear only the sound of the television, which was transmitting a western movie.

I found a hotel, a two-story building with undecorated walls painted a dark red and the words "ALBERGO LAGUNA." In a stationery shop I looked for road maps, and a young woman with an extremely tired look spoke to me very slowly, as if she had to weigh every sentence she uttered. She said, "There isn't much here," then, "Adria is out of the way," then, "As you will have seen for yourself."

In that town there were two or three central streets full of modern shops, bars, and motor scooters, and hidden streets where I found beautiful old villas. Turning around, I saw a gigantic television transmitter, which seemed to me taller than any building in town. In another shop no one knew anything about the place I wanted to go; it seemed forever vanished from people's minds and from the road maps.

Back at the hotel I began reading a novel by Malcolm Lowry. After dinner I watched television, a film with Stewart Granger and Deborah Kerr.

Leaving Adria, open space widened out in all directions as far as the eye could see. A freeway rounded an uphill curve and linked up with another four-lane freeway. That morning it was full of trucks and cars, which were escaping under the rain. From high up on this road I saw the plains with gray fields cut through by canals, and many of those beautiful houses with the tower-shaped chimneys, abandoned and crumbling with the roofs in pieces, doors and windows walled up.

244

From the time that I left Adria I did nothing but follow canals of still water into which the rain fell. All around were old farmhouses, fields of wheat, people bicycling along narrow lanes, and small iron bridges over canals where every so often someone under a large umbrella was fishing. Just before crossing the Po, the profile of the earth behind me became concave as far as the horizon. On a sign with a drawing of the roads along the banks of the river, I read names of places: "TAGLIO DI PO,"[43] "PORTO TOLLE."

The look of the passengers in the bus, along with the dirgelike quality of their voices, was of people who had long given up silliness, the putting on of airs, and saying anything more than necessary. Because the road was full of potholes, the bus creaked continuously.

At a certain point, without knowing why, I got off the bus. Luckily it was not raining any more. Along the long straight road to Taglio di Po, the countryside was sown with power poles that carried the eye to infinity.

The low and long horizon, veiled by a halo that seemed to be rain, was crossed by cypresses and white willows. In the ditches everywhere grew red dock. Scattered in the fields were abandoned houses whose roofs had fallen in, but along the street stood modern houses. The surrounding fields of wheat were yellow and deep. The corn was still green.

When it began to rain, there wasn't a living soul to be seen across the entire countryside. The driver, cornered in a small square, hesitated for quite some time before deciding to pick me up, and gave me long, searching looks. On the dashboard there was a photo of a child, and a little stuffed dog, which continuously bounced up and down, hung on the rearview mirror.

I didn't exchange even one word with the driver. Getting out of the car, what, at a distance had seemed the wall of a fortress, turned out to be a long line of postwar houses with shops of clothing, sporting goods, and electrical appliances as well as many bars. The other side of the village looked out upon devastated lands and ruins up to a far-off point where I saw only rocks and mud. It was like being in a distant outpost. Some dogs were mucking about in a pile of trash.

Just as I attempted to cross the road all the drivers madly honked their horns. I was certain that those drivers were not going anywhere, but just drove around endlessly given the slightest excuse, terrorized of being still. I watched them impatiently waiting at a traffic light in the rain, honking their horns, frantic not to be still.

That village is called Taglio di Po because once the men there had to split the river in order to direct its flow and regulate the mouth. But climbing the embankment to take a look around, I wasn't able to imagine what might have existed differently within the space of my era, the only one I had ever been able to know. All I found on the embankment was a sign that read: "GYPSIES FORBIDDEN TO CAMP." Further along was a field full of scattered garbage: empty cans, the remains of an old suitcase, a piece of a thermostat. Under the embankment sat low houses of ex-fishermen — a countryside dotted with gray, industrial buildings and no one around.

The bridge over the Po, under which I had taken shelter, was a long stretch of cement resting on eight or ten columns. Under it ran the blue tubes of an immense methane pipeline. The rain was pouring down, and some birds were soaring along the riverbanks, almost touching the ground.

Towards mid-afternoon I crossed a bridge in the direction of Piano on straight, very wide roads, which undulated slightly. The dark sky seemed endless with its low horizons, and trucks passed, lifting wings of spray on either side of the road. Then, under the shelter of a gas station, I asked directions for which road to take. The attendant made impatient gestures, as if he couldn't stand anymore to see the faces of other people.

I abandoned the traffic-filled roads and moved towards the bank of the Po Grande by way of narrow lanes, which passed alongside houses with cane-fenced gardens. In one house there was a man who was watching television with his hat on. At a certain point the man called out a woman's name, then turned to look in the direction of the window but did not see me. Two beetles and a line of ants were tumbling about over the gravel between fragments of brick and plaster.

Towards six in the afternoon with the sky getting darker and darker, I turned onto a big, wide road not knowing where it would take me. A sign informed me that the 45th parallel crossed at that point. I was halfway between the north pole and the equator.

Walking with my hood up, I wasn't able to see anything to the sides. I wasn't able to get a lift from any of the cars. All escaped into the mist that had fallen.

The next morning at Goro, where a driver had dropped me off in the night, I was given relatively precise directions to the place I needed to reach. I was told that I had completely gone off on the wrong track. The train on the old local line between Bologna and Portomaggiore took only three hours to get there, and from Ferrara by car it took only an hour.

It was Sunday, the weather had cleared up and it was easier to get rides. I got a lift as far as Ostellato, then another in the direction of Portomaggiore.

At a crossroads, while I was getting out of a car, the driver told me, "It's now time for the beast to go and eat." I thought that he was talking about me, but instead he had meant himself.

In Dogato I asked a man who was out walking with his dog if he knew the village I was looking for. The man was happy to talk, but knew nothing to tell me of that place. So he walked a while with me, making small talk as he went. Then in a bar, where they also sold newspapers and had a long shelf full of pornographic magazines, he offered me a bite to eat. We spoke of the time and the fact that until a couple of centuries ago in that area there had been the sea, and that Portomaggiore had been a large harbor.

By now the land was very rich, with orchards everywhere. The unfalteringly flat horizon was no longer desolate and threatening, as on the day before. The orchards in blossom from far away seemed actual woods, and traced a rose-colored profile along the edge of the earth.

Coming from Ostellato, the long curving road was completely lined with plane trees. Nearby I also saw acacias and many canals where fishermen reminded me of the ways of my people. Above a field a flock of seagulls was flying around something. I heard their cries.

I walked down this road as far as another crossroads. To the right there was a narrow road, and down low, resting on the ground, was a very small sign that read "SANDOLO." In that village my mother was born.

I sat down on a milepost and tried to re-imagine the place. In the background I saw the bell tower of a church, very low, with a metal point, which glistened in the sun. At one time there must have been few cultivated fields, many marshes, nothing nearby, and flat and deserted land all around. When my mother left that village she must have been seven or eight years old.

I tried to imagine something, but had only vague images of haylofts, buses of times past, and cobbled streets. I envisioned a small church with a terracotta façade.

On the other side of the crossroads I saw nothing, only empty countryside and that low bell tower. I couldn't imagine anything else of other times and of other situations. Out of a house on the road emerged a girl who stretched her neck out to see what I was doing, sitting there on the milepost. I then turned back towards Ostello.

Translated by Patrick Barron

MONICA SARSINI
(1953–)

Born in Florence, Monica Sarsini is a writer and multimedia artist. Her colorful paper collages have been exhibited in galleries throughout Italy and Europe. She has taught sculpture and painting, as well as creative writing at the Giardino dei Ciliegi and in schools in Florence. As a set designer, she has collaborated with avant-garde theater groups. Her literary works include: *Libro luminoso* (Luminous book), *Colorare* (To color), *Serenata* (Serenade), *Riassunto* (Summary), *I passi della sirena* (The steps of the siren), *Il mezzo di contrasto* (Means of contrast), *Crepapancia* (Stomach rifts), "Feritoie" (Fissures) in *25 Autori e la Follia* (25 authors and madness), *Crepitudine* (Riftitude), and "Colline" (Hill) in *Prefigurazioni* (Prefigurations). In 1999, Italica Press published *Eruptions*, a collection of her short fiction, which comprises selected translations from two of her books, *Crepacuore* (Heart rifts), her 1985 work on colors, and *Crepapelle* (Skin rifts), her 1988 reflections on the senses. All of these pieces are sensual explorations in Sarsini's experimental, yet concrete narrative style.

PINK *

Pale, gentle, effeminate, sweet-smelling, blushing delicateness. The sunsets on the highway from Rome to Florence with black mountains standing out against a limpid summer sky. Women with their gray hair in a bun, crocheting as they linger in bed, while the house moves along to the pace of the housekeeper's steps, not over-concerned with time. Sled-riding downhill over the snow, or going down the slides in the melancholy city-parks, muddled by an aimless confusion of colored balloons. Pigs, spring fruit blossoms, tongue and gums, tonalities of

*Selections in this section are from Martha King, *New Italian Women: A Collection of Short Fiction* (New York: Italica Press, 1989).

the ear. Heat, warmth, sugar-coated almonds. Apologetic attempts, an oasis, a limbo that falls apart as everything around it closes in. Flamingos, abundance of bourgeois objects, gaudy, affected, wanting to appear lovely, but not even decently passable. Nausea, cotton fluff, fear of solitude, of growing up in silence without accomplices. Unnatural nature, spectacular Epiphanies. To abstain from declaration, to fear judgment, to refrain from argument, to be tired of fighting; to wish to go back and stay innocent. Arms akimbo, listening to the confessions of someone half-reclining, elbow resting on the bed-table, legs all hugged up tight. Bits of Carnival-time, lotions, hair drawn at the back of the neck, making peace, having no one to wait for. Family ideology, some fish, hard candy. Antique but not old laces, cobwebs, soap. Pink with black, pink with orange. Illusions, hopes, mirages, unkept promises, when one wishes to believe that the enthusiasm with which we embrace a cause is genuine. Dazzling angel faces in the clouds, Pontormo-pink, rose-pink. Going on singing when the others in the choir have stopped. A promising future. Habit, unpretentious desire. Black people's palms. Kindergarten girls' collar bows, ribbons on doors and in shop windows when a baby girl's birth is not to be kept a secret. Ostrich feathers, clouds, vapors, fumes, nebulous billows evaporating against the metallic gray of the city. Cactus flowers, dog teats, tender skin in the midst of aged pachydermic roughness. Color without substance, color that does not take wing, does not become a vegetable, does not reach maturity. Rosolio rose liqueur.

LAVENDER

With leftovers from dawn, lavender drew together in a faint light and, from the pavement, gazed on the familiar indifference of places still uninhabited by the devourers of time. Lighting a cigarette, its long tender legs nonchalantly strolled into a puddle and waited there, in that vague position, for the corner cafe to open. It kept disappearing and reappearing, gently vanishing, like someone trying to come into the world although already there — knowing it would not have a voice, but hoping for a sudden joy, like the surprise at a party, long put off because of shyness.

It was up early; the city streets were deserted. At the newspaper stall, the bored vendor waited, looking out from the wall of magazines, for the daily newspapers to arrive by bicycle.

Lavender saw the daylight, the swift dissipation of people addicted to rushing even though no one is chasing them. Habitually lazy, it tried to feign an air of initiative, which quickly faded away because it had no memory for how things should be imitated. It changed its mind again, still keeping that ambiguous peace that comes from knowing we're not observed. Stumbling among the motorbikes that leave a wound in the asphalt as they brake, it slipped into the cafe, to take shape again over the tablecloths covering the newly-dusted tables, and along the glass-divider that keeps the dust off the spongy muffins and crisp cookies.

It lingered there for a long while in a sort of doze, resigned to the wait, indifferent to its haphazard mood, and then went on to idle, void of purpose, over faces that must be re-composed after the secret battle of night, so that no trace of a powerful dream may remain on the vanquished cheeks and burnt-out gaze. It searches for itself in a shop window, surprised to meet itself. Silence intertwines with its fingers like a long thread that is hard to unravel. The fear of death returns, and this feeling dissolves all consciousness of necessity. Its understanding of death is a dispassionate awareness that cannot be shaken off.

The color hovered about and arrived later, within touching distance of the words that were yet to be said.

SILVER

To seek each other, reflect each other everywhere, aglow in the darkness. To get to know objects, to remember where we are, to shine out, catching light, playing with reflections. To soothe, marvel, transmit an exquisite fairy-tale aura to an image, add movement to a glance, prolong a look, become enchanted with superficiality. To be surprised and stupefied, to recall magical associations, suggestive impressions, to slip away from time. To stop and try to see more than what is there, to throw doubt on what we actually see. To exalt luminosity and the essence of angles. To decorate, celebrate, ornament, make things memorable. To wait no longer for daytime to have something of night, for night to be space. To be assured of an opening, a point of escape, a gap in material life that we may pass through, like music. The feeling of cool relief, haste, even disloyalty. Haziness, a mixing of fire and oceans. To do away with surfaces in order to avoid depth. A flight from the impulse to perpetuate.

GREEN

Never still. It breathes, ripples, becomes part of the air, swelling, rocking, trembling. It races, jumps or sneaks about. Deaf, mute, unwary of adversaries, translucent, it has no beginning, no end. Its profundity reaches every niche of the forest, swinging with the trees, shaping the wind. Weaving in and out, it creates mazes in space and a soft musky odor over the cottony oceanic silence.

It is a sign of life among the plants and of seduction for reptiles; it is comforting, cordial, digestive. In shades of various intensity, penetrated by sounds, a rush of freshness that is unripe, flexible, an exceptional dancer not afraid of the world it owns, the energizer of metallic light, opposed to vainglory. It mirrors nothing, neither the tree next to the house nor the lizard on the garden wall. Meadows, pastures, prairies, plum trees, pine trees, parks, pistachios. It moves forever ahead, but never escapes, letting others search for it, mobile and spectacular. Verdi, the national anthem, Maurizio Nannucci, vegetables, Verdiglione. Fertile, frankly sexual, it laughs gurgling, greets you with a wide grin, with open arms, with the firm stance of a mountain climber or a gymnastics teacher. A painstaking seamstress, an expert at embroidering hems and borders, sewing buttonholes. Apparently unacquainted with nostalgia or bitterness, loved by everyone. "Why is green suffocated by black whereas white isn't?" Because it exists outside of itself, always the host. Greenbacks, being in the hills. It has a task to perform, a mission to accomplish, never thinking over past choices, destined for immortality. Long greenish distances are liberated at every passing. Alert and aware, it is young, and although others may try hard not to die or go insane, not wanting to remain in this world, but lacking the courage to leave it, green is contented, fulfilling its duty, aspiring to maturity. Like a person without dreams who laughs and smiles, not too concerned with itself, eating what comes along, out of curiosity for new tastes, uncomplaining, nonchalantly swallowing tranquillizers, closing its eyes when its head aches, calmly dozing at the theater, unmoved by boredom.

WHITE

Disintegrated voices, where all sounds fade away, calls reach their end, and space absorbs them; where words go when they sink to the deep or get thrown ashore. Can anyone express thought without the voice inevitably taking on those characteristics, imposing authority through acceptance of prohibitions, seductions, gestures, and the mazes of propositions that sadden words, forcing infinite repetition like someone who tries desperately to sit down, get up and go away. These are people who talk to each other, seek each other and adopt a pose when they meet. People who are forever late so that they may act as though they had never come, while others cannot remain where their desires lead them because they are afraid to die. Lines of shade, light, pointed angles, openings, ravines, short runs, dense steam and then periods of thin silence. Hands clasping the knees like cradles or hats, warm lips pressed tight that focus ahead. Corners in which waiting is immersed, over the knotty tree branches. A relaxed oval face that crosses hazily above, below and through another face, momentarily as in a port. A glitter of pleasure while glancing about, finally at rest and out of the wind. No need for experience in these seas. At the wedding tomorrow, it will be catapulted among white lilies, rice and sheets. White eyes and teeth stuck in a dark face, with luminously incandescent pearls at the ear-lobes. The fingernails standing out against the tan skin are like shells on the cliffs, whereas the white curves of the nails seem to be ephemeral shields protecting a desire to streak a furrow in the earth. The nails are open shells that embrace in the warmth of the skin. It is the dawn breaking from night's embrace while, on the terrace rail, shreds of curdled spiderwebs swing from the green columns, hanging by a slender thread. The railing has blossomed ephemerous white growths that sway in the wind like sleepwalkers. The baker has set the baskets of warm bread all in a row next to the door, while way beyond, the thoughts of life spread ever wider on the horizon, arching softly, making the end imperceptible, slipping away, never stumbling, like a laugh that spreads, a voice reaching the bed, breath, a high floor, a white ceiling. The distant white whale among the icebergs. The white cliffs of Dover, Siamese cats, polar bears and ghosts, choir-boys, the uniforms of nurses, cooks and sailors. White telephones. Aniseed, milk, fresh almond and walnut kernels, bananas. Salt. Sails over the waves and a white band holding back dark hair. Pelican swans, a bone in a dog's mouth, elephant tusks. Lambs, marble quarries, the moon behind the clouds, dazzling blades, Snow White, snow, canvas for painting, sleepless 'white-mares.' Space suits, zebra stripes on the asphalt, zebras in the savanna, white chessmen and checkers. A starched tuxedo shirt, egg white, cigarette paper. Thin crests of foam that break against the ship's side.

Translated by Gloria Italiano

254

ENVIRONMENTAL WRITING

CHAMPIONS OF NATURE:
THE ENVIRONMENTALISTS

INTRODUCTION
BY ANNA RE

"When we see hills devastated by fires, urban congestion, the gradual disappearance of fauna, rivers contaminated by toxic waste, mountains crumbling down, the human body intoxicated by pesticides, lead, etc., we can't help wondering why technology has been used against humankind's interests instead of being put to its service."*

What is nature? There is no single answer to this question, because nature has always been interpreted differently depending on which historical period, culture or civilization is being referred to; and even today it is difficult to find an answer. One purpose of this anthology is to highlight the approach that science and the arts have towards nature, thus facilitating a wider comprehension. The authors in the first sections belong to the world of the arts, while most of the authors in this section are scientists, social scientists, political activists or journalists. They have created interdisciplinary methods of research on environmental topics — research stemming from personal experiences, often as members of organizations such as the Green Party, Lega Ambiente and the WWF. Thus, not only have they written about their concerns about nature, but they have also tried to solve practical problems. Their work can be compared to that of Americans Edward Abbey on wilderness issues in the West and Rachel Carson on marine ecology and on toxic waste. In the United States there is now a recognized school of literary theory, commonly referred to as ecocriticism, which has sought to identify and theorize

*Giorgio Nebbia, *Le merci e i valori* (Milano: Jaca Book: 2002), 99.

257

a recognizable tradition of environmental literature that articulates the subtle truths of ecology. However, in Italy there have yet to be any major collaborative attempts at consolidating these writers into an organized group. As a collective of individual voices for the environment, many Italian writers have been as involved with political action as with environmental writing. Their work, which can be viewed as a rough-knit, yet unified, tradition is destined to become more and more influential in the future.

This attitude towards nature is derived from many social, cultural, and political events. Starting from the middle of twentieth century, a new sensitivity towards nature has emerged. Nature no longer appears as a constantly renewing reality with infinite resources, but rather as a vulnerable organism already heavily scarred by humanity. Uncontrolled industrial development, atomic bombs exploding on Hiroshima and Nagasaki, open-air nuclear tests and radioactive fallout, and the indiscriminate use of chlorinated pesticides are a few examples of the dangerous and widespread effects humanity has had on nature.

In the past, our creativity never broke the established balance, and nature could tolerate our abuses. Yet the scientific discoveries of the twentieth century applied to an increasingly advanced technology showed how devastating our power could be, consequently altering the relationship between humanity and nature. Thus we are compelled to think of nature in an ecological way, and the word "ecology" has become a household term. Ecological thought emerges from a new "idea of responsibility," * — our responsibility towards nature: if we want to save ourselves and the future generations, we need to take care of nature.

The '60s and the first part of the '70s — up until the first oil crisis in 1973 — are considered to be the years of ecological awareness, the "spring of ecology." In 1962, in the United States, Rachel Carson published *Silent Spring*. Carson warned that the unrestrained use of chlorinated pesticides in agriculture would

---

*Hans Jonas, *Il principio di responsabilità* (Torino: Einaudi, 1990).

bring death to many living creatures, and as an example she used the death of birds making spring "silent."

In 1963, under President John F. Kennedy, a treaty was signed between the U.S.A. and the U.S.S.R. to forbid open-air nuclear tests. The year 1970 was declared the European Year for the Conservation of Nature. Again in 1970, in the U.S.A. ecological protests culminated in the declaration of Earth Day on April 22, producing in a few short years the definition of air standards (Clean Air Act) and the constitution of the EPA (Environmental Protection Agency). In May 1972, the United Nations summoned an international conference in Stockholm on the subject, "Human Environment." Italian environmentalists, Antonio Cederna, Giorgio Nebbia, and Virginio Bettini participated. The conclusion of the conference was collected in a dossier entitled *A Single Earth.*

The concept of sustainable development and sustainable society was developed to safeguard the earth's natural resources for future generations. "The earth is lent to us by our children" became a popular slogan. The need to limit population growth and limit the unconditional use of natural resources was proposed, and people began speaking of "different standards of development." In Italy, the "Club di Roma"— a group of scholars dedicated to possible future social problems — commissioned leading professors of the Massachusetts Institute of Technology (MIT) in Cambridge to research these problems. *Limits to Growth* was also published in 1972 at the time of the conference in Stockholm.

Again in Italy, a group of researchers and scientists started working for the scientific magazine *Sapere*. In 1974 Giulio Maccararo became its outstanding chief editor. Environmental problems, such as nuclear power and industrial pollution, were discussed, and there was also criticism of scientific methods. Marcello Cini, a successful Italian physicist, challenged (as he had already done in his previous writings) the neutrality of scientific knowledge. In 1976, the accident at the Icmesa factory in Seveso, near Milan, launched the problem of industrial "relevant" risk. The moving spirit in those days was a woman, Laura Conti, who later became a great environmentalist. In the national newspapers, articles on the environment started to appear regularly. Every paper had its specialists on the environment, such as Alfredo Todisco for *Il Corriere della Sera*, Virginio Bettini for *Avvenire*, and Giorgio Nebbia for *Il Giorno*.

After the nuclear accident at Three Mile Island in 1979 and the ecological catastrophe of Chernobyl in 1986, the Italian environmental movement began to draw closer to the anti-nuclear movement. Already, in the middle of the '70s, Italian environmentalism had started the battle against nuclear power stations. Two young professors of physics, Gianni Mattioli and Massimo Scalia, founded the "Committee for the Control of Energy Options," with the support of the magazines *Quale ecologia* and *La nuova ecologia*. In Italy, scientific environmentalism began to critique the academic world, which responded to the growing problems with scientific dogma.

The anti-nuclear movement would eventually win approval in France, Germany, Holland, and Sweden. In Italy, a referendum was held to abandon nuclear energy altogether. "Nuke? No, thank you" became a popular slogan in the anti-nuclear movement. It was written on young people's jackets, on backpacks, and on children's strollers. The strong protest against nuclear energy after the Chernobyl tragedy led to a victory in the 1987 popular referendum: Italy definitively broke with nuclear energy.*

∎

The twentieth century embodied both hope and increasing disillusionment. However in the last ten years events also reached a critical mass. The world conference in Rio de Janeiro (1992) highlighted controversies between the countries participating and pointed to the new risks of pollution — among them, the Greenhouse effect, the ozone hole, the melting of the polar ice-cap, desertification, and the reduction both of the rain forests and of biological diversity.

---

*After three years of battles led by a new political party, "I Verdi" (the Greens) the nuclear power stations will be definitely closed.

The Kyoto Protocol of 1997 sought to reduce the emission of carbon dioxide in the atmosphere, but the demanding changes of economic and social organization necessary to achieve this were not accepted by the United States and other powerful countries ("the Umbrella Group"). At the same time, the environmental movement began to address such issues as genetically modified foods, food security, electromagnetic fields, radioactive waste, unequal exchange, the individual's rights, and the global market. The movement began to struggle more and more with a "total" concept of the world and with "a unique line of thinking" on the environment.

■

In a country like Italy, where artistic creation has always played a major role in history, the relationship between the people and nature has distinct characteristics. Italy's environmental resources are fused with its artistic heritage, and both are testimony to a search for harmony and spiritual growth. Aesthetic values are linked to historic values, and art to landscape. Ercole Ferrario writes:

> ...errant knights...men and women, wandering up and down valleys, mountains, forests, coasts, resting in enchanted castles, dreamlike islands, magic gardens... Ariosto's gardens remarkably reflect both the important and the little-known courts that populated Italy...one has the impression of being in a place that humanity has carefully modeled to obtain a unique effect, not like the wilderness that still existed in the dark forests beyond the Alps.*

From the 1950s, organizations for environmental conservation in Italy — ItaliaNostra, WWF, Greenpeace, and Lega Ambiente, — were speaking about "environmental humanism"† where the defense of the environment also includes the quality and even the very meaning of life. As a consequence

---

*Andrea Ferrario, *L'idea di natura nella storia della letteratura*, (Milano: Unicopli, 1989), 1:159.
†Andrea Poggio, *Ambientalismo* (Milano: Bibliografica, 1989).

of economic "globalization" a new outlook has begun to emerge in Italy that enriches local resources, in particular, combining regional specialties (food and wine) with the artistic beauty that can be found in every corner of the country. The name of this movement is Piccoli Comuni (small locally-governed towns). Such leaders as Ermete Realacci, the president of "Legambiente," are particularly keen to see this initiative develop.

■

A deep concern for the future of humanity, a love of nature and a thorough scientific foundation has transformed Italy's environmentalists into nature's spokespeople, with the hope of arousing public interest and participation in our Earth-Home, the defense of which is and remains the greatest challenge of the third millennium.

We have mentioned only a few of the many authors who have contributed to the birth and development of Italian environmentalism. But our objective in the following selections is simply to give an bird's-eye view of the movement as a whole.

LAURA CONTI
(1921–1993)

Laura Conti, scientist and writer, was born in 1921 in Udine and died in 1993 in Milan. In 1944 she joined the partisans and in July of that year was arrested and deported to a concentration camp in Bolzano where she remained until May 1945. In 1949 she received a degree in medicine. Later, she became a town and regional councilor and then a member of the Italian Parliament. She is best remembered for her work fighting for environmental and social issues. *Una lepre con la faccia di bambina* (A hare with the face of a child) tells the story of two imaginary children, Marco and Sara, who experience the environmental disaster that occurred in Seveso, a small town near Milan, in 1976. A cloud of the toxic substance dioxin spread in this densely inhabited area, poisoned and often killed the living creatures it encountered on its way. Marco, who uses the simple language of a twelve-year-old boy, narrates. However, the fact that the story is presented by a child does not prevent it from confronting so-called major "adult problems." With simple words Marco and Sara tell a sad story of pollution, miscarriages provoked by dioxin poisoning, inexplicable illnesses, and money interests winning over human interests. The adults in the story do not want to involve the two children in what is happening, yet Marco and Sara understand more than what the adults around them imagine. Conti's books include *Cecilia e le streghe* (Cecilia and the witches), *La condizione sperimentale* (The experimental condition), *Questo pianeta* (This planet), and *Che cosa è ecologia* (What is ecology).

A HARE WITH THE FACE OF A CHILD*

We sat in a living room where there were prints on the walls of hunters in red jackets riding horses, and started speaking about feminists and those pictures of theirs.

"I know that dioxin hurts babies when they're already born. But those who aren't born yet? That's hard to believe."

"But babies who aren't born yet are already alive. They're in their mother's belly, they get blood from their mother."

"That's true. I knew that. Why didn't I think about that? A baby in his mother's belly doesn't see anything, doesn't hear anything, but if his mother takes in poison it'll hurt him too, make his nose turn into a hare's snout."

"I was told that in that town called Ho Chi Min there were a lot of babies with hare snouts."

"A lot."

"Who knows what it's like in a town where all the babies have hare snouts? Maybe the hares have babies' faces."

"Idiot."

She turned and it seemed that she wiped her eyes with a handkerchief.

"Whatever — what do you care about babies with hare snouts? You sure don't have to have a baby, it seems to me."

"You don't only have to think about what happens to yourself, but also about others."

"Which others?"

She didn't answer, she told me a story of the cows from the seminary, an old seminary that is in our town. The priests' school doesn't exist anymore, because there is nobody who still wants to study to become a priest. There is only a farmer who takes care of the cow stables, the fields, and the feeder.

"The cows of the seminary were all pregnant. Two of them delivered too early, the calves were both dead. One of them had two heads, the other had skin like a fish."

---

*From Laura Conti, *Una lepre con la faccia di bambina* (Roma: Editori Riuniti, 1978). This translation by Patrick Barron and Anna Re first appeared in *ISLE: Interdisciplinary Studies in Literature and Environment* 7.2 (2000): 179–87.

"So also calves, when they're in their mother's belly, can take in the poison?"

"Sure, they're also…"

"What are they?"

"A word like *"fiammiferi"*[44] — a word that means animals with tits. They're animals with tits too, they take blood from their mother before being born, if the mother is poisoned, they get poisoned too, like human babies."

Who knows how she got to know so many things? Actually, when she was saying those things, I remembered that I had heard them at school, but outside of school I could never remember them. But she had brothers who always spoke to each other and with their friends and let her listen to what they were saying. Different from me, she never remembered anything when she was at school, and so she was always the worst in the class. Sure this dioxin was a strange thing, it was related to hormones and tits. Who knows if my cousin in Rapallo knows all these things? If next year I go to Rapallo, I want to check.

Then Sara said to me that Assuntina had fought with her fiancé. That's trouble, because her fiancé is an employee at the social security office, he's a gentleman. Sara's mother's always been happy about their engagement.

"Did they fight very badly? Doesn't he want to marry her anymore?"

"It isn't that he doesn't want to marry her anymore. He wants her to do something that Assuntina doesn't want to. She says that she'd rather kill herself."

"Why should she kill herself? She doesn't have to do what he wants her to, and that's it."

"Well, but she can't help but doing it, that's the thing."

"What is it? If she can't help but doing that thing, her boyfriend is right."

"You can't understand."

"Why can't I understand?"

"Because you're a man."

If my parents are speaking, I'm not able to understand because I'm a kid. If Sara is speaking, I'm not able to understand because I'm a man.

That night I dreamt about a big mess of baby cows with fish skin and fish with baby cow legs, hare snout babies, and hares with baby faces. Sara grabbed a cat with a hare snout in her arms and said, "Here's my little sister, my Carmelina has come back."

I told her, "What are you saying? It's a cat with a hare snout."

She said, "No, it's a kid, a baby with hare's snout and cat's body."

The cat turned and looked at me with her little face like a hare and cried. When I woke up, I realized it was a just a stupid dream, but while I was dreaming I was very scared.

One night the mayor brought a huge map and some men put it up with tape on the huge bulletin board that's in the living room. There were streets marked, and even houses and fields. There was also our house, and Sara's house. It was hard to find them on the map, but Pasquale helped me. Zone A, which is our area, the evacuated one, was drawn as a triangle with the factory at the top, then there was Zone B, under it Zone A and all around Zone C, and everywhere there were little numbers. The men were looking at the map and grimacing:

"Look here. I live where it's 12, and they evacuated us. Here, in Zone B it's 40, and they're all happy at their places."

"To work and nab our customers."

"At your place it's 12. Look here, what about at my place? There's number 6 and 50. Those living in Zone A were pissed off because they got cleared out. Maybe those in Zone B, which is so badly polluted, were angry because they didn't get evacuated. Or maybe they were happy to stay there in the poisoned area — who knows?"

One night the town councilman came to visit and everybody attacked him.

"Why were the people living in Zone A evacuated where there was hardly any pollution and in Zone B, where there was so much pollution, people weren't?"

The councilman said the man was right. Then, he added, "It's not only Zone B that has heavy pollution. Zone C also has heavy pollution. Listen — there are sick babies all over, here alone a hundred and eighty dead rabbits. How is it possible that there isn't any pollution? There's pollution, very high pollution. But lab reports are false, they say there's no pollution. And do you know why?"

They knew, but didn't want to hear it from him: "Because of big industry. If they put this area in Zone A, or even only in Zone B, they would have to close all the factories, this one and that one. Workers on the skids, indemnity to pay, can you imagine? As long as it's only craftsmen's workshops, they close them down and don't give a shit. But, if it's about factories, you understand."

Then everybody cried out, as if it was the first time they were hearing something like that.

"What bullshit!"

"What crap!"

"Sold to industry! Fucking Politicians!"

Sometimes the mistake was to close craftsmen's workshops, other times the mistake was not to close the big factories. Sometimes it seemed that dioxin was dangerous, sometimes it seemed it wasn't. Once an important professor held a conference in Politeama, full of people. He said that he wanted to move into our houses and drink the milk of the seminary cows in order to show us that dioxin wasn't so dangerous. But, how can he drink the milk of the seminary cows if they're sick and don't have milk anymore?

One night a young man in the basement coffee room said something I was thinking of too, "If dioxin isn't that dangerous, who would have cared to spread the word that it was so dangerous?"

A tall, fat man with white hair said, "It's big industry. In order to pay workers so little they need to drive craftsmen out of business. Who dumps dioxin? Industry. Who goes out of business? Craftsmen. It's simple."

Another man started saying that it was the radicals and communists who dumped it because they wanted something. But, then he looked around and saw that we young guys were there. He didn't explain what the communists and radicals wanted, he only said, "we understand each other, don't we?" and the others nodded in agreement. Always things boys can't understand. Who knows then what these great mysteries were?

In the sitting room where there were the women it was even worse. One day I opened the door and there was a woman with red eyes. She was drying them with a handkerchief. All of them immediately said to me, "Go away, go play." Go play!… Did they think I was six?

. . . .

[Sara and Marco are now living in a hotel, having been evacuated from their village. They are speaking about Assuntina, Sara's sister, who was pregnant when the accident happened and is now afraid of having a child with deformities. For this reason, she goes to her aunt's village in the south of Italy to have an abortion.]

We came back to the hotel late. People were already in the dining room, but nobody was sitting at the Di Pasquas's table.

"Oh my gosh, what happened?" said Sara.

She ran up the stairs because she had no patience to wait for the elevator. I ate quickly and then went upstairs to listen at her door, but the voices were low. Then Sara came out a moment and she told me what had happened. Her aunt had called. She hadn't had the courage to go ahead with the operation because Assuntina was too advanced in her pregnancy; she was in her fifth month already. And when she said no, Assuntina became pale and without saying anything ran away from home, ran away without taking her coat. They looked for her everywhere in the village but couldn't find her. They didn't go to the police because they were scared. Her aunt was afraid because the sheriff already had an eye on her, and please, even Assuntina's mom should not go to the police to say that her daughter had disappeared. Assuntina's mom was there, sitting on the sofa. She trembled all over and was crying. But she didn't want to be heard and was crying quietly.

Two or three days later another call arrived. They had found Assuntina. They had found her collapsed in front of the hospital in Messina, and since nobody had helped her, she had done it by herself. She had stuck a knitting needle in her tummy to kill her baby with the hare snout. What courage, my God! Then she had gone to the hospital, perhaps she

268

wanted to be hospitalized, but she had fainted in front of the door. Now she was in the hospital. Her condition was serious, but there was some hope according to the doctor. Their aunt was not in trouble, nobody had bothered her because nobody knew that Assuntina was her niece in Messina. And for the rest, it was clear that Assuntina had done everything by herself, without the help of anybody. Immediately after that the policemen of our town had called and told Sara's dad and mom to go to the police station because there was news for them. They had gone there, and the policemen had told them that their daughter was hospitalized in Messina and in serious condition because of the induced abortion, and that she had asked for her mother.

They said, "Poor girl, obviously she had been abandoned by her man and she was afraid of dishonor."

However, since she was of age and there was no sign that other people were responsible, they denounced only her.

Sara's mother immediately left with Pasquale, and Sara told me to bring her on the crossbar of my bike to the highway bridge, but she made me stop a little before. Since it was foggy, it was hard to find the exact spot she wanted, a place where the net of the barbed wire was cut, and it was possible to get in. We passed through the middle of a cornfield. Because of the fog nobody could see us. We arrived at the street where Sara lived. Nobody was there. All the doors and windows were opened, there was a deep silence. The voices of the reclamation workers came from far away. Then we entered Sara's house. It was dark, the furniture wasn't there anymore, they had disconnected the electricity. Sara told me in a low voice: "Well, you understand, if Assuntina dies, it's nobody's fault, it's only hers. They've even denounced her, because it's her fault."

We were speaking quietly. We were walking on our tiptoes because we were worried that somebody would hear us even though nobody was there. We went upstairs, to Assuntina's bedroom. Sara pulled the rolling shutter up and showed me light squares on the walls:

"Here there was her picture with her fiancé in Venice at Piazza San Marco while they were feeding the pigeons. Here there was a little picture with dried flowers that they bought

269

when they went for a trip to Switzerland. There is nothing left. We didn't even take a picture when they took us away. If she dies, we'll have nothing left of her, nothing."

We went to sit on the steps, where once there were bottles for tomato sauce, and now there was nothing. The plants in the kitchen garden had fallen and were rotting on the ground. It was so foggy that we couldn't even see the fence and the gate.

"Think of those bastard policemen who pretend not to know anything, pretend to believe that she was afraid of dishonor, pretend not to know that we had been poisoned by dioxin. Assuntina was in all the newspapers that time when the bastard doctors let her hear her baby's heartbeats; and also that time that the shit-head priest wanted to take her baby. But, policemen don't know anything. Of course not."

She picked up a little twig from the ground. She started doing drawings on the ground, like that time she touched the dead animal with the twig.

"Do you know why they pretend not to know anything? Because they don't want to deal with the newspapers again, the doctors that let her hear the heart and that priest. That's what Pasquale says.

"He also said, 'if this story gets out, the factory will have to pay, and nobody wants to bother the factory.' And dad and mom are staying quiet too, because mom is afraid of scandals. So, if Assuntina doesn't die, she goes to jail and the factory doesn't have to pay anything. And if she dies, the factory doesn't pay anything anyway and we don't even have a picture of Assuntina. There'll be nothing left of Assuntina, it'll be as if she wasn't even born."

We stayed there for a while without talking. It started raining. The fog faded away, and we could see the chicken yard again, but they had already started to pull down the fence.

"Do you remember Sara? There, that's where the dog house was."

"The dog is dead."

"Do you remember, the cat used to go to sleep on her back."

"The cat is dead too."

"Do you remember the snacks you used to prepare, bread with tomatoes and salt and oregano?"

"Maybe the last tomato was poisoned by dioxin and made me sick. Maybe it poisoned you too."

"But you're all right now. You recovered, Sara. Your face is almost like it used to be."

"I'm not fine. Look at my nails."

"They're clean. You learned to clean your nails."

"No. Look, they're black — not the edges, they're clean. The very nails, where it used to be flesh-colored, it's black."

I put my hands close to hers. My nails were flesh-colored, and her nails had a kind of black shadow.

"What does it mean?"

"Many babies that suffered from chloracne[45] have this black shadow. Nobody knows what that is. Even doctors don't know. They say it's a sign of getting poisoned by dioxin."

Then, that night she came and knocked very softly at my door: "Marco, Marco, open up."

She was wearing her new coat and new shoes.

"I'm leaving. We're all going to get mom for the funeral."

"When are you coming back?"

"I'm not coming back. My dad and brothers will come back because there's work here, but mom and me will stay there. Mom says that she doesn't want to live in this poisoned town any longer, a place that killed one of her daughters."

"Sara, oh Sara."

"Well, bye."

"Sara, what am I going to do without you?"

Her eyes were red but she smiled at me, "You find a girl short like this." And she knelt down. "Or a girl tall like this." And she stood up on her tiptoes.

Now, when it rains and nobody's on guard, or when it's foggy and nobody can see me, I come to Sara's kitchen garden and sit on the steps. I can't hear any noise, only some voices from far away. I look at my nails. Now there's a black shadow on my nails too.

NOTE

Dioxin is a highly toxic substance for embryos. If a pregnant woman is exposed to it within the third month of her pregnancy, her child may be born with deformities. If the malformation is

271

serious, the embryo will not survive and the woman will miscarry. In these cases, miscarriages are improperly defined as "spontaneous abortions." The word "spontaneous," in this particular case, means: "not wanted by the mother but by others." For example, Givaudan.[46]

On July 10, 1976, a dioxin cloud coming from the ICMESA reactor descended on Brianza. It can be inferred that the exposure to the cloud provoked an indefinite number of spontaneous abortions. It would be useful to statistically compare the number of miscarriages that happened in the polluted area "before" and "after" the cloud. That is, it would be useful to be able to compare the number of miscarriages in August 1976 to that in August 1975, the number in September 1976 to that in September 1975, and so on, month by month. However, the statistical comparison has not been done because registrations at the hospital were so approximate that an estimate would be rather difficult. In cases of hospitalization because of spontaneous abortion often the record reads, for instance, "hospitalization to check the uterus," since that is the surgical treatment practiced in spontaneous abortions, and also in other pathological conditions. Or it reads "hospitalization because of endometriosis," without specifying if it was a post-miscarriage endometriosis. The clinical histories of a hundred or a hundred and fifty women would have had to have been reconstructed — a difficult job, but not impossible. Since this was not done, we will never know how many abortions the cloud caused when it spread across the sky and fell to the ground. However, we know other things.

After July 10, 1976 hospitals in Brianza filled out registration forms with more accuracy. After that day hospitalizations because of spontaneous abortions were correctly recorded. Thus it is possible to compare the number of miscarriages in the period after dioxin: although we are not able to compare the number in August 1975 to that in August 1976, the number in September 1976 to that in September 1975, and so on, we are however able to compare the number in August 1976 to the number of in the successive months in 1976 and 1977. While I am writing this note (January 1978) the statistics are available up to June 1977.

272

The statistics highlight a slight increase of spontaneous abortions between August 1976 and June 1977. In the area under the medical jurisdiction of the Desio Hospital, spontaneous abortions, which made up 10% of the deliveries in August 1976, in June 1977 made up 18% of the deliveries: an 80% increase. This phenomenon can be explained by the accumulation of high quantities of toxic substances and by the fact that people continued to live in polluted Zone B, and in the so-called "Zona di Rispetto" (Zone of Respect). Women lived in polluted houses and gardens, and toxic substances slowly built up in their bodies. There was a physician who, for a woman who had asked to have an abortion, listened to the embryo's heartbeats with a phonendoscope. However, it was not technically possible to record the slow fading heartbeats of the "spontaneously" dying embryo, and then send the recorded tapes to the shareholders of Givaudan.

Translated by Patrick Barron and Anna Re

ALFREDO TODISCO
(1921–)

Alfredo Todisco, after university studies in Trieste, began his career as a journalist for *Il Mondo*. He is also a novelist and an ecology scholar, and for the past twenty years he has been a reporter and special correspondent for many Italian newspapers, as well as, at present, the editor of *Il Corriere della Sera*, one of Italy's most important dailies. He has published many works on the environment, like "Breviario di ecologia" (Ecology breviary) in which he offers the reader a survey of the disastrous state of the environment. In *Storia naturale di una passione* (The natural history of a passion), nature, poisoned and polluted, takes revenge on humanity by depriving it of the capacity to love by insinuating a funereal torpor, a disgust for life in all human thought and senses. The love relationship between Delfina and Sebastiano, although projected against a luminous and poetic background rich in passion and erotic ardor, does not escape this universal degradation. The final image of the book is that of the falcon that "destroys with its beak in fury and horror" its own poisoned and prematurely laid eggs — a terrible premonition of the day the sky will become empty, like the heart of man.

FROM: THE NATURAL HISTORY OF A PASSION*

While their friends chose to remain on the shore, Sebastiano and Delfina decided to climb to the top of the mountain, which to the south lined the narrow access to the bay. Oblivious to the fact that the sun was already high in the Turkish sky, they clambered up the steep and rocky footpath scattered with reminders of the recent passages of flocks of sheep.

---

*From Alfredo Todisco, *Storia naturale di una passione* (Milano: Rizzoli, 1976).

274

After the first stretch, relieved by the intermittent shade of pine trees, the footpath led to an opening, banked exclusively by low, bristly, parched brushwood which, as the altitude increased, gradually gave way to a rocky, landslide-prone terrain.

After about an hour and a half, they had only begun the second half of the climb to the summit, which threatened to be even rougher. In fact, the footpath became steeper and more uneven, winding its way up a sort of gorge burnt by the sun, where not a breath of air arrived. They made their way up slowly, at times grabbing any support at hand, their perspiration evaporating immediately, so torrid and dry was the heat.

Although put to the test more than they would have imagined, they continued their climb with youthful stubbornness, determined to reach the top.

Slim in her bathing suit, Delfina walked ahead with an energy and resistance that inspired a growing amazement in Sebastiano. Each time, conscious of the strain he felt in his own limbs, he would anxiously ask her: "Are you tired?"; she answered firmly: "No, I'm perfectly fine."

Gradually, as they approached the crest, the sheep-track became hidden by the debris of a landslide terrain increasingly less practicable. It often gave way as they walked, increasing the effort required. While, breathing hard, they proceeded ever more slowly, they encountered a hypnotic scenario of gleaming flint, with millions of cracks similar to mouths twisted in menacing, enigmatic grimaces.

Every now and then, the flight of a black raptor in the chalk-like sky intimated that hidden somewhere in that desolate landscape there must be some form of life.

Finally, after having got past a last deposit of schist, they found themselves in the midst of a narrow, flat saddle, from which they could see the Bay of Adrasan, and at the center the *Erna* seemed as small as a grain of rice. Beyond, there was the expanse of the outer sea, light and airy and as vast as a second sky.

Satisfied that they had reached the summit, they wanted to rest and enjoy the marvelous scenes offered to them from those heights. Sebastiano and Delfina sat down on a rocky ledge, just a step away from the edge, jutting out from a vertiginous precipice above the open sea.

Suddenly, with a sharp sound, a large bird emerged seemingly from under their feet and rose with lightning speed into the sky. It was a falcon.

After the first moment of amazement, Sebastiano and Delfina crawled along the ground to the edge of the chasm and then leaned over, curious to see the place from where the raptor had risen. At first, they saw nothing, Then, half hidden in a niche in the rock, practically within reach, they saw a nest woven of brush. Inside the nest there were two round white forms that seemed like eggs, and yet didn't.

In the meantime, the falcon had begun flying low around their heads, making threatening sounds, obviously intent on defending its home from the sudden intrusion. All at once, it swooped down onto its nest as though onto a prey, gave two rapid blows of its beak and darted away once more, disappearing in the air as if disintegrating.

As a result of that violent airborne attack, the nest had tipped just enough so that the two could no longer see inside it. Sebastiano, curious to understand just what had happened, cautiously moved so he could see the nest again. And what he saw disturbed him deeply. On the bottom of that rough basket lay two bladders of sorts, crushed, whitish, and each with a gaping wound. They seemed and did not seem to be eggs. Overcoming an instinctive sense of disgust, Sebastiano decided to gather up those strange sloughs to look at them more closely. As he lifted them gently with his index finger and thumb, they hung limply like entrails dripping onto the ground the viscous and luteous mucus with which they were filled.

They could only be falcon eggs. But they had no shell, or better yet, they appeared to have thin, veil-like shells which were fragmented into a thousand small crusts and seemed to be stuck to the layer of tissue inside the eggs, which were reduced by the wound to a mucilaginous, empty container.

While, beside him, a disconcerted Delfina observed the moist placenta he held in the palm of his hand, Sebastiano thought he understood what they had seen by chance on that

276

distant cliff sheer above the sea, as distant from the techno-logical world as a bit of the moon. "It's a sign!" he exclaimed.

Sebastiano had heard of the insidious danger that threat-ened to render extinct many species of raptor that fed on birds that for them were nothing more than poison. The migratory birds, prey of the raptors flying over cultivated fields, absorbed and retained the poisons that the farmers spread abundantly to defend their crops from the increasingly aggressive attacks of armies of parasites.

But these artificial toxins, the product of human ingenuity, had a terrible aspect. Once they entered the food chain of animals, it was practically impossible for them to be elimi-nated. They take the living organism by surprise and accumulate in their bodies virtual "seeds of evil" from this era of advanced technology.

Those predators were destined to suffer the most deleteri-ous effects of those tenacious albeit invisible guests. And that was because they were daily condemned to incorporate as many doses of poison as birds they succeeded in capturing. Thus, they accumulated in their tissue successive increments of toxins which, while relatively innocuous in the individual prey, ultimately became deadly concentrations.

Now, besides the lethal cases often observed in ornithologi-cal laboratories, the insecticides threaten the survival of the raptor by inhibiting hormones. Eggs are destined to be laid prematurely, without a shell. The raptor in turn destroys the offspring.

While he explained to Delfina the meaning of what they had seen, Sebastiano was aware that the danger threatening the raptor, and all species of predators, was nothing more than a superficial indication of the deeper, hidden poison flowing in the lymph of the earth.

Sebastian felt the need to observe a moment of silence. The air had become even more static. Preoccupied, Delfina looked at the sea, which appeared to slumber in the embrace of a calm horizon. Her amber-colored skin, with its tender blue veins, appeared even sweeter than it usually did.

Momentarily bewildered Sebastian looked at her. Then he gazed over the blue summits rising beyond the Bay of Adrasan toward Europe, where he imagined the vast expanses of ploughed fields from which the chirping populations of migratory birds, flying over the statue of Artemis, transported as far as the peaks of the Taurus Mountains those distillates of industrial stores. Those distillates, which if one were to heed the warning of the event he had witnessed, forced nature to turn against the primordial source of its own existence.

The two youths retraced their steps much more rapidly, treading the uncertain terrain, which every now and then raised clouds of dust.

As they approached the *Erna*, which the next day would bring them to Analya, the last stop on the cruise, Sebastiano realized, with the painful resignation, which any encounter with the inevitable produces, that on the summit, in an instant, the moment of the final separation from Delfina had arrived.

When they reached the shore, out of breath, Delfina looked back at the far off peak to calculate with satisfaction the distance they had walked. And then, she asked Sebastiano, "Where has the falcon has gone?"

The sky was empty.

Translated by Anna Re

ANTONIO CEDERNA
(1921–1996)

Antonio Cederna was born in Milan. He received an under-graduate degree in humanities at Pavia and later specialized in archaeology in Rome. He was a leading member of ItaliaNostra, an association created in 1955 for urban protection. Cederna denounced the degradation of old town centers resulting from reckless economic development and property speculation and discussed the future of Italian cities from both traditional and modern points of view. His first articles are collected in the volume entitled *I vandali in casa* (The Vandals at home). As editor of the weekly magazine *Il Mondo*, Cederna explored the achievements of Italian urban planning, comparing them to those throughout Europe.

FROM: THE VANDALS AT HOME *

The "Vandals" of this volume have nothing to do with the real Vandals: the barbarians who arrived in Italy after the fall of the Roman Empire. Historians demonstrate that to demolish a well conserved basilica or a temple in those times would have been an absurd waste of time and energy, especially considering the reasons why they came to our country. Thus, we ask forgiveness to the Vandals' memory, for our slanderous opinion of them. Rome and Italy have been destroyed by the Romans and the Italians. The vandals we are interested in, are our contemporaries, who became a legion after the last war, and owing to their vile avarice, ignorance, vulgarity, or simple bestiality, have reduced, and are continuing to reduce, the legacy of our past to dust. Owners and estate agents, speculators of building sites, building companies, industrial and commercial real estate companies, private businessmen, clerics and

---

*From Antonio Cederna, *I Vandali in casa* (Bari: Laterza, 1956).

laymen, architects and engineers lacking in professional dignity, urban destroyers, powerless and corrupted authorities of state and city, fallen aristocrats, upstarts and plebeians, confused and corrupted writers and journalists, reactionary prophets of the internal-combustion engine, extremely ignorant rhetoricians of canned progress. The artistic and natural wonders of the "Country of Art" and of the "Garden of Europe" are in the hands of these madmen: native squanderers of an outstanding heritage. This is how we show ourselves to the world.

No compromise is possible between civil people and today's vandals....

A long time ago in Milan, there was (and maybe there still is) a church similar to many others. It was not a particularly distinguished church and had no Touring Club stars. It was small, the architect is uncertain, and it was surrounded by recent buildings. Its name is Saint Raphael, and it is next to the Duomo in Via San Raffaele. The façade was built at the end of sixteenth century, the inside around 1600; it has ordinary arches, ordinary columns, and ordinary paintings. Unfortunately Rinascente, a department store selling standard items giving earthly happiness to citizens, is right next door to the church with no stars. One fine day, Rinascente, in order to adjust to the growing needs of the "Lombard metropolis," decides to enlarge its space. Can the church of Saint Raphael hinder its project? No problem: Rinascente quietly plans its demolition. In cases like this, it is usual to override the authorities and go to the Curia to see what can be done. The Curia of Milan is very fond of its old churches in Milan, almost as fond as the Curia in Rome is of its old churches in Rome. Thus, halfheartedly — and for a modest payment of only 500 million lira — the descendants of Saint Charles Borromeo, founder of Saint Raphael, are persuaded to sell Saint Raphael to Rinascente. The worthy prelates claim that those 500 million lire will be used to build new churches in the suburbs to convert new souls to the faith. Another Milan institution, the national newspaper, *Corriere della Sera*, quickly aligns with Rinascente and the Curia. This is the mouthpiece of common sense in Milan. Out of spiritual affinity it first supports the demolition of the church, then, reflecting its pragmatism, responded to the psychological effects produced by the demolition with silence.

Voices of protest rise from a couple of papers and from some cultural associations. The authorities silently tremble, torn between their duty to preserve the buildings and the pressure of economic powers (Rinascente, the Curia, *Corriere della Sera*). A commission from Rome arrives, secret documents are written. Nobody knows anything. In an almost Kafkaesque reality, uncertain, generic, ambiguous, obscure, contradictory news circulates throughout Milan. For instance, the church "will not be touched," "it will be moved somewhere else," it will be demolished but the façade will be re-built "elsewhere," it will be "reduced" and transformed into a chapel in the enlarged store, etc., etc. Silence follows.

It doesn't matter that the old church of Saint Raphael was temporarily saved, because of some fortuitous and temporary set of circumstances. The fact is, for similar reasons, dozens of monuments fell in the past, others will fall in the future. This vile church market is a typical case. The powers that have been destroying Italy for decades, and will continue to do so, are in total agreement: the greed of the big business, the mundane and demagogic spirit of the ecclesiastic hierarchy, the weakness of the authorities designated to preserve our heritage, the insensitivity of respectable "educated people," the opportunism and conformity of the important newspapers who proclaim to be independent, are all equally responsible.

Translated by Anna Re

FROM: THE DESTRUCTION OF NATURE*

Rural Italy has become urbanized and depressing in many respects. The dehumanization of the cities is often confused with progress, carbon dioxide with civilization, smoke from chimneys with well-being, the elimination of any sign of nature with the affirmation of freedom. The worst economic

*From Antonio Cederna, *La distruzione della natura* (Torino: Einaudi, 1975).

forces, connected to speculation and land rent, are the only ones who have profited from this.

Nature, for the poor immigrant from the south of Italy, is more often than not associated with subsistence agriculture. Parks and gardens have always been a privilege for the rich, to be admired from the outside, beyond walls and barbed-wire fences. An uncivilized legal directive has reduced private property to a cult, preventing Italians from conceiving of their territory as a public and collective property. Even countries that had to "fight" against nature (fear of forest fires, the severity of climate, the violence of floods) have, finally, learned to love and respect it, and nurture it. Whereas the Italians, who had always lived in harmony with their environment, have gradually acquired an equivocal familiarity with it, leading to incomprehension, hostility, underestimation, and contempt.

Now, we are paying for the damage inflicted by a culture that has theorized the pre-eminence of man as an "artist" over nature; of a philosophy that has objectively denied nature's existence; and of a religion that, at its lowest and most commonplace levels, has always regarded nature with suspicion and incomprehension.... As you see, everything can be explained and justified. But it is against these distortions, against this immaturity that we have to keep on fighting day after day: in order to oppose this lethal, and by now widespread idea, that the territory and its resources are waste land, *res nullius,* marketable goods or land to be conquered — and so can be indiscriminately divided up, made suitable for building, and privatized for exclusive interests.

Translated by Anna Re

DANILO DOLCI
(1924–1997)

Danilo Dolci was born in Sesana, a village near Trieste, to an Italian father and a Slovenian mother. In 1952 he moved to Sicily, where he began his work with the poor and his life-long struggle for social and environmental betterment. He soon gained recognition for his efforts to organize nonviolent resistance to corrupt local government, the mafia, and flagrant abuses of the land and sea. His many awards include the Premio Viareggio, the Lenin Peace Award, and the International Gandhi Award. His published works, which range from works of investigative journalism and essays, to poetry and collections of folklore, include *Creatura di creature* (Creature of creatures), *Racconti siciliani* (Sicilian tales), and *Gente semplice* (Simple folk). The following story of a Sicilian farmer, collected by Dolci in the 1950s, is taken from *Waste*, an examination of the damaging social and environmental effects brought by corruption.

AN EXPROPRIATED FARMER*

I lived there always; I kept the animals there too. Three *salme*[48] of land, it was. I had a vineyard and large trees growing; I'd planted everything, right down to nut trees. I'd walnuts as well, poplars, and ever so many willows. There was a four-roomed house, cow-stalls, a large byre that reached from here to that fireplace. There was a room with a trough for tramping out the grapes. The house had a courtyard and a shed with a sloping roof. Originally, the farm belonged to Baron

---

*From Danilo Dolci, *Waste: An Eye-witness Report on Some Aspects of Waste in Western Sicily,* trans. R. Munroe (New York: Monthly Review Press, 1964).

Planeta, but he sold it as it had become a nuisance and we liked the spot so much that we paid him what he asked for it.

I spent about forty years there. I lived there with my brother, as we kept cows. It was while I was there that we planted all the trees, because there weren't any there before. Whenever I came across young saplings, I would transplant them, hoe the ground and weed around them to give them a chance to grow. There were fig-trees that produced more than two quintals of figs. The river ran by the land and the freshness from the water kept the trees from drying up. There were always chickens there.

Some engineers appeared and when they got to the farm they started calling from one to the other. They were surveying the land; but it wasn't as if we knew that they were going to make the reservoir here. After a bit, I began to hear rumors that they were going to build a reservoir. Everyone was saying: "They're going to build the reservoir; they're going to build the reservoir." There was nothing we could do to stop them and we began to be afraid. The people said that that was what they were going to do, but we didn't believe them. We'd never seen an artificial lake before. Everyone who had land that was due to be flooded had murder in his heart, but what could he do? They'd never seen a dam before. We none of us had. We didn't know what it was. It didn't seem possible that all the land would be lost.

Then the expropriation notices arrived and it turned out that all the land to be covered by the reservoir was to be expropriated. They sent along a form for one to sign, which gave all the details. It didn't mention any figure for compensation. "The reservoir's going to be built just the same whether you signed or not," the people were told. People said that they'd have to pay through the nose for the land. "It makes no difference whether you sign or you don't, because the land is going to be taken over all the same." Nearly everyone signed; only a few didn't. Lots signed before me. They gave me the form and I signed it. But we never saw any money. They made us sign whether we liked it or not.

When they began to make the road leading up to the site we tried to stop them. We all went and stationed ourselves on the main road to prevent them; because we knew that without the road they couldn't make the dam, as they needed the road to get the material up. And we didn't want it. But the police appeared immediately and then what could we do? At the least move, they'd have turned on us. They were armed and we had to be careful not to get killed — as that's their trade. A lorry crammed full of police, and some police cars as well, had arrived by then; and the whole outfit appeared on the scene, right down to the police colonel. So we couldn't stay where we were. There were masses of police. "Stand back! Stand back!" they shouted at us. "No one can stay here. Move on all of you." They had rifles and revolvers. And I don't know how many lorries there were, and clerks and workmen, all on the job. Hundreds of workmen building a wall wide enough to take a lorry. What was I to think? Could I kill them? We were overwhelmed and confused by it all; and the folk felt frightened.

They had machines to do everything. They mixed the cement with machines and tipped it all out there, into the dam. You've never seen so many machines, one for one thing and another for another; and they went on mixing and tipping, night and day. And all the time the wall went up and up. It was more than a hundred meters long. Each day the workmen went up higher. They quarried the stone with dynamite. They laid charges under the rock and blew the stone into the air. And day by day the wall grew higher. Before they started you could see right into the cleft in the mountain, from our house, but gradually the wall rose and cut out the view, until, in the end, all we could see was the wall itself.

Then one day the water began to form against the dam; it was winter-time. The quantity of water grew and grew and the level rose. Those whose houses were nearest had to leave, abandoning their land. Bit by bit, the level rose, according to how much it rained. As the water submerged the trees, those, who could, cut them down and took away the wood. At times the water rose so quickly that a person would leave a tree there one night, and in the morning he would find it gone, swallowed up by the water; and then it was too late to get the wood.

We had even planted corn, thinking that the water wouldn't get so high that year and we lost it all; the water covered the lot. It should have been a good crop, too, because we'd had the land ploughed by tractor. Bit by bit, the water became a lake. It was such good land that we could get two crops a year off it. I was very fond of the land and the place. At last, the water rose so high that my nephews came and took me away before I was imprisoned by the waters. The house was on a little knoll and, as the land was low all round, it was becoming a little island standing up out of the water that was flooding round it. All the others round about watched the water rising, rising, and said to each other: "One day the water will cover Uncle Felice, too." "The water's bound to wash him away one of these days," they would say, and in the end they came and took me away. I tried to refuse to go with them at first, because I was anxious about the cows; but my nephews drove them off and I had to follow. What else could I do? I could see what was happening to the house, but what could I do about it?

I went on watching the house from here. If the water were a little lower you could see what it looked like. Day by day, the water rose, one meter, two meters, until at last only the roof was showing. We had a well with lovely fresh water to drink. All the neighbors came there to drink it. Lovely spring water, it was. We were never short of water. The neighbors came to drink from all around.

At last, only the tops of the olives and of a walnut tree remained to be seen. And then nothing at all. The more it rains, the more water there is.

We were left without land or money. The authorities paid ninety thousand lire a hectare for second-grade land — to those they paid — and seventy-five thousand for third-grade land. One year they paid us five per cent interest on the expropriation price. We've been backwards and forwards — and are still at it — after this or that document. We've worn ourselves quite thin doing it. When they took the land, they didn't need a lot of documents. Now we've been sent to Girgenti, Palermo and Sciacca. We've been arguing the question for the last four years. After three years, they gave us seventy-five per

286

cent of half the price of the land. We did have a lawyer, but even he got sick of hunting up documents and gave it up.

The total area covered by the reservoir was 190 *salme* of land, more than 300 hectares. More than two hundred families lost their land under the water. We're all in a mess: we haven't any land any more and are looking to replace what we've lost. Now the price of land is too high; you can pay a million lire a hectare if it's near the town. If there are trees on it, they're asking a good deal more, more than two hundred thousand lire the *tumolo*, which means nearly a million and a half a hectare. Everyone who received the compensation bought land with it, and so the sellers thought to themselves: "These people need my land." And so the price went up.

Every now and then, when they think of it, the authorities send us a demand note for the taxes on the land and the houses which are under water. Sometimes we pay; but there are other times when we haven't the money, and so how can we pay? Once or twice I've had the bailiff in the house. They were going to take away everything and so we had to pay up whether we liked it or not. What else was there to be done? Lots of people have been forced to pay taxes on the land that's been submerged for the last ten years.

I was left with two *tumuli* of land that were not touched by the reservoir. Then they went and built the new road which cut right through the middle and they haven't paid me a penny for that. I was left this bit of land by my father and mother and they want to see all the documents of a hundred years ago. We haven't got them; they're in the records offices somewhere and they don't put themselves out to find them. We go to Girgenti and they say: "You must go to Palermo." You go to Palermo and they say: "You must go to Sciacca" or "You must go to Girgenti." Or else they say: "There's no money." They want to see papers that are a hundred, two hundred, years old. I can't read or write. My brother and I were always together; we each worked harder than the other. Now he's dead. He couldn't get over the sorrow of losing the land. He couldn't bear the sight of the lake. My nephew looks after our affairs now.

One day, about a hundred of us assembled at Sambuca, in the town, and marched to see the police sergeant. "Don't make a fuss," he said, and sent off a telegram. After that, we got some money. A lawyer and an engineer appeared on the scene and brought some money orders with them, with which they paid some people.

As we were without land, we had to sell the cattle, and now we are working here as *mezzadri*[49] and dividing the profits. We even had nut trees. I was always finding saplings and transplanting them. I would ask permission from the owner first. There were cherry trees. There were also three mill-wheels down there. The engineer told the miller that he'd treat him as a friend. The mill had been modified; there was a large house with a loft, a little room and a byre with fourteen stalls for the oxen that turned the wheels. The mill went on working right up to the moment when the water reached the door. Not that there was any corn to grind; it was just that the miller wouldn't give way. The technicians had said to him, jokingly: "We'll soon see Serafino with his feet up and a cigar in his mouth," meaning that they'd have to pay him such a lot of compensation. And then. . . . It cost him one hundred and forty thousand lire in lawyer's fees before he could get anything out of them at all.

The mill fell down and only the bridge was left. Now the mill works down there, near the bridge with five arches, which used to carry the water for the mill. When the miller's wife goes out into the countryside, she turns away so as not to see the ruins. They'd been there for fifty years. She was screaming so much when she left the mill, you'd have thought they'd murdered her husband. They'd found the place in a rotten state when it belonged to the prince of Gamporeale, and they'd put it in order with their own hands. The mill was already half under water when they came away. She threw herself on the ground, weeping. There was water underfoot, but what could they do? Even now she still dreams that the mill is working.

The dam has come to stay; I don't see anything moving it. When the water drops, there's a branch of an olive tree which acts as a landmark and you can see where the farm was. But the roof of the house has fallen in. You can see it above the water in the summer when the level of the dam is low. I didn't want to pick the olives. My heart was in the land and we thought to ourselves: "When the water drops, we'll pick the fruit." We didn't want to take the doors off the house even. Not that you can recognize any of the houses; they're just stones.

When my nephew was called to settle the compensation, Baron Tomai, who worked for the Land Reform Authority, said to him: "Why didn't you pick the olives? It was stupid not to." There were nineteen olive trees belonging to his wife. They were twenty years old and the olives were just coming on.

We stayed right up to the last. When the water had reached our knees, my nephew took me away on a mule. We couldn't get the doors off because of the water. The roof beams floated afterwards; and seeing that they were still floating two or three days later when the water had dropped a bit, we tried to get them away. But the ground was too soft and we couldn't manage it. Then it began to rain again, there was a storm, and that was that.

We have no land of our own. All the farms are occupied and no one wants to let. We haven't any money to buy a farm. Baron Tumminelli had some land for sale, but we hadn't the money.

They say that every now and then the houses appear above the surface; but my eyesight's not what it was and I can't see them any more.

Translated by R. Munroe

GIORGIO NEBBIA
(1926–)

Giorgio Nebbia was born in Bologna. He received a degree in Chemistry and was a professor of economics at the University of Bari from 1959 to 1995. In 1998 he received a "laurea honoris causa," and he is now emeritus professor. Nebbia has been a senator of the Italian Parliament for many years. He is the author of various works — *L'enerigia solare e le sue applicazioni; Risorse, merci, ambiente; Il problema dell'acqua: sete!* — on the relationship between human behavior and the land, the production cycle, and the disposal of waste materials. He developed the thesis, central to his work as a whole, that "it is not true that goods are produced by money, and it is not even rigorously true that they are produced by goods: goods are produced by nature."

THE CRISIS IN THE RELATIONSHIP BETWEEN MAN AND THE ENVIRONMENT*

> *I brought you into a plentiful land*
> *To eat its fruits and its good things.*
> *But when you entered you defiled my land,*
> *and made my heritage an abomination.*
> Jeremiah 2.7

Recently a public outcry has arisen over the irrational use of natural resources. Environmental damage caused by pollution, overcrowding, and the gradual extinction of animal and plant species have contributed to a new awareness. Rivers are covered in foam and transformed into drains; land-slides caused by erosion have progressively dislodged some cities;

---

*Selections in this section are from Giorgio Nebbia,"Il punto di vista cristiano sull'ecologia," *ItaliaNostra* (Milano, 1972): 12–15.

even our bodies have been poisened by pesticides, lead, mercury, and chromium in the drinking water. Such is the reality in which we and our children live today.

In Italy, as in many other modern countries, a re-examination is underway of today's technological and consumer society, which thoughtlessly exploits nature and, in turn, risks becoming a victim of the degradation it causes.

Underdeveloped countries have unwittingly altered the environment by gradually exploiting their natural resources. In advanced societies that wear and tear has taken its toll much more rapidly. The technical process of transforming natural resources: air, water, forests, soil, minerals, animals, and vegetation into commodities ends up damaging everything necessary to the physical, psychological, and moral well-being of humankind, not to mention its survival.

The sense that something was amiss in this production frenzy and in the race for material well-being has often been raised by scholars and philosophers; but the apparent success of technology has silenced this voice of conscience and reason. Moreover, as long as the production of goods, exploitation of natural resources, and pollution remained at low-levels, it seemed that nature could cope with the waste products from cities and industries. It "digested" them in its large biological geo-chemical cycles; and even though there was squalor in the big cities and filth in the rivers and on the beaches, nobody thought that nature would rebel and that an *eco-catastrophe* was imminent. The growing population has increased the demand for goods and technical perfection. Atomic bombs and radioactive waste from nuclear energy is a threat hanging over the heads of all living organisms. Also, the discoveries of synthetic products — detergents, pesticides, and plastics — were greeted enthusiastically because they offered solutions to problems of everyday life, and also generated substantial profits. However, after a few years, it was clear that the chemicals resisted natural biodegradation, thus increasing the toxicity in the environment.

Translated by Anna Re

THE LESSON OF ECOLOGY

By reexamining the models that we believed to be the very basis of our progress, we can now see why ecology has assumed such importance. Originally seen as the study of the relationship between living organisms and the environment — today ecology has become global: studying the relationship between human society and its home ("oikos"), the entire planet, Earth.

There are other aspects that I would like to consider. We can take resources from the Earth into space. But from no other planet or star, reachable by technological means of transport in a reasonable number of weeks or months of space travel, can we receive energy, minerals, soil for cultivation, or food. On Earth, natural resources are available in huge, but not unlimited quantities. In certain areas of the planet, such as in highly populated and industrialized countries, the exploitation of resources is reaching a crisis point: the progressive lowering of the water table under Milan is the result of the excessive use or even the waste of water for urban and industrial purposes. The destruction of the agricultural environment is a consequence of an increase in productivity; the heavy traffic in the cities is a consequence of productivity and so on....

Furthermore, the "goods" produced by technology do not disappear when we throw them away. Sooner or later they are transformed into waste that has to be disposed of "somewhere." And what's better than the storage chambers of nature — rivers, lakes, sea, soil, air — thus creating pollution. Increasing population and increased production means we will have fewer resources available for the future, especially if we continually damage the quality of our remaining resources by dumping waste materials. For this reason, I suggest that our society no longer be called the consumer society, but the *waste society*. The biosphere has limited means for regeneration or for dealing with pollution if this exploitation of more and more of its resources continues.

Earth is like a space capsule that keeps a limited supply of air for itself, and water and food for its astronauts, who have to deposit their own waste materials in the same capsule.

Unlike a space capsule, Earth does not have any place to go either to stock up on other resources or to discharge waste.

Ecology teaches us that there is a close interrelationship among all natural resources and that an action in any single place on the planet has an effect on the balance of the whole biosphere. One of the most significant examples of this is the use of DDT. It was introduced on a large scale as an insecticide during the Second World War; it contributed to wiping out of malaria in many areas of the earth — even in Italy — and it helped increase agricultural production. However, since 1950, it has been observed that DDT accumulates in animal fat, and recently even in the Antarctic, DDT was found in animals. This means that when a farmer uses this insecticide, it is washed away by the rain into the rivers. From there, DDT reaches the sea, it is absorbed by the fish, and working its way through the food chain, it comes back to man, even thousand of miles away from where it had been sprayed.

Hundreds of other similar examples demonstrate how a new sense of solidarity is necessary among all the inhabitants of the biosphere, both animate and inanimate: the ocean, the earth's surface, the atmosphere, the soil, and the minerals.

The words of Saint Francis assume a particular meaning in the light of all that has been said. He put nature on the same level as man and he called air, water, earth, and wild animals, his brothers. The Creator, showing His greatness, asked that they be loved and respected, along with man. That is why I suggest that Saint Francis — the patron saint of Italy — be nominated as the patron saint of ecology.

Translated by Anna Re

FULCO PRATESI
(1934–)

The naturalist Fulco Pratesi was born in Rome. After beginning a career as an architect, he later decided to devote himself to nature conservation. He was president of Lega internazionale per la protezione degli uccelli (LIPU, or International League for the Protection of Birds) and a consultant for *ItaliaNostra*. In 1966, in collaboration with friends, he founded the Italian chapter of the World Wildlife Federation (WWF); since 1979 he has been its president. He has written many books dealing with nature and has often contributed to two newspapers, *Il Corriere della Sera* and *L'Espresso*, as well as to many nature magazines. He draws animals, especially birds, and illustrates the books he writes. *I cavalieri della Grande Laguna* (The knights of the Great Lagoon) recounts the mysterious and fascinating annual migration of birds around the world, in particular that of the *cavalieri d'Italia* (*Himantopus himantopus*, black-winged stilts or avocets). The name "cavalieri" (knights) probably comes from the long claws that give this species an aristocratic look. These birds nest in Italy from March to September, after wintering in Africa.

FROM: THE KNIGHTS OF THE GREAT LAGOON*

Durante raised a claw (they were coral red, and he was very proud of them) and he looked worryingly into the distance. Far away on the horizon shimmering in the heat, the eucalyptus and some low white buildings could barely be made out; the landscape was unchanged: dry cracked mud stretched into the distance. You could see the small dark slicks of it churned

---

*From Fulco Pratesi, *I cavalieri della Grande Laguna* (Milano: Rizzoli, 1979).

up by the skittering of thousands of birds, and here and there wisps of grayish glasswort.

The drought was here to stay....

Continuing to peck, partly because of hunger and partly to maintain his self control (when intimidated, black-winged stilts eat, or pretend to, or clean their plumage), Pallino turned to Durante: "It seems to me that things are getting bad. If it continues there is no way one can start nesting." Vista nodded, looking questioningly with his ruby eyes at the old leader. "It's a bad situation. If it doesn't rain, we will have to leave."

"To go where?" Pallino asked always frightened by hasty decisions.

"In the extreme north the rich soil water comes to an end." (rich soil water, for the knights of Italy, are lagoons, ponds, and marshes where a thin layer of water covers rich and black banks of mud full of food, as opposed to the sea, which is poor soil water).

"That means we will have to cross the poor soil water again," said Durante carelessly. "We already did this several days ago when we came here."

"That was different," Vista intervened. "We knew that route well. We've been crossing it for years and years, and we know what can be found on the other side and where we will end up. To leave like this, towards the rising sun, seems to me imprudent; especially now that many females are almost ready to lay eggs."

Durante did not answer.

Far away, in another puddle, the rest of the group stood out against the darkness of the lime. You could see the young, still not perfectly black. Some females and males were looking for food, while others were sleeping on one leg with their head under their wing. Others were taking care of their plumage after a day's work. A homogeneous and determined group, Durante thought, which he had successfully led from the lake in the deep south, without loss or defection. "Thanks to my experience and the right decisions," he muttered. "But this time it's different, as Vista said. This time it's serious business. We have to decide as soon as possible if we want to start this uncertain crossing or if we want to risk it, and make our nests here, hoping rain will pour from the sky."

He took off for a short flight. The black and brilliant wings lifted him easily. He stretched his long legs beyond his tail and immediately afterwards, with a quick movement, he planed down springing close to the others.

"So, what are we going to do?" Beccostorto asked in an acid tone. "It seems we have come back to poor soil here." (In their language "poor soil" meant the Sahara Desert.)

Beccostorto had been like that since he was born: the upper part of his beak joined to the lower jaw with a rather large and ugly malformation. This defect made eating difficult and didn't contribute to his character. He was always ready to criticize others in the group, he was intolerant to collective decisions, and he didn't respect the authority of the leader — even though groups of Italian black-winged stilts — around fifty individuals — did not have real leaders. Unlike most animal communities where a strict and severe hierarchy almost always exists, in a group of knights, only the oldest and most expert has some ranking above the others, in this case Durante, or his partner Sette (Seven, so-called because once, instead of laying four eggs as everybody else, she laid seven).

Durante looked eastward in the direction from which the great poor-soil-water rain clouds usually came.

On the bank, in the distance, a cart loaded with salt seemed to float on the flickering layers of air because of the heat. A long line of curlews directed north marked the sky.

"Others are leaving" he thought. "They don't want to be without water either."

Years before, when he was young, he made a trip to the very far north, following a little group of royal godwits. After the long adventurous trip he nested down with an older female in a large inland marsh. Everything went well till the hatching period. Then, an endless period of rain raised the level of the water and all the baby birds died.

"That's not a place for us.... It's better to stay around the great water."

He was interrupted from his thoughts by the shrill voice of Beccostorto. "What are we going to do? What shall we do? We can't stay here. We are not stone curlews....."

The decision was his responsibility. Entirely. A mistake, an incorrect evaluation and the broods of the year would be lost. Maybe with the risk of not returning to the deep south. Anyway, it was impossible to stay. The couples were going to nest, and it was not sensible to postpone the hatching. The danger of having the baby birds unable to fly at the moment of departure, just before the autumn storms, was too serious. It was better to lose broods than already developed young birds.

"I think it is better to leave" said Durante to his mates. The group of elders that was resting with him in the almost dried up puddle nodded. "Maybe to avoid the dangers of the great water, we could go north. In the very far North, rain is more frequent," Durante said, "but we must always travel along the coast, as we did to come here. Even if in the last few years we have been fine, it seems to me this time the situation is different. Eat well all day. Tomorrow morning, we'll leave."

Translated by Anna Re

GIANNI MATTIOLI (1940–)
AND MASSIMO SCALIA (1942–)

Gianni Mattioli and Massimo Scalia are both professors of physics at the University of Rome. They have long been leaders of the environmental organization Lega Ambiente and of the anti-nuclear movement, which helped eliminate the use of nuclear energy in Italy. They are frequent contributors to environmental magazines, such as *Quale energia*, and are currently members of the Italian Parliament for the Green Party. The article that follows, "Prometeo è caduto a Cernobyl" (Prometheus fell at Chernobyl), was written the day after the meltdown of the Chernobyl nuclear power station's reactor on April 26, 1986. Mattioli and Scalia's revised myth contrasts vividly with the inscription under the statue of the young Prometheus at the Rockefeller Center in New York City, symbol of "human progress": "Prometheus / teacher in every art / brought the fire / that hath proved / to mortals / a means to / mighty ends."

PROMETHEUS FELL AT CHERNOBYL*

Chernobyl marks the end of the Prometheus myth. In the dark recesses of time, Prometheus stole fire from the gods and gave it to men to brighten their miserable lives. In modern times, Prometheus must somehow assume the role of a scientist. Now he has stolen the innermost secret of nature, of matter's cohesion — nuclear fire — and has given it to mankind.

Certainly something profound and terrible was shattered when the myth was reduced to mere rhetoric, to a metaphor for the crude and false equation: "technological and scientific progress equals social progress." Prometheus stole nuclear fire not to deliver it to humankind but to the general staff of

*From *Il Manifesto* (May 1986): 20.

298

armies. It is true that those were terrible times and the extraordinary "squadron" of European brains coordinated by Oppenheimer delivered the first atomic bomb to the American army under the obsessive conviction that Hitler's insanity might beat them. How can we condemn them?

However, it should also be said that Heisenberg, who remained in Nazi Germany and was certainly capable of creating the German atomic bomb, gave this reason for staying behind: to hinder and distract attention from the atomic bomb project. This he was able to do with courage and intelligence.

Faced with the rise of the insanity variable — Nazism — Prometheus split himself into a dual personality. He stole the fire, despite the awful certainty that he would not be able to give it to humankind, but would have to give it to the Titans. The other ego, the separated one, gave up the idea of stealing it because he knew there was no one to whom he could give it. And now nuclear fire represents a real possibility for the self-destruction of the species. But the revenge of the gods is terrible. The eagle with the bronze beak gnawing at Prometheus's liver is no longer necessary. Prometheus has become the Titans' puppet. The military/industrial system and its inexorable logic has had a profound impact on the attempt to veer attention away from the inhuman image of nuclear fire at Hiroshima and Nagasaki by trying to emphasize the promise of growth and well-being from the "peace atoms": electronuclear energy.

Today, Prometheus, confused, hears the shouts of the multitudes that followed him and believes it is possible to establish a heaven on Earth for the unlimited growth of humankind's power and knowledge. Today Prometheus has risen again, to remind us that in his language "atom" means "inseparable." There is no nuclear fire for the peace of mankind....

But Chernobyl calls us all, all people. No more challenges or aggression, away with exasperating dominion, away with disintegrating violence, there is a complex and difficult harmony to be re-created.

Chernobyl has made us all aware of the bitterness of Einstein's thoughts on the difficult years. He argues that our world was facing a crisis, which those with the power to make decisions had not understood. The uncontrollable power of the atom had changed everything except our way of thinking. Humankind was thus being dragged towards a catastrophe without comparison.

Today, however, many of us understand, today we dare to think and dare to hope the catastrophe can be halted. We ourselves can change to conform with the world in which we *want to live.*

Translated by Anna Re

GLOBAL CLIMATE CHANGE*

Already twenty years ago, most climatologists agreed that the increasing concentration of carbon dioxide in the atmosphere would cause of an increase in the temperature in the atmosphere. This phenomenon became known as the "greenhouse" effect, and the mechanism is similar to what we witness when tomatoes, strawberries, and flowers grow under glass. Various gases, and in particular carbon dioxide, reduce the amount of solar energy that the earth's crust reflects into the atmosphere. Climatologists pointed out that with the advent of the Industrial Revolution and the increasing use of coal, gasoline, and gas, physical parameters were visibly changing. The concentration of CO_2 in the atmosphere that had maintained a value of 280 ppm[47] up until the end of the nineteenth century, climbed to a value of 320 ppm at the end of the 1950s and an all-high of 370 ppm at the end of the 1990s. The alarm of the climatologists was well-grounded. The IPCC (International Panel on Climate Change), a United Nations body, established physical-mathematical models that were able to predict variation in global effects. The model predicted a scenario of what would come about in the next decades as a result of the progressive increase in the temperature; in particular, the melting of the polar ice-cap, the rise of sea levels (adieu Venice!), intense rainfall in some areas and droughts that accelerated desertification in others.

*From *Avvenimenti* 20 (May 24, 2002): 35–36.

But actually how reliable was the forecast from these models? Given the extreme complexity of the bio-geo-chemical cycle of carbon and its irreducibility to conform to models that were even more sophisticated than those already proposed, the accent was put more on the "trends" and on the irrefutability of the correlations (the "Planet's fever" resulting from the increase of the concentration in the atmosphere of greenhouse gas), rather than on quantitative data. For instance, some North American scientific reports went as far as providing figures that were totally lacking in balance and caution.

The scientific community (the "v.i.p." science), for the most part, had little interest in, if not downright skepticism about, the problem, except for a few authoritative voices. Carlo Rubbia, for example, swore that Enrico Fermi would have made the battle against the greenhouse effect a priority in scientific research. Therefore it is not difficult to understand how an agreement between governments on reducing emissions of anthropogenic gases is problematic, as we saw at the conference in Rio in 1992, when the proposal of a carbon tax by the European Commissioner for the Environment, Ripa di Meana, was not supported. In '94 the beginning of a more concrete commitment to the problem led to the Kyoto Protocols in '97, an important step forward, although some of the ambiguities in the agreements were strengthened by the uncooperative attitude of some governments even in recognizing the gravity of the problem.

The American Academy of Science, once it recognized the scientific basis of the problem, obliged the Bush Administration to change its attitude, receiving only formal acknowledgment, which in concrete terms has produced little or nothing, but at least it is a significant step towards a correct scientific approach. For this reason we believe it is of utmost importance to continue to discuss the theories at the heart of climatic change, and not merely treat them as sterile academic dissertations.

From a scientific point of view, the depiction of a greenhouse effect predicting dramatic events extending over a long period of time (50–100 years) is wrong. Moreover, the correlation between the increase in greenhouse gas and gradual climatic change does not particularly preoccupy the attention of the public; since it does not face abrupt changes in life style, it isn't committed to putting pressure on politicians and seems to put its future into the hands of science and technology to find the solution. The inundation of Venice can wait.

In our opinion, the *theory of stability* provides a more rigorous model, without creating unnecessary alarm, only that perhaps it has the flaw of not providing a gradual and comforting answer to the phenomena. The situation it portrays is more in line with the facts as we know them today, not those of a distant future.

The theorems and the methods of the theory of stability, founded at the end of the nineteenth century by Poincaré and Liapanov, provide an irrefutable framework for understanding what is happening today.

What exactly is this theory able to show us? It demonstrates how *changes in the structure of a physical system induce changes in the stability of the equilibria,* thus allowing a situation of stability to become unstable. The system will undoubtedly find other configurations that have a stable equilibrium, but that doesn't mean that the new stability will necessarily benefit the whole ecosystem (after all, dinosaurs had no responsibility for their extinction whereas our survival depends on us!). Above all, we mustn't neglect the fact that changing from one stability to another results in a phase of imbalance and readjustment that, more often than not, is dramatic.

Today we are looking at a situation that has come to a head. For instance, serious flooding takes place ever more frequently compared to the past.

The theory of stability demonstrates that critical events can come about according to parameters, among which time is not necessarily a present factor; there is no foreseeable zero hour when the change in stability will come about. It's sufficient that one of the parameters indicates a significant variation in the structure of the physical system.

So much for the idyllic predictions in the next ten years of seeing "walls of water" attempting to inundate San Marco in Venice, and held back by splendid, technological mobile

302

barriers (an innovative ingenious system called M.O.S.E.) that hopefully Moses would have been proud of!

But if the application of the theory of stability is the case, then decisive steps must be taken. In other words, the Kyoto Protocols must become a reality in order to re-establish the conditions for stability in which we will have much more likelihood of survival — unlike the dinosaurs.

Translated by Deberah Catts

VIRGINIO BETTINI
(1942–)

Virginio Bettini is an associate professor of urban geography at the University of Venice. In 1970 he founded the magazine *La nuova ecologia* (The new ecology), one of the most influential proponents of Italian environmentalism. He has written extensively on the environment, including his book *L'analisi ambientale* (Environmental analysis), an inquiry into the methods and techniques for evaluating environmental impacts. *Cap Chat* is a novel born from a journey in Canada, when Bettini was a member of the European Parliament, and deals in part with the use of wind as an alternative energy source and also explores the complex problems related to pollution and politics in Italy. Cap Chat on the Canadian side of the St. Lawrence River is the largest wind power station in the world. The huge wind farm in Cap Chat is also the dream of Paolo Dell'Acqua, the novel's protagonist as well as a representative in Italy's parliament. The novel *Cap Chat* is a thriller with intrigues, blackmails, and terrorist attacks woven throughout.

BLOWIN' IN THE WIND *

The old Victorian-style Windsor Hotel in Montreal, in Rue Peel, opened in 1878 — read a shiny brass plate — it could be the ideal place.

He liked it because he loved historic buildings and categorically refused to stay in places like the Hilton, Sheraton, and Holiday Inn. "Never patronize a hotel built after 1901," was his motto. Carmen was of the same opinion. That's why she booked him there. She knew the Windsor Hotel, she had described the large halls, which in the past were ballrooms and

---

*From Virginio Bettini, *Cap Chat* (Teramo: Interlinea Editrice, 1993).

now had become backdrops for the conjurors, illusionists, and clowns of the large traveling circus of congresses and symposia.

Paolo found himself in the light-well that illuminated the lobby–garden. He walked towards the vast monumental Peacock Alley corridor. His room was in Liberty style and helped him relax. He stretched out on one of the twin beds and half-opened his eyes to imagine the bamboo and teak of Carmen's room, the window frames eaten by the salty air of the sea, the paint peeling off the noisy air conditioner. He had such a dreary memory of the hotel rooms where he'd been during his Caribbean trips — Havana, Cienfuegos, Managua — when he was searching for the first American city, La Isabela in Santo Domingo.

He did not know San Andrés, but he could imagine its outline. The Caribbean Islands were all drawn up by computer. The same, basic elements, the same schemes, designed with the aid of a mouse and a large Mac in the hands of chaos: a coral reef, a lot of white sand, immaculate beaches, wooden homes among the palms, several tower buildings made of cement, which gave the idea of the improbable existence of a pitifully poor Central Business District, the din of car horns, the scrap iron of the rusty car shells, and humidity, a lot of humidity, relieved with frequent showers.

He got up slowly and went to the window.

The city was bathed in a sweet and clear afternoon light. The taxi run from the Dorval Airport had been quick and silent over the big expressway, with the Lachine Canal on the right, running into a vertically built landscape.

The main attraction of the skyline, which rises in the heart of Montreal, between Mont Royal and the old historic city, once surrounded by walls, is the bold and futuristic Trade Center. This is where the World Congress on Wind Energy would be held, in a sort of no man's land, which none other than some advertising agent with no sense of the ridiculous had termed a "geographic link between the old and the new city." Once he arrived in the hotel's hall, he was greeted with the usual politeness. He had a day's lead over the parliament delegation, or at least he thought so. His peace of mind nevertheless had already been shattered by a message from Nicole who had asked him to meet her in the lobby at eight o'clock. The phone rang. He jumped between the two twin beds to take the call. It was Carmen.

The Trade Center rises up between Place d'Armes and Place-des-Arts. Paolo approached the monstrous building with awe. It was erected on cement pillars above an underground high-way. An immobile spaceship in the middle of the city, invisibly anchored and connected to the telecommunication satellites. In the large hall where the 6,000 congress participants were seated, a debate with one of the more prestigious guests, James Lovelock from England, the inventor of the Gaia theory, was underway....

Paolo reflected on the lecture he would be giving the next day. He always had problems with "wind farms." He was not contrary in principle, but he believed that the wind-farms logic was the same one that had guided the choice of locating two large plants in Italy, one on the Molise mountains at Frosolone, foreshadowing the transformation of an wind survey station into a wind factory (a plan that — because of bureaucratic obstacles, jurisdiction conflicts, and the stupid opposition of environmentalists themselves — was not taking off), and the second in Sardinia, in the Monte Arci Sanctuary. Paolo's dream — how he conceived of the Wind Island in Sardinia — was rather more complex and specific. His plan for energy transition started with the theory of large wind rotors, Gamma 60, with a 1.5 megawatt power, placed in groups of two or four close to the coastal towers built by the Spanish and the Piedmontese populations between the fifteenth and eighteenth centuries. The landscape of the island would be slightly transformed by these wind towers, but they would replace the petrochemical horrors. What Paolo planned, went beyond the concept of the wind farm. An interconnecting coastal network would bring electricity to over half a million people spread around the island, and not only to one village of three thousand inhabitants. It was time to stop the do-it-yourself....

Paolo slowly got up from the armchair of the large amphi-theater, which had seated 6,000 and where no more than 200 people like little ants in a structure large enough for dino-saurs, were left milling around. He noticed a familiar face, Tullio Regge, an Italian physicsit with an international repu-tation. With astuteness and curiosity he was looking back at Paolo from his wheelchair. If Tullio were here it meant that the congress held a certain importance even for those who were not strictly "soft." He picked up his portfolio of abstracts and went over to him.

"You seem surprised to find me here," said Tullio with his bright feverish eyes. "I also want to fight in the name of the famous Dell'Acqua theory where the role and importance of parliament is based on the irreversibility of the cosmos. So, I prefer to actively live in the irreversible cosmos than to be-come mummified in parliament."

Paolo received a slap on his arm in welcome. It was a sign of affection from Tullio, who started to push his wheelchair forward implying that he expected some help. Paolo already knew this gesture, gripped the handles, and pushed the wheel-chair towards the elevators.

Tullio seemed euphoric.

"I'm staying in the same hotel. I know everything about you, since you made the mistake of hiring an extremely efficient and sensible assistant."

"Have you converted to soft energies?"

"No, no, you know my position. I am all for the intrinsi-cally safe nuclear energy and I have a moderate trust in fusion. I do not run after the DIY bit. We still need to study those papers related to the possibility of recycling all the pluto-nium left by the bombs in the civil plants. Don't tell me that environmentalists prefer to leave the plutonium in the hands of military bases instead of disposing of it in safe and super controlled nuclear plants?"

"No, that's not the case, and anyhow it's hardly the point."

"Well young man, you are probably wondering why I came so far. I'll tell you why. I believe that before devoting oneself to this expensive do-it-yourself wind farm, it is important to immediately switch on the only plant available, to compare energy savings. *Negawatt* against *Megawatt*. They invited me to tomorrow's lecture. Perhaps I am not as brilliant as Lovelock, but I still have some cards to play."

. . . .

"Listen to my version of the problem," said Tullio after making sure that the shoulder belt was well hooked to the chair. He was squeezing his weak legs with both arms, as he always did when he wanted to concentrate. "Specialized operators lend the sum of money necessary for reconverting energy plants in companies or apartment buildings; they have been working with profit for several years now, recovering the investment from the percentage on energy savings. We should start from there."

"In that case, the energy saving products should have strong tax relief and minor planning costs. Look, I have digested your steps on transition a long time ago," said Paolo pushing the wheelchair faster now.

"But what do you expect from Europe in the year 1993? A sharp turning point insofar as energy policies are concerned? You know the lobbying parties who pound us each day. Our electricity board is nothing compared to the tough European electrical oligarchies"

"That's why we should push for other things, for transition, or soft energies."

By now they were approaching the Windsor Hotel along the wide footpath. Tullio turned towards Paolo in a flash, his face lit up in a cunning and teasing smile, the same one he puts on when he wants to challenge something: "There's a woman waiting for you in the lobby. It is not your Spanish lady. I met her at the restaurant at noon, and she asked me if she could have breakfast with me. I believe she's an interpreter. I thought I had made a conquest. Then she asked me if you were coming, and so then I understood. Can I pay you a compliment? Your reputation as a lady killer is still alive."

Nicole was sunk in a red couch. The light make-up that she wore over tiny lines made her childlike beauty even more alluring.

"Well, I was right" moaned Tullio. "At least introduce her to me and pretend that you don't know that I've already met her."

Nicole got up and moved towards them. She bent slightly over Tullio and whispered almost sighing, "Thanks, professor, for bringing him to me."

Tullio half turned his wheelchair towards Nicole. He took her hand and looked at Paolo with astonished incredulity, and shaking his head, he moved off towards the restaurant.

Paolo and Nicole did not have much to say to one another. She knew of the story with Carmen, and Paolo knew of her old but renewed passion for a Spanish deputy who acted both as lover and father. The child Nicole with her husband could only reach an incestuous type of love. Perhaps they could talk about that.

They wandered around Place d'Armes, Rue Saint Sulpice, Rue de la Commune, Place Royale, and the old quais for a long time, until Paolo chose a restaurant next to the dock where the boats left for the Lachine Falls.

Nicole seemed only to have thoughts for her summer plans: the Escorial course, a stay in Paris with her mother. She also spoke of how boring Holland was, without even mentioning Petit-Pierre.

The subject was brought up by Paolo.

"Do you know that I met your husband in Kourou?"

Translated by Anna Re

NICOLA LICCIARDELLO
(1943–)

Nicola Licciardello was born in Sicily, took a degree in philosophy in Trieste, and then worked as a researcher at the University of Padova in the early 1970s. After years spent traveling abroad, which included studying yoga in Asia and teaching Italian in Australia, he returned to Italy, where he has since taught literature in high schools, worked as an editorialist for the newspaper *Il Mattino* in Padova, and organized poetry readings for peace and the environment. His publications include essays on utopian thought (in reviews such as *Angelus Novus* and *Contropiano*), the book of poems *Il Ballo Immune*, the CD *Grazie alla Terra* (Give thanks to the earth), and many interviews and translations. Recent years have been dedicated to travels in Central America and the study of Latin American poetry, especially in relation to shamanism.

GIVE US OUR DAILY WILD[*]

When under the great mulberry of Pratale, Etain Addey[50] launched the proposal for a collective book of stories by all of us on the "wild in my everyday life," she also responded to my question, "what do we want to communicate of bioregionalism in the city, and in what way?" The first revelation of that encounter was that myself, that I, and no one else, was the bioregionalism in the city in which I lived; I could not wait for some "guide" to come and bless an initiative for the wild in the city — because there are no guides. Examples certainly exist — Snyder and others — but it is no longer enough to translate them. It is here that each person must rediscover the wild, where he or she lives, whether it be a

---

[*]From an unpublished manuscript.

metropolis, village, or forest: contact with a non-codifiable, undeniable space. There where each one of us lives, this encounter has already taken place, more or less consciously all along (or it will never happen): thus, one must rediscover it and communicate it. Only by communicating it does it become real. In this way I found myself relating the open space of my Tai Chi at sunset.

This space is at the end of a wide cul-de-sac that passes through a field; at its end on the right is a little clearing, closed off from the sidewalk by hedges, so that from far off you couldn't tell it existed. On a bicycle, you can get in with a jump. To the left and front is a cornfield, and all around a hedge of large trees, which in the lushness of summer hides the hills. This hedge was always dear to me, I might say with Leopardi, as the sun plunges into it and the space on the right, fallow for so many years. This extreme corner of civilization, or rather of cement, this fallow space — where in the years a shrub has grown as big as an oak — is my wild space, only a few hundred meters from home. I go there to do Tai Chi at sunset — from April or May to October — but return even in the most disparate hours: in winter, in the rain or snow, at midnight or noon, to look at the sky and meditate. I also go to smell the odor of the earth in September when it is exhausted, pungent, and gaping, and the clods are at rest — or in the fog, or on moonless nights when I can recognize the constellations, and when all space is a uniform skin, lightly reddened by the city.

In this way, here innumerable poems were born, here I unwound the film of my life, here I took the most difficult decisions. For a long time it was a space frequented by no one, an extra space, even for mopeds, whose antics finished at the end of the road. In all truth, there have always been signs of other presences: bottle shards, bits of plastic, cardboard boxes, table legs. Someone at sometime now comes here to toast or smoke (not to kiss), but almost never when I come, and never in my corner. I keep this space clean — near which now looms a postmodern barracks under construction. There are also the noisy tourist airplanes — the small airport is just over the river — that take off in waves, exactly at sunset; they pass over me, almost directly overhead, in their anxious trip in hunt of the last ray.

On certain summer afternoons I lay down to sunbathe on the grass of the field, in a bathing suit. Once someone called 113,[51] but since I had fallen asleep with ear plugs to block out the noise of the crane on the barracks, when I opened my eyes I saw an ambulance on the road, and people discussing what to do with me. A young man approached me to ask how I was feeling, and if everything was okay: "Yes, why?" "Oh, nothing — we thought that you weren't well." As I left, the group dispersed. On the road I found out who had called 113: two young men with their dogs — black war machines that would have rushed me if their breathless owners had not forcibly held them back. "My dog sniffed you, but you didn't turn," one of them apologized. "Since you were nude...we thought something had happened." Nude, not exactly. Then I explained that I go there often, and worriedly asked, "But your dog might have bitten me...can it wander around without a leash? Are you insured?" "Yes, but if it bites you, it's your own damn problem," the other aggressively responded. Paradoxically he was kept from lashing out by the need to control his dog: the tough guys and their war machines neutralized one another, I thought in satisfaction.

By and by I returned to my place and, like other times, redefined the territory by urinating along the borders of the fallow area, round the young oak. I did it almost without thinking, but remembered that no dog has ever come so far as my corner — and not even the mastiff would, even in the following days when I found it again in front of me.

This sort of language is not, however, understood by young boys, who came rushing up once on bikes, almost running me over: "Hey there mister, what are you doing? Yoga? Taigiuan? Hey mister, what is it?" This was a difficult test: I could have stopped to politely respond to them, begun a conversation, perhaps gotten them to join in...even taught them. Or else, I could have continued, unperturbed, and ignored them — in the face of this close-range threat of distraction. Their obstinacy and anger at not getting a response grew. I was almost able to transform this force into the energy for a more concentrated performance: they were, after all, an audience. Or rather, they were at the moment the world, with its urge to eradicate diversity — attention itself. They were like a sixth destructive element that assaults the "five elements" of dance. At the same time there formed in my mind an awareness, an acceptance of the possible failure of my resistance — that it could succumb at any moment. And again, the paradoxical balance of forces revealed itself as intolerable exactly to those who "want" to break it: I did not turn to look at them, and they eventually left.

Other times I invited friends to join me at sunset for a free course of Tai Chi: but all, sooner or later grew tired of the endeavor — perhaps because it is informal, and so out in the open. For a while an old man watched me in contemplation from afar. Little by little he came closer. Taking him almost by the hand, I explained a bit, told him to observe, to follow my movements — inside, his body, his balances....

Fireflies at the edges of the cornfield are the only light in spring; with the mosquitoes of summer, I use the same strategy of estrangement as with the boys. Swallows, on the other hand, who come often during the fall, observe me from high up at the beginning, then glide down, dance overhead, almost greet me with a shout, and then fly off. When a cat comes it stops to watch, seemingly seeing beyond movement: its form of nonintention, asking of it the reason while understanding it.

But clarity doesn't always come. It is born of superabundance, of being and being here — including every co-present thing. From its richness, which manifests itself for every unknowable grace — the choral shaking of distant leaves, the breathing of the corn, the separation of colors — there is something that cannot be disrupted, for it is already the never equal to itself, even in this patch of valley: the irreplicable sky every evening, every unstoppable instant, the slow fantasy that no human art can ever reproduce. And now: "move your hands like the clouds," swim in the air at its same frequency, without ever cutting, not even shaking, the thread that invisibly connects to the Shen.[52] Evermore slowly and rounded, flowing in the shape without passages, with no more attention to figures, freedom caused by following, until the rhythm of your unfolding coincides with the entire rhythm of the light of the sunset — in which all skies seen and unseen light up, and their glory unites the continents in peace, Heping[53]; the last full, circular gesture with the arms, and the star Venus appears.

Should I offer, and share, all this? Should I propose to someone in the neighborhood to make a little garden or orchard out of this fallow space? Should I protect it from the future owners of the neo-barracks by creating a public area, dedicated to Tai Chi and poetry? But, once planted with new species, crossed with various paths, and perhaps even given a bench or two, who would come to visit this place, if not kids with their mopeds and cell phones — who might befoul it without even enjoying its "wildness." This question is a challenge to my "bioregionalism": perhaps only an infinite compassion can respond.

Translated by Patrick Barron

LOREDANA LUCARINI
(1946–)

Loredana Lucarini lives and teaches in Milan, where she received a degree in foreign languages and literatures from Bocconi University. She has taught workers for many years and has actively been involved with many social and ecological issues. Among her writings is a study of the idea of nature in medieval troubadour literature and a homage to Laura Conti in the year of her death (1993). *Una storia ecologica* (An ecology story, 1998) describes the fight to reduce the air pollution caused by the car maker Alfa Romeo.[54] In the late 1980s and the early 1990s this problem grew gradually worse, especially at the Arese plant near Milan. Citizens and workers gathered forces to oppose the use of paints containing chemical solvents, which at the time were being dispersed into the air in very high quantities — up to 15 tons a day. As a consequence, for the first time in Italy TAR[55] denounced the firm and forced it (and the automobile industry in general) to switch to water-based paints.

ALFA ROMEO *

Alfa, *Anonima Lombarda Fabbrica Automobili,* (literally, Anonymous Lombard Car Factory) was born at the beginning of 1900 after the shut-down of the French-Italian Darraq. Alfa (which would be renamed Alfa Romeo) became established in the Milan neighborhood of "Il Portello." The organization bought more space than it needed at the time, but not so much as to influence the future development of the area around it. It didn't really have a particular political strategy concerning the development of the urban areas adjacent to it.

During the First World War the engineer, Nicola Romeo, bought the organization and renamed it Società Anonima Ing.

---

*From Loredana Lucarini, *Una storia ecologica* (Milano: FrancoAngeli, 1998).

Nicola Romeo &C. In a few years it was given its current name: Alfa Romeo. In the 1920s, Alfa Romeo continued to be a handcraft organization, with a limited number of cars produced on commission. The success of the sports models and the excellent engines were not enough to prevent an economic crisis. In 1928 engineer Romeo quit as director. Since Alfa Romeo had become famous all over the world, the government saved it by putting it under the control of IRI (Istituto per la ricostruzione industriale).

Up until 1950, car production didn't represent the main activity of Alfa Romeo. Its basic activity was manufacturing aeronautical engines. It produced sport cars primarily for competition. Very few cars were built as they were very expensive to produce; the car engines were tested in aeronautics.

During the Second World War car production was interrupted.

After the Second World War production started up again with the Alfa 2500, a luxurious, expensive car. However, producing luxury cars didn't guarantee a market and did not compete with companies like Fiat and Lancia. It was time to leave the handcrafted-production of sport cars and cars for the élite and start mass production. With production of the 1900 model Alfa Romeo introduced the assembly line.

The passage to new technologies was neither immediate nor complete.

Alfa Romeo continued for a number of years to mix the traditional ways of production with the latest technology. Mass production reduced the cost of production and, as a consequence there was a substantial demand for a car that was still of high quality even though it was mass-produced.

The increase of production necessitated enlarging the factory in Portello. This was impossible because of lack of space in the area and high land costs. The Milan town-planning strategy in 1948 designated the Portello area, occupied by Alfa Romeo, for residents, craftsmen, and parks, encouraging industrial decentralization towards the suburbs, or even right out of the cities....

Public opinion in Milan — because of the organization's prestige and the public's sentiment — was against moving Alfa Romeo outside of the city. And when the actual dismantling of Portello began — it was gradual and the production never entirely ceased — not only the people in Milan, but also the public administration were worried that they had insisted too heavily on decentralization, and the move was considered the loss of a prestigious tradition.

The new location fell on Arese because it was north of Milan, close to the North Train Station; it was close to the highways, the lakes, and Turin; it was also close to Portello. Moreover, it wasn't too expensive and it was possible to start building the factory immediately.

On February 27, 1959, the executive board approved and the area was bought.

THE ARESE COMMITTEE FOR ENVIRONMENTAL PRESERVATION

In 1987 when Alfa Romeo was bought by Fiat, becoming Alfa Lancia, Fiat increased its car production without making improvements at the Arese factory. Soon noticeable paint fumes began to affect the health of the inhabitants of Arese, who organized the Comitato di Arese per la conservazione dell' ambiente (Arese Committee for Environmental Preservation).

When I heard about the committee in Arese, and about the reason for its creation, I found it impossible not to go to its meetings. In the winter of the year 1987, I went for the first time.

I remember that it was a foggy night, so common in our area. It was quite hard for me to go to Arese from Milan, but I was really eager to get to know the committee and understand more about the whole situation.

There were about 15 people, mostly businessmen and freelance professionals, middle class people who had moved to the gates of Milan looking for countryside and, ironically, clean air (!!!). They founded a new settlement in Arese in the 1970s and it was growing constantly. Some of them had some political background from the 1968 student revolution.

I was struck by Mr. Tagliabue, because of his inspired attitude; and Mr. Umberto from Abruzzo, an alpine guide, now converted to the urban Lombard neurosis and to the plea-sures of good food. Mr. Vittorio with his amazing skill of being able to put air pollution coefficients into chants. Mr. Scarbelli, a lawyer who never arrived without wine and salami from his area around Pavia. Mrs. Vittoria, an ambitious manager, who continuously reminded the group to be pragmatic. Carla, our cherished secretary and coordinator (without her, we would not have been able to find anything). Ernesto, representing the unions in Milan who, with his intuition and his impetu-ous passion, was able to galvanize everybody.

The atmosphere was combative, but we were united. Initia-tives were proposed like fireworks, and I ended up with massive amounts of documentation.

I was really involved in the general excitement. I had al-ready been taking part in all the initiatives to protect the environment for more than a year — in particular, the initia-tive to stop the use of nuclear energy in Italy. I had re-written some famous fables in an "ecologically correct" way. I had been a sandwich woman going around with two wonderful panels of Sleeping Beauty in Chernobyl: when the princess wakes up she does not find the prince but "nano-curies" (a pun, since "nano" in Italian means dwarf.)

Here in Arese, I was also making myself useful for a good cause. For a green suffragette it seemed like an occasion not to be missed. Here was an environmental message that would shake people up, like it had shaken me, making them under-stand that the great challenge of the third millennium would be the environment.

THE CONCERTS

Among the various initiatives of the Comitato di Arese to de-fend their rights to a healthy environment were creative ones such as Christmas concerts.

It became a tradition for the committee in Arese to organize a Christmas concert. One year it was held at Villa Litta in Lainate — one of the towns where the Committee for Envi-ronmental Preservation was constituted.

Villa Litta is an imposing building, like many others in Lom-bardy. But, Villa Borromeo-Litta in Lainate has something unique: its wonderful park. The park has a building called

"Ninfeo" composed of many rooms with mosaics. This building conceals a series of unexpected and spectacular fountains, in part still working, and in a niche among its grottos a "Venere al bagno" by Canova can be admired.

A very beautiful fountain rises in the center of a garden in the Italian style: the fountain of Galatea. The group of "Ratto delle Sabine," attributed to the school of Giambologna, forms a stage. Nymphs, putti, and mermaids stretch themselves in the air creating delightful crossover fountains.

"The conservation of the entire complex from the scars of time and negligence will be a heroic deed," Enrico Benzo, town councilor in Lainate, told us. Continuous attention, care, and love for his "creature" determined the start of repairs at the villa, thus enabling cultural events during the Milan summers to be held there.

The night of our concert, Enrico Benzo was present, and we were fascinated by his charming conversation. He recounted a story about Foscolo,[56] who often used to spend time in the villa. During a reception offered by Duke Litta at the closing of a hunting tournament, in which Milanese noblemen and the viceroy Eugenio Beauharnais[57] had participated — he suddenly became jealous of Countess Antonietta Fagnani-Arese's flirting and lashed out at her with a whip.

We could imagine the poet wandering through the splendid rooms and in the gardens at sunset or on warm summer nights. It's the feeling of suspended time and stillness that makes the beauty of Villa Litta unique.

AND WHAT NOW?

After five years of legal battles, the TAR ruled in favor of the citzens of Arese, forcing Fiat Lancia to restructure. In December 1991 water-based paints were introduced into the Arese factory.

Tonight the white moon shines on the terrace of my apartment. It illuminates the pergola, the scented oleanders in bloom and the quiet deserted streets below.

The Alfa story has come to an end for now. Alfa Lancia installed combustion chambers; renewed, in part, the painting system; and eventually introduced water-based paints.

319

Was our victory true glory? It is difficult to say. Difficult to say if the restructuring of the firm or the gradual drop in production was responsible for the reduction in pollution. Fiat has opened a new Alfa Romeo factory in Melfi. Today, when we speak about Alfa Romeo, it is to discuss the future of the abandoned area.

Many questions remain unanswered. Why, for instance, did the real estate market in Arese never collapse but, on the contrary, continue to maintain its high prices, and why did Arese continue to be one of the most sought after residential areas around Milan?

Why did such a consistent number of citizens from Arese never notice anything and continue to consider Arese a pleasant place to live, close to Milan?

Would the prestigious Alfa Romeo company have had a different destiny under the control of Ford?[58]

Sensitivity towards the environment, like every kind of awareness, results from a slow cultural process. What seemed unthinkable yesterday, is today part of our civilization. Environmental Departments are present in many Italian universities, university students ask us for interviews on our experiences for their theses, and a graduate student from the American University of Reno, Nevada, has been teaching a course on literature and the environment in Italy. The Government and Parliament are studying proposals for laws introducing "environmental crimes."

Appeals to establish a historical archive of Italian environmentalism are being made in order to conserve the history of the movement; ordinary citizens who left their private lives to dedicate precious time to the environmental movement will not be forgotten.

All the dear friends of these long years are around me tonight, witnesses to the story of Alfa Romeo in Arese, a fundamental case for the introduction of water–paint in the Italian car industry.

Translated by Anna Re

GIUSEPPE MORETTI
(1948–)

Giuseppe Moretti is a life-long farmer and has always lived in the place where he was born, Basso Mantovano in the Po River Basin Bioregion of northern Italy. Since the 1970s he has been actively searching out change, as much personal as societal, rooted in the principles of bioregionalism. In 1992 he founded the newsletter *Lato Selvatico* (Wild side) in order to provide a forum for the discussion and spread of bioregional thought and practice. In 1996 he and many other dedicated individuals created the Rete Bioregionale Italiana (Italian Bioregional Network), which acts as a "common ground" for a wide range of similarly minded organizations and people — from environmental groups and newspapers to teachers. Their publications include *La Terra Racconta: il bioregionalismo e l'arte di disegnare le mappe locali* (The storytelling earth: bioregionalism and the art of drawing local maps) and *Ri-abitare nel Grande Flusso* (Re-inhabiting the great flow), a selection of the American poet Gary Snyder's work translated into Italian. Currently the network is working on a book, edited by Etain Addey, dedicated to the practice of the wild and the re-inhabiting of place.

WILD AND CULTIVATED*

I live in the Po River Valley — the Pianura Padana or Padania — and work the land on a small farm that once belonged to my parents. Ecologists define the Pianura Padana as an "ecological desert." Where once there existed immense forests of oaks, elms, and linden trees, and rivers free to meander and form extensive wetlands, we now find geometric fields cultivated with grains,

---

* From an unpublished manuscript.

fruit trees, grapevines, and hay. Deer, wolves, and bears disappeared long ago; in their place are less demanding species. Everywhere there are roads, houses, smokestacks, factories, antennas,…and cities ever more crowded, while the quality of life, air, water, and soil dramatically diminishes. Undoubtedly, apart from the need to lead a dignified life, human beings in this bioregion have not known how to set themselves limits and have not known how to recognize the worth of a healthy and diverse environment. We can say that the Pianura Padana today is the result of a choice — already of remote times — to domesticate all wild nature, including humans and their connections with it. There comes the urge to leave.

But what happens if you decide to remain and shout your own howl of the wild that is disappearing? You rediscover yourself…because the wild is a part of yourself. It is the essence of that which we truly are — beyond the codes and models that we set down and impose upon ourselves. Rediscovering your own (wild) self cannot be separated from appreciating what is other than your (wild) self — which means comprehending necessities and needs, and also means making the effort to achieve an awareness of yourself as part of the common walk in which animals, plants, and the human mind interweave in a sinuous and mutual, reciprocal exchange. The first act in the progression is thus to go towards the wild…and it doesn't matter how humanized the place is: a small wood, an impenetrable thicket, the meanderings of a river, a marsh, a hedge, or an abandoned field. These are the borders and contours where wild nature's reign persists. Climbing plants, tadpoles, hawthorn berries, the hooting of a tawny owl, the darting of a weasel, and the inviting shadow of an old oak are part and expression of the spirit of place and the farmer — as well as the woodcutter, beekeeper, fisherman, and anyone having direct contact with nature. These people have a primary responsibility towards nature because, beyond societal conventions, they interact with a place of relations of an order greater than the sum of their individual interests, necessities, and urgencies. To meet the wild inside and outside of yourself means to cultivate patience, and to learn where to look, and how long to wait…until one day you truly see it.

322

It was in this way that I decided to stay, and not only to farm — it goes without saying — according to the principles of organic agriculture, but primarily to regain a sensibility, responsibility, and attention towards the rhythms, ways, and limits of wild nature. My idea was to live this mindfulness — concretely — in the life of all my days, by means of the simplest possible existence, the greatest possible self-sufficiency, and accepting every guiding bird, plant, or animal in order to gradually bring the farm back to a type of porous equilibrium between the wild and cultivated.

At that time, in the early seventies, the agricultural landscape that contained the small farm of my parents was still (for a short time) essentially the landscape of our grandparents — large hay fields for dairy cows, grain for bread and polenta, and a variety of grapevines for wine; all this was intermingled with long hedges running along ditches, and especially along property lines. My father — with a life dedicated to his family, two years spent in a prison camp during the Second World War, and much work in the fields — was, like many of his peers, incredibly efficient in the use of the earth's resources. The trees, for example, had to be species useful to the family's economic welfare and to the farm itself. They therefore had to efficiently regrow after being cut and produce plenty of firewood in the shortest time possible, as well as poles suitable for supporting vines. Because of this the hedges along the ditches and property lines were often nothing more than well-ordered rows of pollards — almost always of a single species — poplar, plane, willow, or mulberry. Here and there grew a few larger specimens for making grape-boxes, trellises, or beams. The most farsighted let a few impressive English oaks or walnut trees grow, in order to provide "piggybanks" for their children. But their efficiency went beyond this — even the wild plants that grew between one pollard and another and along the banks of the ditches were periodically mowed. There were no shrubs to be seen, apart from the odd patch of dogwood for making brooms or indigo dye for baskets. Yes, the efficiency and the care with which they managed their fields would today be a source of admiration. But if we would try for a moment to see with the eyes of the woodpecker, the snipe, or marten, all this would appear terribly inhospitable. In my mind it was clear that if there is no habitat — sufficient and coexistent food, water, and refuge — the wild has very little chance of prospering.

I began with the plants — the first ring of the cycle of life. I still clearly remember the unending discussions with my father when I discovered the seedlings of oaks and elms, or of shrubs such as alder buckthorn or hawthorn, in the hedges along the ditches. "Make sure you don't cut these!" I told him. "But why," he countered, "the oak is a tree that grows too slowly...and then it creates shade, and nothing can grow underneath...and these (hawthorn) are just a bunch of thorns." Sound pragmatism, it might be said, that was born from a life of scarcity and hardship...but one that also clearly reflects cultural assumptions, by now well rooted, according to which all must be sacrificed for the good of the family and of society. But for myself, one who "cultivates" a certain interest in existence, it is impossible to conceive of a relationship with the earth that does not take into account the richness and diversity of nature and thus, I repeat: those who work the earth have a primary responsibility to make certain that their actions do not negatively affect the larger ecosystem, but instead must work to achieve a balanced relationship with it.

The question was: "how can one manage to revitalize, in an ecological sense, a small farm, while also safeguarding its ability to support a family?" "Do with less, and improve the quality of the spaces." The hedges were ecologically very poor — almost a monoculture. I began to research in books what the former landscape of this bioregion was like, investigated on foot every hedge, little woods, clump of bushes and marshy zone in the surrounding area, and asked the older people in the village what plants and shrubs used to grow, what the most common consociations were, the most frequently occurring species, the indigenous varieties, and what the woods were like along the nearby Po River. I remember one old hunter who seemed to come back to life when I asked him the questions. "There were oaks as big as a house," he told me, "and the white poplars grew together thickly with the elms, and also maples and ashes and clumps of blackthorn, elder, and alder buckthorn. Around

324

the oxbow lakes the alders mixed in with the willows on the highest spots. There were quails, hares, and 'native' pheasants everywhere, and also buzzards, jays, and woodcocks — and it wasn't uncommon to see a mink or marten."

Gradually mowing stopped beneath the hedges and along the banks, and the young saplings of oak, field elm, and field maple were left free to grow; new indigenous plants of white poplar, ash, alder, hazelnut, and above all shrubs, such as dogwood, alder buckthorn, buckthorn, and hawthorn, were added to create a "woods effect" and to increase the biodiversity. Stopped too was the pumping of water from the pond to irrigate the fields, even if it was the best; in reality the severe lowering of the level of water jeopardized the life of the fish and intensified infilling. All around, the woody border was thickened and enlarged, and the old, dead pollards were not replaced, but left as places of food and shelter for a multitude of insects and for woodpeckers, ravenous for goat moths. The planting of new hedges along the borders of the fields, in effect, increased the number of nesting birds: nightingales, blackbirds, starlings, blackcaps, and shrikes; the bees were crazed in the spring for the precocious blooms of cherry plum and wild cherry trees; the hedgehog and hare took shelter under the shady boughs during the sultry summer heat. And it isn't true that all this invites damage to the crops. On the contrary, in my experience, the enlargement of the natural habitat prevents incursions into the cultivated one. Also, I've noted a greater balance, and that the crops grow healthier.

Much has changed in these last thirty years — the dairy farms have almost completely given way to monocultures of corn, beets, and soybeans, which are often managed by owners who now live in town. Increasing wealth has brought heating to houses, and the poles that support grapevines are now made of cement; as a result, hedges and large trees have been felled for "one extra square inch of ground." On the other hand, the abandonment of the countryside and the neglect that has left the few remaining hedges untouched is a source of a surprising return of the wild. Foxes have come back to dig their dens in the maquis, buzzards and harriers soar above the fields in search of prey, and a few handsome field elms or English oaks wave their tops over the horizon. But one cannot be deluded by a recovery: the motors of bulldozers, backhoes, and hedge trimmers are always ever more efficient. To slow them down, a law of the European Community has allocated funds for the maintenance of the hedges. But as soon as the need prevails — in a sense legitimate — to clean the communal ditches in order to drain the surface waters — or, as is happening precisely in these days, that a magnificent hedge is being totally annihilated for no reason but the voraciousness of a new landowner — all disappears in the passing of a few hours, and without even the slightest regard for, or attention to, what it represented.

As regards my place, the trees are free to wave their boughs and the shrubs to create habitats. All this has not gone unobserved: new sounds, smells, and colors are everywhere. The most conspicuous and satisfying effect has been the extreme reduction in the distance at which birds escape in flight from my approach. At first, the songs of the oriole and nightingale, the hammering of the green woodpecker, and the call of the kestrel were rare and always very far away, but now are right outside the house. The pond, a true green oasis, is home to green tree frogs, ring-snakes, grey herons, mallards, moor hens, penduline tits, magpies, and buzzards — and in winter the tracks of foxes and the scratches of the wings of owls who swoop down upon their prey are impressed upon the fresh snow. But my presence in all this is not that of a spectator. I have never thought of making a museum piece out the wild, of considering it as something other than myself. To live the wild is not only a need of the spirit, but is above all a practice necessary in order to truly meet the spirit of the place. Every time that I choose a tree to fell and chop up for wood to heat my house, I express gratitude and enter into the direct cycle of existence; every time that I find aromatic mushrooms I consider them a gift; every time that I gather berries and edible herbs, I recognize their energy; every time that my hands rest on animal meat it is to renew the cycle of life.

"Good," cries the jay upon the old oak, "now it's time to start!"

– Dedicated to Gary Snyder

Translated by Patrick Barron

STUDIO AZZURRO
(1982–)

In 1982 Fabio Cirifino (photographer), Paolo Rosa (visual artist and cinematographer) and Leonardo Sangiorgi (graphics and animation artist) founded Studio Azzurro, a center for artistic experimentation and video production. In 1995 they merged with a group formed by Stefano Roveda, an expert in interactive systems. Studio Azzurro views itself as an artistic language deriving from a wide variety of artistic sources. Their first retrospective, "Videoambienti 1982–1992," presented a journey tracing the path of a search towards the integration of electronic picture, surrounding space, and viewer interaction. The group's current activities are aimed at creating "sensitive environments" in which technology is joined with narration and space. These interactive environments are supported by "natural interfaces" that allow audience interaction without technical tools, but through "natural" actions such as touching, stomping, or talking — a process that stimulates dialogue and spontaneous immersion in sensorial experience. Their many activities have included installations, exhibitions, documentaries, educational workshops, and various publications, including: *Ambienti sensibili: esperienze tra interattività e narrazione* (Sensitive environments: experiences between interactivity and narration), *Interattività — Studio Azzurro: opere tra partecipazione e osservazione* (Interactivity — Studio Azzurro: works between participation and observation), and *Studio Azzurro: percorsi tra video, cinema e teatro* (Studio Azzurro: pathways between video, cinema and theater). Khaled Fouad Allam, the author of the following "postcards," holds the chair of Sociology of the Muslim World at the Universities of Trieste and Urbino. An essayist and columnist for *La Stampa*, he is also the author of *L'Islam contemporaneo*.

THE EARTH THAT GENERATES THE AIR *

Postcard

I sometimes feel as though I were in the film *Traffic* by Jacques Tati: we are overwhelmed by a chaos that stretches out like dust in the desert. Every morning I see these people, people of the shadows, humble, torn from their roots, submit to world time in our building sites of hope. Our cities have become barriers to the beauty of the earth, where one feels one is living in a permanent state of war. The noise of the traffic is not so different from the crashing thunder of war. The noise of our Mediterranean cities is a deafening racket: and the silence, the last wisdom of the sea, is but a memory for the poet. What will become of our cities, of our wind, of our waters, of our trees, of our shouts and of our pain? The earth is tired, tired of us, of our footsteps, of our very bodies. It has become fragile. Have we entered the winter of the world?

The combination of conflicts and climate changes has such a domino effect that the word catastrophe is insufficient to express the reality: of the 135 million people seriously suffering from desertification, more than half are concentrated in the Mediterranean and in sub-Saharan Africa. Desertification causes the progressive and relentless loss of thousands of square kilometers of agricultural terrain, setting off a spiral of conflicts and migrations. The factors that contribute to the environmental degradation generate and kindle civil wars and other forms of conventional conflict: since the Second World War, one hundred and forty other wars have caused over fifty million victims in the developing countries alone.

This scenario also includes the complex demographic issue, and here the forecast is worrying and tends to scuttle any dialogue between Europe and other Mediterranean countries. Here, too, the dividing line is evident: on the northern shores of the Mediterranean, between 1950 and 2000, the population rose

---

*Selections in this section from Studio Azzurro, *Meditazioni Mediterraneo: A Journey through Five Unstable Landscapes* (Milano: Silvana Editoriale, 2002).

from 158 to 212 million; the countries to the east and south, instead, have tripled their populations, going from 73 million in 1950 to 244 million in the year 2000, so that today in the southern Mediterranean 50% of the inhabitants are under 25 years old. Egypt has 68 million inhabitants, Turkey 67, and Algeria 30 million, like Morocco: these countries have a strong migratory potential, and they numerically approach the populations of France (59 million), Italy (57), Spain (40), where the average age of the population is typically rising. From 2000 to 2025 the inhabitants of the southern Mediterranean will increase by 48%, while that of the European Union will only rise by 3%.

The events of the last two decades of the XX century have determined a geopolitical picture that is as yet unresolved. The world-wide uncertainty emphasizes the dividing lines that bisect the Mediterranean in all directions: the island of Cyprus is still divided; the cohabitation in the Balkan states is still unsteady, the city of Mostar continues to be divided between the Croatian and Muslim administrations; the question of the ex-Spanish Sahara thwarts any real communication between the Maghreb countries; the Israeli-Palestinian conflict is emblematic of the unstable Mediterranean equilibrium. The Gulf War was just the preface to this foreseen catastrophe.

PERFUMES CARRIED BY THE WIND

Postcard

Not a day goes by without a present day Noah's Ark crying to the wind and to the earth. Their eyes cry out against our silences, but we are mute, paralyzed by the novelty, the incomprehensible; we're too tired to think, to foresee, what the future will hold. They are biblical journeys, that these naked people face: a whole humanity seeking refuge. These are hard times, in this postmodern era, with our politics: we even call them illegal immigrants, intruders, refugees, non-Europeans. But have you seen the look in the eyes of these women? They have the same age-old look as the Virgins of the fourteen hundreds: they have something of the face of the Virgin Mary — this is where the sacred expression of desperation hides today. Sometimes they have given birth in the hold of the ship, pushing life to the limit; they escape from destruction, but they still know how to create what we are no longer able to, they are able to build hope. They are the only architects of hospitality that are left, they hold no office, they tell no story, no one writes the screen play to explain this thing, but they live it. Their strength is just in this: to lead action back to hope, to leave the tragic struggle that prevents us from being real human beings.

If the Mediterranean basin is one of the central points of the world today, this is because it is situated at the heart of the global phenomenon of migratory flows. It is characterized by generalized mobility: from the Middle East, from North Africa, and from the Balkans, a new generation of immigrants is arriving — often with diplomas or degrees, but from countries experiencing deep political crises or serious ecological disasters, or where their rights as ethnic or religious minorities are denied — and they have triggered a long-term chain of events that is being engraved in the heart of our society. A tenuous border separates the immigrant and refugee categories, and today we also speak of environmental refugees: even if this term does not yet have a legal basis, it nevertheless represents a reality.

These migratory flows, a real challenge for the new century, also stem from the dramatic economic disparity between the north and the south of the world: for example, the average GNP per person in the European Union is 14 times higher (20 times greater in Germany and 19 times in France) than in the countries of the Maghreb. And in these countries, the money transfers coming from immigration represent an important source of income; it represents 6.3% of the GNP of Morocco, and 4.1 of that of Tunisia. The Mediterranean today is slowly becoming a dividing zone, a border that people try to breach. The number of routes continually increases, the domain, in recent years, of a real black market economy revolving around immigration. Cities like Melilla and Ceuta, the Canary Islands and the Balearic Island, the Islands of

Sicily, regions like Puglia and Calabria, and the Gorizia area are today the capitals of a new geography of immigration, breaches in a new wall that is no longer that of Berlin, but one separating the Mediterranean from the rest of the World. Many observers and experts have warned that if demographic control is not instated within the framework of sustainable development, by the year 2025 a series of disasters are inevitable.

NOTES

1. Hermione is the daughter of Helen of Troy and Menelaus of Sparta; here the name may refer to D'Annunzio's earth deity (the earth and its animate life forms who speak to the poet), as well as his companion (perhaps Eleanora Duse).

2. "Pianto," translated here as rain, may also mean crying or weeping.

3. "Molle," translated here as wet, may also mean soft or yielding.

4. "Chiome," translated here as hair, may also mean foliage.

5. Demeter is the Greek goddess of agriculture.

6. Persephone is the daughter of Zeus and Demeter who was abducted by Pluto to reign with him in the underworld.

7. The three Gorgons are snake-haired women whose gaze turns the beholder to stone.

8. Hesperis is one of the Hesperidies, the guardians of the tree of golden apples; Erinys, the Furies, divinities of the underworld.

9. Pan is the Greek god of flocks and shepherds, often shown with horns on his head and the legs of a goat, playing a double flute or syrinx.

10. A psyche, or cheval-glass, is a full-length mirror set in a frame in which it may be tilted.

11. The araucaria is a tree of the pine family from South America and Australia.

12. "Intenzioni (Intervista immaginaria)," *La Rassegna d'Italia* 1.1 (January 1946): 84–89.

13. Menicanti's epigraph refers to a letter that John Keats wrote to Richard Woodhouse, dated October 27, 1818: Letter 118 in *The Letters of John Keats: 1814—1821*, ed. Hyder Edward Rollins, vol. 1 (Cambridge, MA: Harvard University Press, 1958), 386–88.

14. "Not of gods not of princes…" is an allusion to fifteenth-century forms of bucolic poetry dedicated to elevated themes and personages.

15. The "butterflies" is a reference to Dante's *angelica farfalla* (angelic butterfly) (see *Purgatorio*, Canto X, 125).

16. Urania is the muse of astronomy.

17. In his dream, Jacob's ladder joined heaven and earth (see Gen. 28.12).

18. "Oh kites" is a reference to Giovanni Pascoli's poem, "L'Aquilone" (The kite).

19. "I do not curb my lips" ("le mie labbra non freno") is from the Latin: "Ecce, labia mea non cohibui" (see Psalm 39.10).

20. The Lazarus here is the one of the Parable of Dives and Lazarus (Luke 16.19–31), not the one raised from the dead.

21. "Cortese donna mia" (my gracious lady) is a standard rhetorical formula in chivalric poetry; "sidera feriam vertice" is a paraphrase from Horace's first book of *Odes*, the full phrase meaning "I will touch the stars with my head, and be exhalted."

22. "Qui omnia vincit" (see Virgil's *Tenth Eclogue*, line 69).

23. See n. 16 above.

24. Fiumicino is a coastal suburb of Rome.

25. Insana seems to be playing on two meanings of *occhio*: "eye" and "bud." The former meaning is evoked by the images of seeing — blinded, shortsighted, and narcissistic sight, or visionary and dreamy perception — which recur throughout the book. The latter meaning becomes apparent in "The Rooting" and is also evoked by metaphors of planting, growing, and harvesting developed in other poems.

26. A baldachin is a canopy projecting or suspended over an altar or a throne.

27. Also translated by Frances Frenaye as *Revolt in Aspromonte* (New York: New Directions, 1962).

28. "Cafone" is a term whose original, regional connotation of "peasant" or "farmer," is now overlain by the far more common and pejorative meaning of "boor" or "ill-mannered person."

29. The carabinieri are members of a special Italian police force, associated with the military.

30. Fucino, once an extensive inland lake of central Abruzzo, was drained in the nineteenth century to create farmland.

31. "A day of land" refers to the amount of land that could be worked in one day by one person.

32. *Pulenta mitunà* is polenta cooked slowly in milk over an open fire.

33. The father of Dalmazzo Giraudo.

34. Payment in the form of small gifts.

35. Literally, "midnight" — the north-facing slope.

36. Telling tall tales, or light trickery

37. A neologism of Stern's deriving from the German *eisenbahner* (railway worker).

38. Calvino published the first of these stories in the newspaper *Unità* during the early 1950s. He based the main character of Marcovaldo on a warehouse keeper who worked at the same publishing house as he did. As in the story "Mushrooms in the City," (below) the man once collected mushrooms along a city road, ate them, and was poisoned. (See "A colloquio con Italo Calvino," *Queensland Dante Review* [April, 1982]: 15). The city where the stories are set is never named; most likely, it is based on either Milan or Turin – where Calvino lived for many years.

39. "Per qui si va, chi vuol andar per pace," Sinus says, quoting Dante a little freely; the text actually begins, "Quinci si va..." Purg. XXIV, 141. The translation is Lawrence Binyon's: *The Portable Dante* (New York: Viking, 1947).

40. The title gives the impression of authenticity, since it is made up of a well-known Latin title, *De amore* (On love) and a common expression, *mutatis mutandis* (appropriate changes having been made), but is nonsensical.

41. A meter (ἐνόπλιος) employed in warlike poetry, or for a war dance.

42. Also translated by Robert Lumley as *Voices from the Plains* (London: Serpent's Tail, 1989).

43. "Taglio di Po" literally means "Cut of the Po (River)," or in other words, where the Po River divides.

44. In Italian the word "fiammiferi" ("matches") sounds similar to the word "mammiferi," which means "mammals."

45. A skin eruption caused by exposure to chlorine or its components.

46. A chemical company located in Seveso.

47. ppm = parts per million, a standard measure of the amount of contaminants present in air or water samples

48. One *salma* (*salme*, pl.) is two hectares, or approximately four acres.

49. A *mezzadro* (*mezzadri*, pl.) is a sharecropper.

50. Etain Addey is the editor of this forthcoming book of the Rete Bioregionale Italiana (Italian Bioregional Network), dedicated to the practice of the wild and the re-inhabiting of place.

51. 113 is the public emergency telephone number for the police in Italy, equivalent to 911 in the U.S.

52. "Shen" in Mandarin means ancestor spirit.

53. "Heping" in Mandarin means peace.

54. Alfa Romeo was acquired by Fiat in 1986 and was renamed Alfa Lancia.

55. TAR stands for: Tribunale Amministrativo Regionale (Administrative District Court of Lombardy).

56. Ugo Foscolo, a famous Italian poet of the nineteenth century.

57. Prince Eugenio Beauharnais was appointed by Napoleon viceroy of the Regno d'Italia in 1805.

58. Ford competed with Fiat to buy Alfa Romeo.

PERMISSIONS

THIS BOOK WAS COMPLETED ON APRIL 21, 2003
AT ITALICA PRESS, NEW YORK, NEW YORK.
IT WAS SET IN GILL SANS AND
GIOVANNI AND PRINTED ON
60-LB. NATURAL PAPER
BY BOOKSURGE,
USA/EU

Made in United States
Troutdale, OR
08/06/2024

21745832R00228